teach yourself...

Microsoft Works for Windows 3.0

Judi Fernandez

MIS:
PRESS

A Subsidiary of
Henry Holt and Co., Inc.

Table of Contents

Part II: Word Processor   81

Part IV: Database   375

Part V: Communications   451

CHAPTER 19: THE COMMUNICATIONS TOOL 453

Preface

Microsoft Works for Windows version 3.0 is an exciting tool for computer users who want one coordinated product that provides all the features they need to get their work done quickly, easily, and attractively. Works incorporates Word Processor, Spreadsheet, Database, and Communications software in one package, all with the same easy-to-use interface, and all integrated with each other so that transferring data among them is simple. Built into the package are a treasure-trove of bells and whistles—lots of color and graphics to make all your output more attractive and more impressive, as well as a wealth of professionally designed forms and documents for those whose graphic design skills need some serious help!

Each of Works' four tools is not as sophisticated as stand-alone products like Microsoft Word for Windows or Lotus 1-2-3. But Word for Windows costs much more and doesn't include spreadsheet, database, or communications tools. Likewise, Lotus 1-2-3 doesn't give you a word processor, a database, or communications. Works' big advantage is that it offers a well-balanced, comprehensive package that includes perhaps the most important 80% of the big stand-alone products. For most users who aren't interested in becoming professionals in the field of word processing, spreadsheets, and so on, that's more than enough capability to meet all their needs. And surprisingly, Works surpasses most of the bigger and more expensive products in the graphics department.

This book will help you become familiar with Works for Windows. It starts at the beginning, with Windows itself. You'll learn how to use your mouse to start programs, choose commands from menus, select options in dialog boxes, and so on. Yes, you can use your keyboard with Windows, but your mouse is usually much more efficient and intuitive. This book emphasizes using your mouse to accomplish most of your tasks.

After you learn how to use Windows and your mouse, you learn the basics of Works for Windows. And then, because you're probably anxious to get started producing all those colorful, graphical documents, Chapter 3 shows you how to use an exciting Works feature called *WorksWizards*. WorksWizards will walk you through the process of creating a sophisticated-looking letterhead, address book, and other documents with very little work on your part. All you have to do is select from a list of options and enter your own individual data (such as the name and address for the letterhead). You can be producing great-looking documents in just a couple of hours!

Parts 2 through 5 of this book deal with Word Processor, Spreadsheet, Database, and Communications. Each part shows you how to use the tool at a basic level, then introduces the bells and whistles that make it exciting. In each case, you learn how to integrate each tool with the other ones so that you can accomplish tasks such as printing form letters and mailing labels, including part of a spreadsheet or a chart into a report, and sending a document file to a friend via your modem.

By the time you have finished this book, you'll be an accomplished Works user. You'll know all the basics and many extras. When you're ready to learn a few advanced topics, you'll know how to use Works' Help system to look them up.

PART I

Getting Started

CHAPTER 1

Working with Windows

If you have never used Windows before, you need to know some Windows basics before you can begin learning about Works for Windows. If you have used Windows before, you can probably skip this chapter. (Scan the list of topics below to make sure you know how to do all these things.) This chapter shows you how to:

❖ Start Windows

❖ Click, double-click, and drag with the mouse

❖ Manage windows: open, close, move, activate, resize, minimize, maximize, and restore

❖ Start up programs

❖ Pull down menus and choose menu commands

❖ Use dialog box elements: text boxes, list boxes, checkboxes, drop-down lists, radio buttons, and command buttons

❖ Configure Windows: change mouse settings, move program icons, establish a StartUp group

❖ Exit Windows

❖ Use the Windows Help facility

Why Windows?

Most IBM and IBM-compatible personal computers run under an operating system called the *Disk Operating System* (DOS). DOS provides the essential facilities that make your personal computer work. It manages memory, controls data storage on disks, and communicates with your keyboard, monitor, and printer. But by itself, it's dull, difficult for a nontechnical person to learn and to use, and it lacks many features that today's user expects. Windows makes up the difference.

The Graphical User Interface

Windows superimposes on DOS a *graphical user interface* (GUI) that simulates a desktop as your main work area. Figure 1.1 shows an example of a Windows desktop. You see pictures of objects (called *icons*), and you manipulate them with your mouse in much the same way as you handle the objects on your real desk with your hands. You can drag them around, open them, close them, put them away, and so on.

Programs designed to work with Windows all use the same interface. Once you're familiar with the interface, using a new Windows program seems almost intuitive. When you install a new program, you already know how to start it, stop it, select items, delete items, open and close files, and so on. The only thing you have to learn is how to apply those techniques to the subject matter of the application. So it takes a lot less time to get up and running with new applications

You also don't have to tell new applications about your hardware. You set up Windows with the correct information about items such as your printer, your monitor, and your mouse; Windows manages these items for all applications. This is particularly helpful when you change a piece of equipment. For example, if you buy a new printer, you have to configure it only once. (People who use DOS without Windows have to reconfigure every one of their applications separately when they install a new printer.)

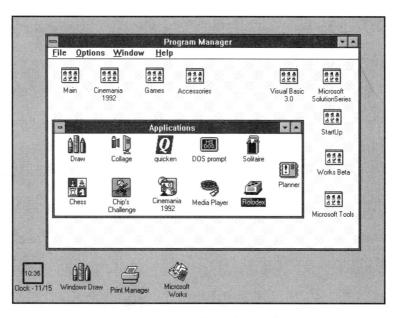

Figure 1.1 *A typical Windows desktop*

Multitasking

Another Windows advantage lies in letting you run several programs at once. You can open an address book, for example, and copy a name and address to a letter in your word processor. And you can refer to a spreadsheet while you write the letter. At the same time, another program can be displaying a clock in the corner of your screen so you can keep track of the time while you work. If you receive a phone call, you can pop up your appointment book and schedule an appointment without losing your place in your word processing document. While your word processor is performing a long print job, such as preparing and printing a set of form letters, you can work on another task or play chess. Figure 1.2 shows a desktop with four programs running: Microsoft Works for Windows, Calendar, Media Player, and Clock.

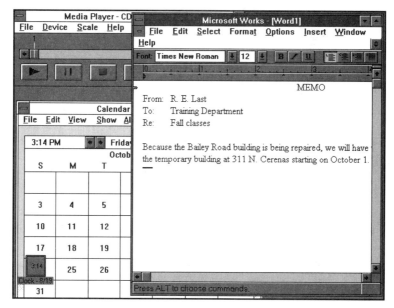

Figure 1.2 *Windows desktop with several programs running*

Getting More out of Memory

Today's personal computers have huge memories, but DOS can't take full advantage of them. Windows can. Although you can't see it happening directly, Windows makes your complete memory range available to programs. This means that programs written to work under Windows can be bigger: They often work faster and do more than similar programs that run directly under DOS.

Starting Windows

If your system isn't set up to start Windows automatically when you boot, it will display the DOS command prompt. To start Windows, type the word **WIN** and press **Enter**.

You can type the **WIN** command in any combination of upper-case and lower-case letters.

N O T E

You should see the Windows logo screen followed eventually by the desktop. (It takes a while, so be patient.) The mouse pointer initially looks like an hourglass, meaning that Windows is not ready for your input yet. The hourglass is Windows' symbol for "please wait." When it changes into an arrow, Windows is ready for you.

A Tour of the Desktop

Figure 1.3 shows a typical Windows desktop. You can see the desktop itself, that is, the gray background on which all other objects lie. If you remove everything from the desktop, you'll be left with this background.

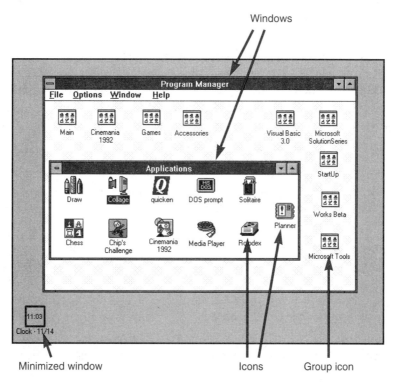

Figure 1.3 *The Windows desktop*

Windows communicates with you through objects called *windows*, which are rectangles used to display information. You can see three windows in the figure: the Program Manager window, inside that the Applications window, and down in the corner, the Clock window. (You'll see a little later why the Clock window looks different from the others.)

Program Manager is one of Windows' most important functions because it gives you access to all the other programs that you run under Windows. Its window contains a collection of icons.

Take a look at the icons in the Applications window for a moment. Each icon represents a program: drawing tools for **Draw**, a deck of cards for **Solitaire**, a corner of a chess board for **Chess**. You learn to recognize a program's icon very quickly and to respond to the picture rather than the label underneath it.

Now take another look at the Program Manager window. All the icons are the same! This is Windows' group icon, which represents not an individual program, but a group of programs. Program Manager organizes your programs in groups; otherwise, there would be so many program icons in one window that you wouldn't be able to find the one you want. In the sample desktop in the figure, you can see several groups that are common to all Windows installations. The Main, Accessories, and StartUp groups are described as follows.

❖ **Main** The Main group contains programs that manage your computer system and Windows itself. You'll find programs there such as File Manager, which lets you see and manipulate the files on your disks, and Print Manager, which manages your print jobs.

❖ **Accessories** The Accessories group includes a wide variety of programs that help you with your daily work. The Clock program, which displays the clock you can see in Figure1.3, is located there. Other interesting accessories provide a calendar, a calculator, a notepad, and a CD player (if you have a CD ROM drive).

❖ **StartUp** The StartUp group is empty when you first install Windows. Any program that you move into this group is started up automatically whenever you start Windows. You might want to move Clock, Calendar or your appointment book, File Manager, and Microsoft Works into the StartUp group. You'll see a little later in this chapter how to move a program into the StartUp group.

You have to open a group window in order to see the programs it contains. The Applications window is an example of an open group. When closed, it is represented by a group icon just like the others (you can see the gap in the top row where it belongs). Before you can learn how to open a group window, you have to know how to use your mouse with Windows.

Mouse Basics

The four basic mouse actions are pointing, clicking, dragging, and double-clicking:

- ❖ **Point** To point, move the mouse pointer so that the tip of the arrow touches the desired object. (Sometimes the pointer changes to another shape when it is over an object or an area; that depends on the program you're working with.)
- ❖ **Click** To click, point to the desired object and press the left mouse button once.
- ❖ **Double-Click** To double-click, point to the desired object and rapidly tap the left mouse button twice *without moving the mouse.*
- ❖ **Drag** To drag, point to the desired object, press and hold down the left mouse button, and move the pointer so that it drags the object with it. When the object reaches the desired new location, release the mouse button.

Windows includes a tutorial that demonstrates these basic mouse actions and lets you practice them. To start the tutorial, start Windows, then hold down the **Alt** key and press **H** followed by **W**. After you have the basic actions, one of the easiest ways to become proficient with your mouse is to play a few rounds of the Solitaire game that comes with Windows (see Figure 1.4). To start the Solitaire game, double-click the **Games** group icon to open the Games window. Then double-click the **Solitaire** icon.

Click here to
turn up the next
three cards.

Drag the nine of
spades to play it on the
10 of hearts.

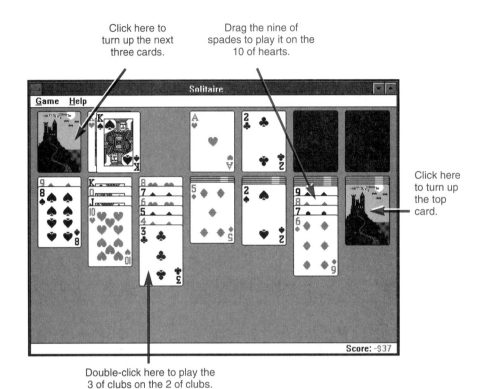

Click here
to turn up
the top
card.

Double-click here to play the
3 of clubs on the 2 of clubs.

Figure 1.4 *Using the mouse to play solitaire*

Swapping the Mouse Buttons

If you prefer to use the mouse with your left hand, you might want to reverse the effects of the left and right mouse buttons. The following procedure walks you through the process.

❖ **To swap the mouse buttons:**

1. Double-click the **Main** group icon.

    This opens the Main window (see Figure 1.5).

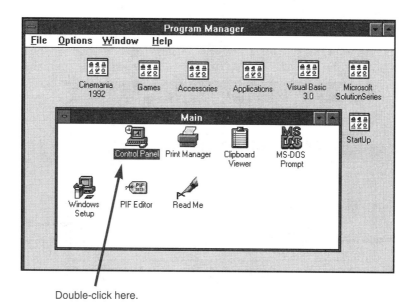

Double-click here.

Figure 1.5 *Main window*

2. Double-click the **Control Panel** icon.

    This opens the Control Panel window (see Figure 1.6).

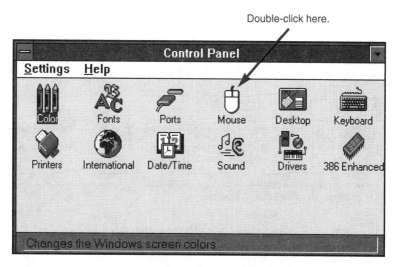

Double-click here.

Figure 1.6 *Control Panel window*

3. Double-click the **Mouse** icon.

    This opens the Mouse window (see Figure 1.7).

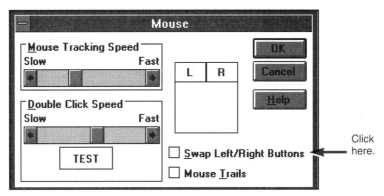

Figure 1.7 *Mouse window*

4. Click **Swap Left/Right Buttons**. (This immediately reverses the buttons. In Step 5 and all subsequent steps, you must use the other button to click, double-click, and drag.)

5. Click **OK**. (This closes the Mouse window, leaving you with the Control Panel window.)

6. Double-click the box in the upper-left corner of the Control Panel window to close the Control Panel window.

7. Double-click the box in the upper-left corner of the Main window. to close the Main window.

Setting the Double-Click Speed

If you're having trouble double-clicking, you might be doing it too slowly. You can tailor Windows to recognize your double-click speed. The following procedure shows you how.

❖ **To set the double-click speed:**

1. Follow the previously listed Steps 1 through 3.

2. In the box labeled **Double Click Speed**, find the button in the middle of the bar. Drag the button to the left (toward **Slow**). Just drag it a little bit; if you set it too slow, Windows might treat two single clicks as a double-click.

3. Double-click the box marked **Test**. If your double-click is successful, the box inverses color.

4. Repeat Steps 2 and 3 until you find a setting where you can successfully double-click every time.

5. Follow Steps 5, 6, and 7 from the previous procedure.

Managing Windows

A nice feature of Windows is that you can arrange your desktop to suit your own convenience. Once you have opened some windows, you might want to rearrange them. You can move a window, change its size, shrink it down to an icon, expand it again, and hide it behind another window. And, of course, when you're done with it, you can close it.

Opening a Window

To open a group window such as Applications or Main, simply double-click the group icon. The group window is a *child* of the Program Manager window. You can move it and resize it within the Program Manager window, but you can't move it or expand it outside of Program Manager's workspace. (In Figure 1.3, the Applications window isn't sitting on top of the Program Manager window, it's *inside* the Program Manager window.)

N O T E

You can change the position of icons within a group window by dragging them. Rearrange the icons to suit your personal style.

In addition to group windows, you can also open *program windows*. Many programs run in their own windows. When you start up such a program, its window opens automatically. When you terminate the program, its window closes. (Some programs take over the whole screen instead of running in a window.)

Windows gives you several ways to start up a program, but the easiest and most common is to double-click the program's icon. Works for Windows provides a typical example. When you install Works, it creates a group item called **Microsoft Works for Windows**. (You can see it in Figure 1.3.) Opening the group window reveals the **Microsoft Works** program icon (see Figure 1.8). Double-click that icon to start up Works and open its first window.

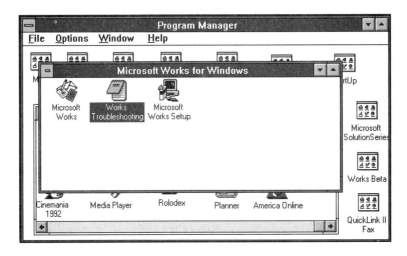

Figure 1.8 *The Microsoft Works for Windows window*

Closing a Window

Various programs provide various ways of closing windows, but there's one method that always works: double-click the **Control Menu** icon (see Figure 1.9). If the window is the primary window belonging to a program, this action also terminates the program. (You might have to respond to questions about saving data and closing files before the program actually terminates.)

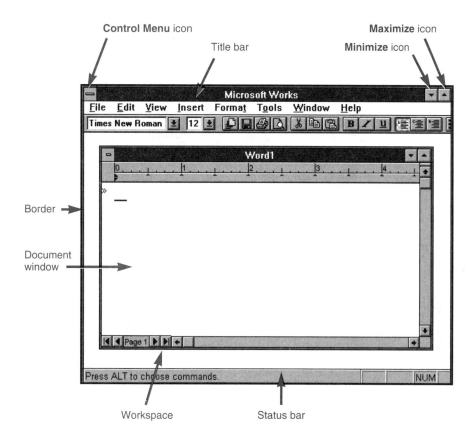

Figure 1.9 *The anatomy of a window*

Activating a Window

There's always one window on your desktop that contains the *focus*, any actions you take apply to this window. You can tell which window has the focus because its title bar (see Figure 1.9, which identifies important window features) is highlighted. In Figure 1.10, the Calculator window contains the focus. If the active window includes child windows, one of them may contain the focus; in that case, both the parent window and the active child window have highlighted title bars. In Figure 1.3, the Applications window within the Program Manager window is active.

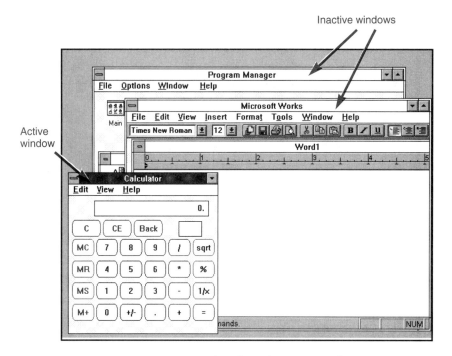

Figure 1.10 *Identifying the active window*

A *cursor* often appears in the active window to indicate where you are within the window. It might take the form of a typing cursor if the window lets you edit text, or it might be a highlight of some kind indicating the currently selected object. In Figure 1.3, you can see that the label under the **Collage** icon is highlighted. This is the cursor. If you pressed **Enter** right now, the Collage window would open.

Click a window to activate it. The window pops to the top of the pile of windows, and the cursor appears in the position you click. (If you don't click a valid position, the cursor probably resumes its last position in that window.)

If you have so many windows open that you can't see the one you want, double-click a blank space on the desktop or press **Ctrl+Esc** to pop up a list of all the open windows (see Figure 1.11). This is called the Task List. Simply double-click the name of the desired window to bring it to the top of the pile and activate it.

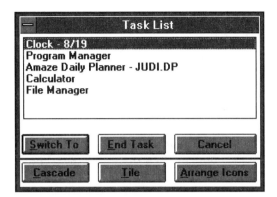

Figure 1.11 *The Task List*

Moving a Window

You can move a window simply by dragging its title bar. As you drag it, only a gray border moves with your pointer. Move the border to the desired new location. When you release the mouse button, the window moves to fit the border.

If a window has no title bar, it can't be moved.

N O T E

Sizing a Window

If a window has a border (see Figure 1.9), it can be sized. Drag the border in or out to shrink or expand the window. When the pointer is positioned correctly over the border, it becomes a two-headed arrow. This shape indicates that you can drag the border. If you drag a side or top border, you change the proportions of the window. You can also drag a corner to resize the window without changing its proportions. When the two-headed arrow points diagonally, you're positioned over a corner.

Maximizing a Window

You can expand a window to fill the entire screen by maximizing it. Click the **Maximize** icon (see Figure 1.9) to do this. (If a window doesn't have a **Maximize** icon, it can't be maximized.) If the window is a child, it expands to fill its parent window's workspace. The maximized window covers any other windows that are open.

The maximized window can't be moved or resized; in fact, it has no border. The **Maximize** icon becomes a **Restore** icon (see Figure 1.12). Click the **Restore** icon to restore the window to its former size and location.

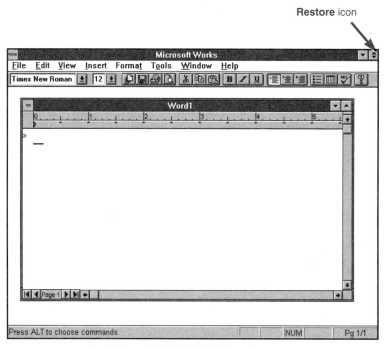

Figure 1.12 *The **Restore** icon*

When the active window is maximized, it covers all the other open windows. That makes it a little more difficult to activate another window. You can't click another window, nor can you double-click the desktop to pop up the Task List. But there is a solution: Press **Ctrl+Esc** to pop up the Task List.

Minimizing a Window

If you want to put aside a window for a while, without actually closing it, you can *minimize* it. Minimizing the window changes it into an icon that is parked in the lower part of the desktop. In Figure 1.3, the **Clock** icon at the bottom of the screen represents a minimized window for the Clock program. Click a window's **Minimize** icon (see Figure 1.9) to minimize it. Double-click the minimized icon to restore the window to its former size and location.

What's the difference between minimizing a window and closing it? The program in the minimized window continues to run. If it's working on a long task, such as sorting a database, it continues that task even while you're working in another window. In the case of the Clock program, its minimized window continues to show the current time.

NOTE

Clock is in the Accessories group. Many people keep the minimized Clock window on their desktop to see the time while they work.

If a minimized window contains some data, the data file remains open, and you don't lose your place in it. When you restore the window to its former size, the cursor is in the same position it was in before. But if you close the window, the program terminates, all tasks are stopped, and all data files are closed.

NOTE

Minimize a window when you want to put it aside for a while. Close a window when you're done with the program and its data.

A minimized window retains many of the characteristics of a regular window. You can activate it by clicking it, and you can move it by dragging it (even though it doesn't have a title bar). You can't, however, resize it while it is minimized.

Moving a minimized icon affects the location of the icon only; when you restore the window to its regular size, it is restored to its former location.

N O T E

Menu Basics

Most windows contain a *menu bar* directly under the title bar. A menu lets you use your mouse to execute commands. The window in Figure 1.13 includes eight menus: File, Edit, Select, and so on. In the example, the Edit menu is pulled down. Click a menu's name in the menu bar to pull it down.

Figure 1.13 *A sample menu*

Each line on the menu is a command; click the command to execute it. In the example, you would click the word **Delete** to delete something. If the name of a key appears next to the command, you can also press that key to execute the command. This is often called a *shortcut key* because you don't have to pull the menu down to use it. In other words, in the example, you can delete something in one step by pressing the **Del (Delete)** key. Or you can do it in two steps by pulling down the Edit menu and clicking **Delete**.

N O T E

In talking about menu commands, this book includes the name of the menu as the first word of the command. The expression **Edit Delete** means the **Delete** command on the Edit menu. **File Page Setup & Margins** refers to the **Page Setup & Margins** command on the File menu.

Commands displayed in light gray text are not available at this time. In the example, the **Cut** command is not available because no text is selected, so there's nothing to cut.

Commands ending in ellipses (...) need more information before they can be executed. Selecting such a command opens a *dialog box*, where you must provide the extra information. In the example, the **Headers & Footers** command leads to a dialog box where you tell Works, among other things, what text you want to include in the header or footer.

Dialog Box Basics

Figure 1.14 shows an example of a dialog box. As you can see, it looks something like a window. It has a title bar and a **Control Menu** icon, but it doesn't have a border or **Minimize** or **Maximize** icons. Thus, you can move it, but you can't change its size. It also doesn't have a menu bar.

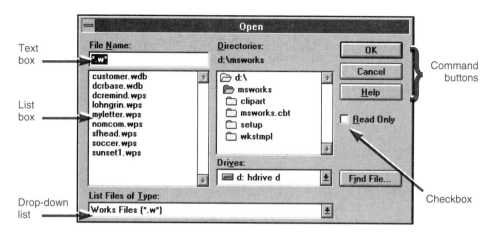

Figure 1.14 *Sample dialog box*

When a dialog box appears, you must deal with it. Most applications won't let you do anything else until you close the dialog box. (You might be able to activate another window, but when you come back, the dialog box will still be there.)

The sample dialog box in Figure 1.14 has several types of *controls*: a text box, list boxes, drop-down boxes, a checkbox, and some command buttons, which are defined as follows:

❖ **Text Box** A text box lets you type information. To use it, click the text box to place the cursor in it. Then start typing. You can move the cursor and delete and replace text just as you do in any Windows text situation. (You'll learn more about how to do this when you study Works' Word Processor.)

❖ **List Box** A list box contains a list of items to select from. Click an item to select it.

❖ **Drop-Down List** A drop-down list is a type of list box, but the list appears only when you request it. To drop down the list, click the arrow at the right end of the box. Then select the desired item. When you select an item, it appears in the box at the top of the list. Click the arrow again to remove the list.

A closed drop-down box looks similar to a text box, but you can't type text in it. If you place the cursor in the box and try to type something, the list drops down and the cursor moves to the item that starts with the last character you typed.

- ❖ **Combo Box** A combo box looks just like a drop-down list except you can type in the text box at the top. You can either select an item from the list or type its name in the box.

- ❖ **Checkbox** A checkbox represents an item that can be turned on or off. When an X appears in the box, the item is on. Otherwise, it's off. Click a checkbox to toggle its status on or off. You can click anywhere in the box or its associated label.

- ❖ **Command Button** A command button causes an action to take place. Most dialog boxes have at least three command buttons: **OK**, **Cancel**, and **Help**. The **OK** button closes the dialog box and executes the original command using the information you have provided. The **Cancel** button closes the dialog box and cancels the original command; any changes you made are dismissed. The **Help** button opens a Help window that explains the items in the dialog box. Many dialog boxes have additional command buttons, such as the **Find File** button in Figure 1.14.

If a command button ends with ellipses, such as the **Find File** button, it causes another dialog box to open.

- ❖ **Radio Button** Some dialog boxes include radio buttons (see Figure 1.15). In a group of radio buttons, one and only one item must be selected at all times. Click an item to select it.

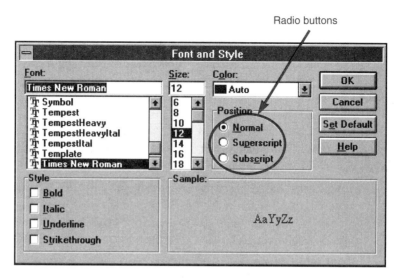

Figure 1.15 *Another sample dialog box*

In the example, **Normal** is selected, as indicated by the black dot in the circle. If you click **Subscript**, **Subscript** becomes selected and **Normal** becomes deselected. The difference between a group of checkboxes and a group of radio buttons is that any number of checkboxes in a group can be selected, or they can all be turned off, as they are in the Style group in the example.

Setting Up a Few Windows Parameters

You don't have to live with Windows' default setup. You've already seen how to tailor the mouse for your own style. And you know how to resize and reposition windows. If you want Windows to remember the changes for future sessions, turn on the **Save Settings on Exit** option. The following procedure shows you how to do this:

❖ **To save Windows settings:**

1. In the Program Manager window, pull down the **Options** menu (see Figure 1.16).

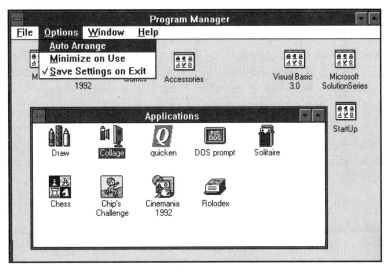

Figure 1.16 *Options menu*

2a. If a check mark appears next to the **Save Settings on Exit** command, it is already turned on. Click **Options** again to close the menu.

2b. If there is no check mark next to **Save Settings on Exit**, click it. (This selects the option and closes the menu.)

If you want to make sure the option is on, pull the menu down again. You should see the check mark. Click **Options** again to remove the menu without changing the setting of **Save Settings on Exit**.

Turning on this option causes Windows to record the size and position of all open windows and of icons within windows when you exit Windows. The next time you start up Windows, the desktop will look the same as it did when you exited.

You don't need to turn on **Save Settings on Exit** to record the configuration changes you make in dialog boxes such as the Mouse dialog box. Those are remembered automatically.

The StartUp Group

One of the standard Windows groups is called *StartUp*. Any programs placed in this group are started up automatically whenever you start up Windows. By default, the group is empty. You might want to place such programs as Clock and Microsoft Works in the StartUp group.

You can move a program from one group to another simply by dragging its icon. Open the group window containing the program's icon, grab the icon with your mouse pointer, drag it so that it's over the new group's icon (you don't have to open the new group's window), and drop it.

When the mouse pointer is over an area where you can't legitimately drop the program icon, it changes into a "no" symbol. When it's positioned properly over a group icon, it changes back into icon of the program that's being dragged. Then you can drop it.

N O T E

To move a program to the StartUp Group, simply drag its icon to the **StartUp** group icon. For example, if you want to start up the Clock program every time you start Windows, open the **Accessories** group, find the **Clock** program icon, drag it to the **StartUp** group icon, and drop it. If you want to move the Works for Windows program to the Startup group, open the **Microsoft Works for Windows** group, drag the **Microsoft Works** icon to the **StartUp** group icon, and drop it.

If memory is limited in your system, don't try to run too many programs at once. If you get frequent "Out of Memory" messages, or if your applications run exceptionally slowly, close as many programs as possible to free up memory space. You might want to remove some programs from your StartUp group if this happens often.

N O T E

Minimize on Startup

When you place a program in Windows' StartUp group, you might want it to start up with its window minimized. For example, the Clock program displays a small clock that continues to show the correct time and date when minimized;

there's very little reason to open the full Clock window except to access its menus so you can configure it. The following procedure shows you how to set up a program such as Clock so that it will be minimized on startup.

❖ **To minimize a program on startup:**

1. Click the program's icon once to select it without opening it. The icon's label should highlight.

2. In the Program Manager Window, click the **File Properties** command. The Program Item Properties dialog box opens (see Figure 1.17).

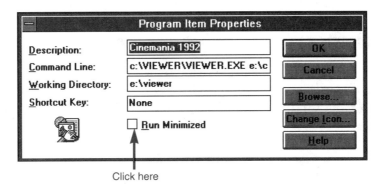

Click here

Figure 1.17 *Program Item Properties dialog box*

3. Click **Run Minimized**. (An X appears in the checkbox.)
4. Click **OK** to close the dialog box.

If you change your mind about minimizing on startup, repeat the above procedure to undo it. In Step 3, the *X* should disappear.

N O T E

Exiting Windows

To exit Windows, double-click the **Control Menu** icon in the Program Manager window. If any programs are still running, you might have to respond to messages about closing your files.

How to Get Help

No matter what you're doing in Windows, on-screen help is always available. You can access it from a Help menu or by pressing the **F1** key.

The Help Menu

Most Windows applications include Help on their menu bar. Figure 1.18 shows Program Manager's Help menu, which is fairly typical of the ones you'll find in applications. Most of these commands open the Help window, which is independent of the application's window. Once the Help window is open, you can get to any part of the Help library. The command you select on the Help menu merely determines the initial information in the Help window. The commands are briefly described as follows:

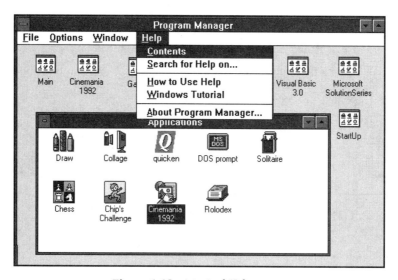

Figure 1.18 *A typical Help menu*

❖ **Contents** This opens a table of contents for the current application's help library. (Each application has their own Help library, although they all use the standard Windows Help window.)

❖ **Search for Help on** This command opens Help's Search dialog box so that you can enter a phrase, such as "exit," and see a list of topics that include that phrase.

❖ **How to Use Help** This command opens a table of contents of topics about the Help system itself. Use these topics to learn how to use the Help window and the Search dialog box.

❖ **Windows Tutorial** This command starts the Windows Tutorial program, which guides you through your first steps in using your mouse and Windows. (This command does not access the regular Help window.)

❖ **About Program Manager** This command opens an About dialog box that shows you the version number, copyright information, and other information for Program Manager (see Figure 1.19). Most applications include an About dialog box. If you call the vendor's product support staff because you're having problems with an application, they might ask for information from this dialog box so they'll know exactly which version you're working with. (This command does not access the regular Help window.)

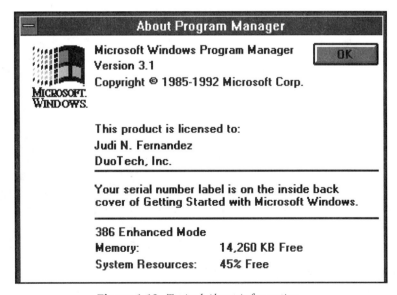

Figure 1.19 *Typical About information*

You'll learn more about using most of these Help facilities in Chapter 2, when you start working with Works for Windows.

Summary

In this chapter, you have learned how to:

- ❖ Start and stop Windows
- ❖ Use your mouse to control Windows
- ❖ Manage a window
- ❖ Start up a program
- ❖ Use menus and dialog boxes
- ❖ Access on-screen help

Now you're ready to start learning specifically about Works for Windows. Chapter 2 introduces you to Works.

Installing and Starting Works

If you haven't yet installed Works, the first part of this chapter guides you through the process. It's a good idea to install Works before continuing with this book so that you can practice new techniques as you read about them. If Works is already installed, you can skip to the section titled *Starting Works*. The remainder of this chapter shows you how to start Works, use a variety of on-screen Help features, and exit Works.

Specifically, this chapter shows you how to:

- ❖ Install Works for Windows 3.0
- ❖ Start up Works
- ❖ Exit Works
- ❖ Start up and use the Works Tutorial

❖   Start up and use the Works Help library

❖   Open and use Cue Cards

Installing Works for Windows

If you haven't yet installed Works for Windows, this section guides you through the process. Installation is fairly easy, especially if you have experience in installing other Windows applications.

The biggest decision you must make is whether to install all of Works or just a part of it. If you decide on a partial installation, you must also decide which part. You can choose the minimum installation or the minimum plus some optional facilities. These choices are more fully explained shortly.

System Requirements

Your PC needs to include at least the following features before you can install Works for Windows:

❖   An 80386 or higher microprocessor

❖   At least 2 M of RAM

❖   A VGA or better monitor

❖   A floppy disk drive, which must have a higher capacity than the old 5.25-inch, double-density (360 K) drives

❖   MS-DOS version 3.1 or later

❖   Microsoft Windows version 3.1 or later

A mouse is not actually required but is strongly recommended. Like all Windows applications, Works was designed for mouse control.

For a full installation, you'll also need at least 14 M of free space on your hard disk. If you have less than that, you can install part of Works for Windows, but you won't be able to install all of it. (You need about 4 M for the minimum installation.)

Starting the Installation

The following procedure shows you how to start the Works installation program, which is named Setup.

❖ **To start Setup:**

1. Start Windows.

2. Close all open applications; the only open window should be the Program Manager window.

3. Insert the Works floppy disk labeled Setup in the appropriate disk drive.

4. In Windows' Program Manager window, pull down the File menu. (See Figure 2.1.)

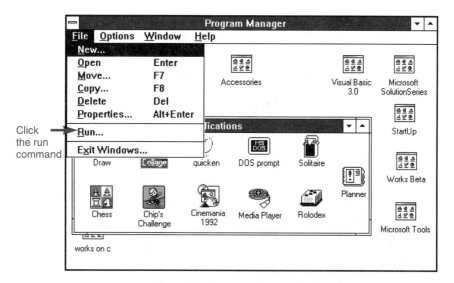

Figure 2.1 *Program Manager's File menu*

5. Choose the **Run** command. The Run dialog box opens (see Figure 2.2).

Enter **A:SETUP** or **B:SETUP**

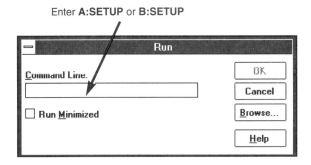

Figure 2.2 *Program Manager's Run dialog box*

6. Type **A:SETUP** or **B:SETUP**, depending on whether the Setup floppy disk is in drive A or B.

7. Click the **OK** button. The Setup program starts up.

The next thing you'll see is the Setup window (see Figure 2.3) containing a welcome message. Click OK when you're ready to continue.

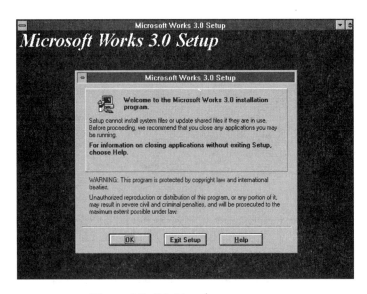

Figure 2.3 *Setup's welcome message*

Eventually, you'll be asked what directory you want to use for Works (see Figure 2.4). By default, Works creates its own directory as a child of the root directory on drive C; the new directory is named C:\MSWORKS. If you want to install Works on a different drive, change the drive name in this window. For example, if you want to install Works on drive D, change the name to D:\MSWORKS. There's very little reason to change the name of the directory itself.

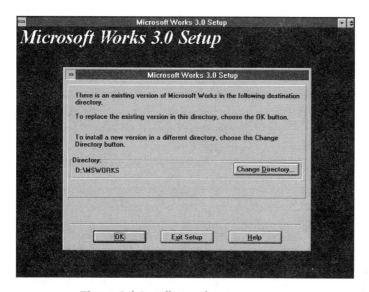

Figure 2.4 *Installation directory message*

If you're installing over an older version of Works, Setup will find the older version and ask if you want to replace it. Installing over the older version won't delete or otherwise harm any data files you have developed with the older version. It just replaces the program files. If you choose not to replace it, you'll end up with both versions of Works in your system.

Next, Setup asks if you want to do a *complete* installation, a *custom* installation, or a *minimum* installation. These options are explained below.

Complete Installation

When you choose to do a complete installation, all of Works is installed in the directory you have designated. You will need about 14 M of space on that drive.

Works examines the drive and warns you if you don't have enough space. If not, you'll have to select a different drive or install less of Works.

If you have more than one hard drive and are installing Works on a different drive than Windows, about 8 M will be installed on the Works drive, but about 5 M will be installed in various Windows directories on the Windows drive.

N O T E

Works is aware of disk compression programs, such as DoubleSpace, and adjusts its space estimates on compressed drives accordingly. When Setup says that you have 10 M of available space on a compressed drive, it means that you can probably install up to 10 M of Works features on the drive. (Don't mentally double the space shown; it's already doubled.)

N O T E

Don't forget that you'll also need some space to store the files that you create with Works. If you fill your only hard drive with the Works program, you'll have to erase something else or keep your data files on floppy disk.

Custom Installation

If you choose to do a custom installation, you must next tell Setup which features to install (see Figure 2.5). Even though it looks like an option, the first item, Program and Setup files, is required. This is the core of the Works program.

When the dialog box first appears, all the options are selected. Uncheck the ones you don't want. When you move the focus to an option, the **Description** box to the right explains that option. The number following each option shows the amount of disk space it needs. Works keeps a running total of the selected options at the bottom of the dialog box.

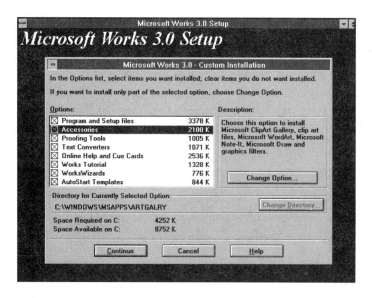

Figure 2.5 *Custom Installation dialog box*

If the **Change Option** button is available, the current option has suboptions. Click the button to see what they are. For example, the suboptions for Proofing Tools are **Spell Checker, Thesaurus**, and **Hyphenation**. You can uncheck any of these that you don't want to install. When you return to the main dialog box by clicking **OK**, the space requirement for the option reflects only the selected suboptions.

Minimum Installation

When you choose to do a minimum installation, Setup installs only the program and setup files. The minimum installation needs about 4 M of hard disk space; Setup warns you if the selected drive doesn't have that much room. In that case, you won't be able to install Works on that drive unless you free up enough disk space.

Completing the Installation

When you have told Setup how much of Works to install and Setup has determined that there is sufficient space on the hard disk, the rest of the installation is automatic. All you have to do is insert disks when requested.

Setup installs Works in a group called Microsoft Works for Windows (unless you specified another one during installation). Figure 2.6 shows what the group window looks like when it is open. You can see that, in addition to Microsoft Works, the group includes Works Troubleshooting. Double-click the **Works Troubleshooting** icon to read suggestions for dealing with problems in Works. To restart Setup so you can review and change your Works installation, double-click the **Microsoft Works Setup** icon.

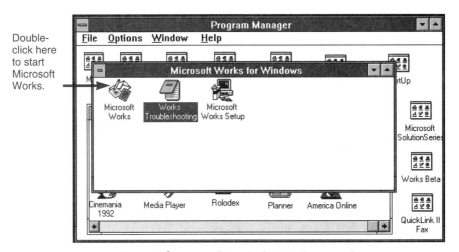

Figure 2.6. *Microsoft Works for Windows window*

Starting Works

To start Microsoft Works, open the Microsoft Works for Windows window by double-clicking its icon in the Program Manager window. Then double-click the **Microsoft Works** icon, as shown in Figure 2.6. The first thing you'll see is a copyright screen. Then the window shown in Figure 2.7 appears. As you can see, you can choose to start a tutorial or to start right in with Works.

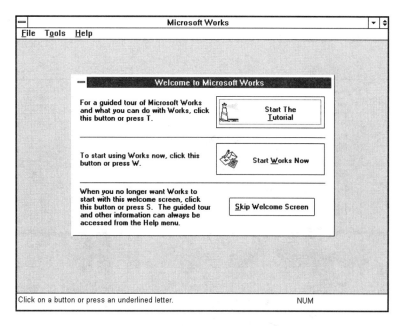

Figure 2.7 *Welcome dialog box*

Using the Tutorial

The Works Tutorial can help you get started with Works, especially if you've never used a word processor, spreadsheet, database, or communications tool before. The first part of the Tutorial is a guided tour of the four tools. (See Figure 2.8 for a sample.) You'll see examples of each tool and how they all work together to accomplish work tasks. The guided tour also contains an overview of what's new in version 3.0. To see the guided tour, click the button labeled **Start The Tutorial** in the Welcome dialog box.

After you have finished the guided tour, the main part of the Tutorial walks through some details on using the four tools. You learn, for example, how to type data in a word processor document and how to enter data in a spreadsheet. You don't have to go through it all. The Tutorial offers menus so that you can pick the topics you want to view. To start this part of the Tutorial, press **Shift+F1** while the Welcome dialog box is showing. (That is, hold down **Shift** while you press the **F1** key.) Notice that you can't access this more detailed part of the Tutorial with your mouse. As long as the Welcome dialog box is showing, you have to press **Shift+F1** to reach it.

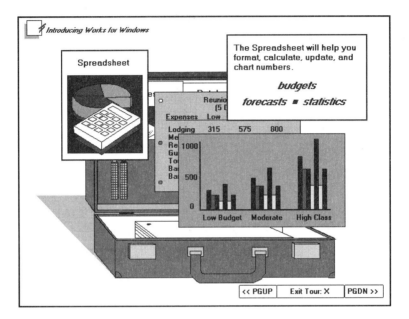

Figure 2.8 *A sample screen from the guided tour*

Once you're in the Tutorial, follow the directions on the screen to get around. Your only options might be **PGDN** to go to the next screen, **PGUP** to go to the preceding screen, and **Exit** to quit the tutorial. (You can see these three buttons in Figure 2.8.) Sometimes you have the option of returning to a menu so that you can choose another topic.

In the Tutorial, you make all your choices by clicking buttons. Or, if you're not comfortable working with your mouse yet, you can press equivalent keys (such as **Page Down**) on your keyboard.

Once you've finished with the Tutorial, there's really no further use for the Welcome dialog box. Click the button **Skip Welcome Screen** to eliminate the Welcome dialog box from future sessions. (You'll still be able to access the Tutorial, as you'll see a little later.)

The Startup Dialog Box

Figure 2.9 shows the Startup dialog box, which appears when you press **Start Works Now** instead of **Start the Tutorial**. This box acts as your main menu for Works. As you can see, you can choose to create a new document using one of the four tools, to open an existing document, to use an Autostart Template, or to use a WorksWizard. You'll learn more about each of these options in later chapters. The **Instructions** button displays instructions on how to use the Startup dialog box.

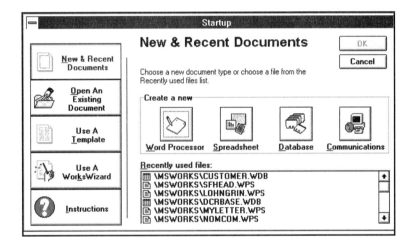

Figure 2.9 *The Startup menu*

Whenever you close a document, this dialog box returns so that you can select your next activity.

Exiting Works

Assume now that you have started Works, created a document, used it to print a form letter, and perhaps transmitted some data to a friend. Now you're back at the Startup dialog box and you're ready to exit Works. You must close the Startup dialog box before you can exit.

❖ **To exit Works:**

1. In the Startup dialog box, click **Cancel** (or press **Esc**). The Startup dialog box closes, leaving the Microsoft Works Window on your screen (see Figure 2.7).

2. Choose **File Exit Works**. (That is, pull down the File menu and choose the **Exit Works** command.)

If you left any unsaved documents open, Works asks if you want to save them. Then it terminates and you return to the Windows desktop.

Getting Help

One of the ways that Microsoft has made Works easier for you is to provide plenty of on-screen help. When you can't figure out how to accomplish a task, you almost never have to turn to a manual; help is at your fingertips.

In addition to the Tutorial, there's detailed documentation available using the Help menu. You also can call up **Cue Cards**, which will guide you through a particular task.

The Help Menu

Figure 2.10 shows the Help menu. You won't be able to pull it down when the Welcome or Startup dialog box (or any dialog box) is on the screen, but it's available at other times. The figure shows what the Help menu looks like when the Word Processor is active; it looks slightly different for each Works tool.

The menu items are as follows:

❖ **Word Processor overview** Provides a one-page introduction to the Word Processor's features.

❖ **Contents** Displays a complete list of Help topics for you to select from (see Figure 2.11)—not just for the current tool, but for all of Works. Just click a topic to select it. Many of the topics on this screen lead to more detailed lists of topics, which in turn might lead to more detailed lists, and so on.

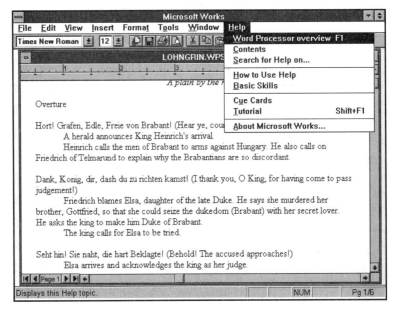

Figure 2.10 *The Help menu*

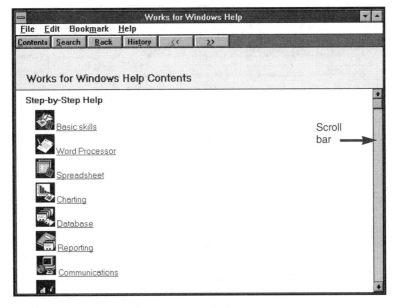

Figure 2.11 *Help Contents*

❖ **Search for Help on** You can often get to a desired topic more quickly by searching for it rather than working your way through several levels of contents. This command opens a dialog box where you can type a word (or phrase). Works displays a list of topics concerning that word. You'll learn how to use this feature a little later in this chapter.

❖ **How to Use Help** Displays a list of topics that explains how to use the Help system, such as Printing a Help Topic, Copying Help Information, and so on.

❖ **Basic Skills** Displays a list of topics concerned with basic skills such as exiting Works, using the Help system, opening a document, and closing a document. The basic skills represent a subset of the complete table of contents. As with the complete contents list, any particular topic might lead to a more detailed list of topics.

❖ **Cue Cards** Cue Cards are quite different from the rest of the Help system. They display a small box at the side of the screen that provides specific steps on how to do something (see Figure 2.12). You'll learn how to use Cue Cards later in this chapter.

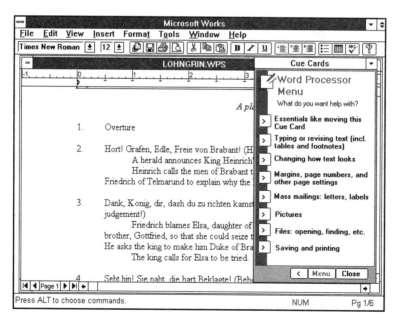

Figure 2.12 *A sample Cue Card*

❖ **Tutorial** Displays the Works Tutorial. Notice that you can access the Tutorial at any time by choosing this command or simply by pressing **Shift+F1**.

❖ **About Microsoft Works** Displays copyright and version information about your copy of Works (along with other information).

How to Scroll in a List Box or Window

When a window or a list box includes a scroll bar, there will be information that won't fit in the window. In Figure 2.11, a scroll bar appears in the window because there are more topics at the end of the list that you can't see right now. You must scroll to see. You can scroll by using your mouse with the scroll bar, as shown in Figure 2.13, or you can simply move the cursor through the box using the cursor keys (**Up Arrow, Down Arrow, Home, End, Page Up**, and **Page Down**). The text in the box scrolls automatically to show the cursor.

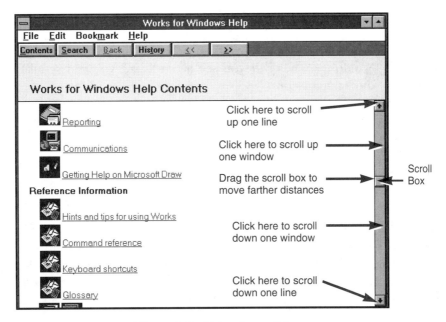

Figure 2.13 *Using the scroll bar*

The amount of text that can be shown at once is called a *page*. (Don't confuse this with the amount of text that can be printed on one page, which the Word Processor calls a page.) The **Scroll Box** shows the position of the current page within the entire text. In Figure 2.11, the **Scroll Box** is at the top of the Scroll bar, indicating that you're looking at the beginning of the text for this topic. But in Figure 2.13, the scroll box is about halfway down, indicating that you're looking at the middle of the text.

You can scroll rapidly by holding down the mouse button on the scroll bar or the scrolling arrows. Scrolling repeats until rapidly until you release the button or there's no more to scroll.

Some windows also have horizontal scroll bars because the text in the window is too wide to be displayed all at once. A horizontal scroll bar works similarly to a vertical one.

When you scroll using the mouse and the scroll bar, the cursor does not change its location in the text. It scrolls with the text. When you find the area where you want to be, you must click the location where you want to place the cursor.

Scrolling is available not just in help windows but throughout Windows. Whenever you see a scroll bar, you can scroll to see more information.

NOTE

Other Ways to Get Help

You don't always have to use the Help menu to see a help topic. There are several other ways to access Help.

The F1 Key

Whenever you press the **F1** key, Works tries to select the best Help topic for what you are currently doing, based on the location of the cursor. For example, if the cursor is currently in the text of a Word Processor document, the **F1** key brings up the word processor overview. But if the cursor is in a Spreadsheet cell, **F1** brings up the Spreadsheet overview.

You can press **F1** at any time, even when a dialog box or menu is showing. With a dialog box, **F1** usually leads to an explanation of that dialog box. (Many dialog boxes have a **Help** button that does the same thing.) With a menu, **F1** usually leads to an explanation of the currently highlighted command.

Learning Works

Works also includes a graphical menu of the Help features called Learning Works. You can access Learning Works from any Works window. Figure 2.14 shows a typical Word Processor window. Notice the **Learning Works** icon. Click this icon to open the Learning Works dialog box (see Figure 2.15).

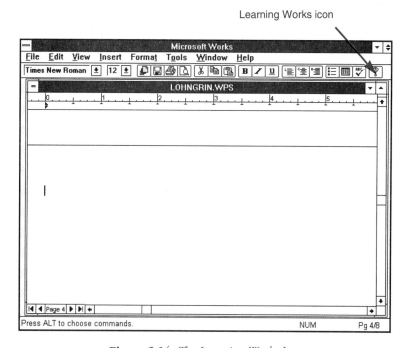

Figure 2.14 *The Learning Works Icon*

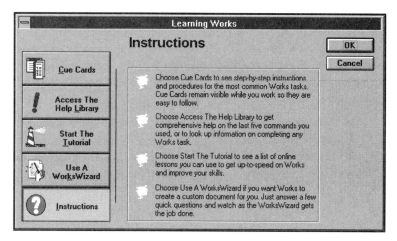

Figure 2.15 *The Learning Works dialog box*

Down the left side of the dialog box are five command buttons. Click **Cue Cards** to start up Cue Cards, click **Access the Help Library** to see the table of contents from the Help library, and so on. The **Instructions** button is selected when the dialog box first appears. It displays the general instructions shown in the figure.

Click **Cancel** to close the Learning Works dialog box.

N O T E

The Help Window

Figure 2.16 shows a typical Help window. This window is mostly independent of the Works window. You can move it, maximize it, minimize it, resize it, and close it without affecting the Works window. Conversely, changes you make to the Works window don't affect the Help window, with one exception: If you close the Works window, the Help window also closes.

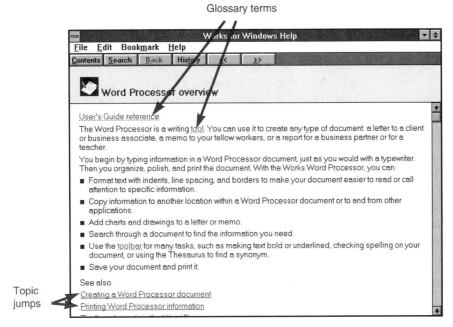

Figure 2.16 *Help window*

Maneuvering in the Help Library

The Help window displays topics from the Help library, which is the main source of documentation for Works. The Help library has longer, more detailed explanations than the Tutorial or Cue Cards. You can also search it for information and switch around from topic to topic.

Once you're in the Help library, you can use the features of the window to link to other parts of the library. The **Contents** button, for example, takes you to the same contents list that the Help menu's **Contents** command accesses. The **Search** button takes you to the same Search dialog box that the **Help Search for Help On** command does. If you click a **Glossary Term**, a glossary box opens to define the term. (Click anywhere to close it again.) A special glossary term, called *User's Guide Reference*, at the beginning of many topics shows you where to read about this topic in the Works for Windows 3.0 User's Guide.

At the end of most topics is a list of related topics labeled "See also". When you click one of these entries, you jump to the indicated topic. And again, you can scroll through the new topic, view glossary terms, and jump to related topics.

Help keeps track of the topics you view. There are two ways to return to previous topics. The **Back** button redisplays the preceding topic. You can back up all the way through your list, one topic at a time, by repeatedly pressing **Back**. The History button opens a dialog box that lists all the topics you have viewed. You can return to any former topic by clicking it in the History dialog box.

Help also maintains a list of all the topics in the Works library, in its own order. The two buttons marked << and >> travel through this list. You might call these buttons **forward** and **reverse**. The >> (**forward**) button links to the next topic in order. When it is dimmed, you're looking at the last topic in the library. The << (**reverse**) button links to the preceding topic in the suggested order. It's dimmed when you're on the first topic in the library.

By the way, the library includes a complete set of topics on how to use Help, so if you're interested in some of the more advanced Help features, such as creating and using **Bookmarks**, you can read about them in the Help library.

The Help Window Menus

The Help window includes several menus. Most of the menu items provide advanced features, but there are a couple of features that you might find handy from day 1:

❖ **File Exit** This command closes the Help window.

❖ **Help Always on Top** This command causes the Help window to stay on top, even when another window is active.

Let's look at how you might use **Help Always on Top**. Suppose you have found the Help topic you want and you want to keep it on the screen to guide you while you work on a document. When you click the document, its window jumps to the top, covering or partially covering the Help window; you might not be able to see the Help text you need for guidance. But if you choose **Help Always on Top**, the Help window stays on top when you return the focus to the document window. You can move the Help window around, of course, so that you can see the area on which you're working.

Help Always on Top is a *toggle* command; click it once to turn it on. (A check mark appears next to it in the menu.) Click it again to turn it off.

NOTE

Searching for Help Topics

Figure 2.17 shows the dialog box that opens when you choose **Help Search for Help On** or when you press the **Search** button in the Help window.

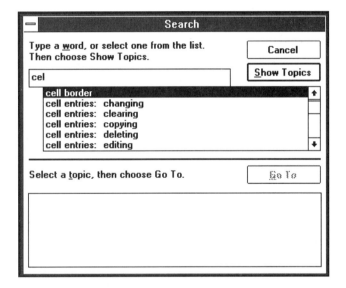

Figure 2.17 *The Search window*

When the dialog box first opens, the text box at the top is empty. You type a phrase, such as **cell**, in the box. With each letter you type, the list box scrolls to show the closest word that starts with the set of letters you have typed so far. You could also scroll through the list of topics until you find one that interests you.

When you find a topic that you want to view, click it and click the **Show Topics** button. A list of topics appears in the lower box. Click the one you want and click **Go To** to view the topic.

When you click **Go To**, the **Search** box closes. You can return to the **Search** box by clicking the **Search** button in the Help window.

The following procedure summarizes the search process.

❖ **To search for a Help topic:**

1. Choose **Help Search for Help On** in the Works window or click the **Search** button in the Help window. The Search dialog box appears.

2. Type a word or phrase in the text box. The upper list box scrolls to show topics starting with that word or phrase.

3. Click the subject you want and click **Show Topics**. A list of topics appears in the lower list box.

4. Click the topic you want and click **Go To**. The Help window opens showing the selected topic.

Cue Cards

Another form of help is provided in Cue Cards, which are not part of the Help library. These cards provide on-screen guidance in common procedures for Works beginners. You might find yourself relying heavily on Cue Cards at first. (They're automatically on when you start up Works for the first time after installation.) You can turn them off when you don't need them anymore.

Figure 2.18 shows an example of a Cue Card on a Works screen. As you can see, the Cue Card is small enough so that you can keep it showing while you work on your document. It stays on the screen until you close it again. (You can minimize it by clicking the **Minimize** icon.)

You must have a mouse to use Cue Cards. If you don't have a mouse and you accidentally open a Cue Card, choose **Help Cue Cards** or press **Shift+F3** to get rid of the Cue Card again.

Open the initial Cue Card, shown in Figure 2.18, by selecting **Help Cue Cards**. You must click **I want help from Cue Cards** to continue. The next card offers a menu of choices such as **Typing and Revising Text**, **Saving and Printing**, and so on. Keep clicking your menu choices until you arrive at the Cue Card you want to work with. Detailed Cue Cards actually walk you through a process. For example, the Cue Card shown in Figure 2.19 explains how to change the margins in a document.

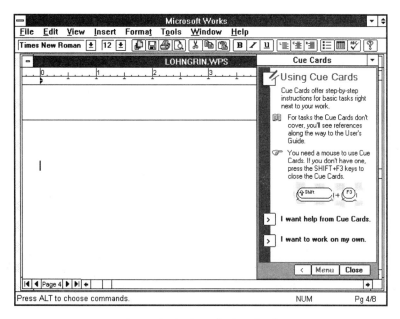

Figure 2.18 *Sample Cue Card*

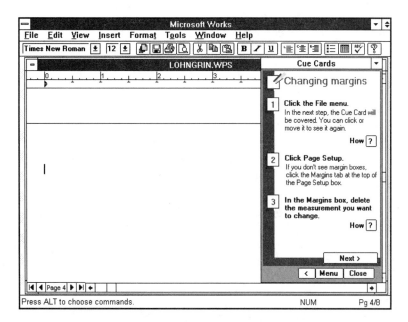

Figure 2.19 *Using a Cue Card to change margins*

This particular process involves more than three steps, but since the Cue Card must be small, only the first three steps show up on the first card. When you have completed these three steps, click **Next >** to see the next Cue Card.

 Click **How ?** to see more details on how to do a particular step.

N O T E

When you're done with a task and want to find another Cue Card, click < to back up one card or click **Menu** to start over with the first menu. If you keep pressing <, you'll back up through all the Cue Cards you have seen so far until you get to the initial card again.

When you don't need Cue Cards any more, the easiest and fastest way to remove them from the screen is to choose **Help Cue Cards** again.

Summary

In this chapter, you have learned how to:

❖   Install Works

❖   Start and exit Works

❖   Use the various Help facilities: the Tutorial, Learning Works, Cue Cards, and the Help Library

In the next chapter, you'll develop an address book and some professionally designed letterhead, then create and print a form letter.

CHAPTER 3

Start Fast with WorksWizards

W hen you install Works, you will probably want to begin immediately. But if you've never used it before, it could take you a couple of days to create your first database or your first letterhead, and even then, they might not look very professional. Works gives you a way to start in using databases and letterheads almost immediately—WorksWizards. With WorksWizards, you add your personal information to professional designs, and you're ready to go.

In this chapter, you'll learn how to:

❖ Start a WorksWizard

❖ Create and use an address book

❖ Create and use your own letterhead

❖   Create and print form letters

❖   Create and print mailing labels or envelopes for your form letters

Starting a WorksWizard

There are three major ways to start a WorksWizard. You can press the **Use A WorksWizard** button in the Startup dialog box (see Figure 2.9) or in the Learning Works dialog box (see Figure 2.15). Both buttons have the same result: The WorksWizard list box takes over the center portion of the dialog box. Figure 3.1 shows how it looks in the Startup dialog box; the Learning Works dialog box is similar. If neither dialog box is open, you can choose **File WorksWizards,** which opens the Startup dialog box with the **Use A WorksWizard** button already selected.

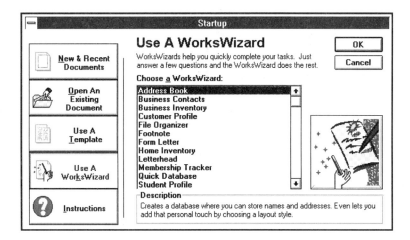

Figure 3.1 *The Startup dialog box with* **Use a WorksWizard** *selected*

Now all you have to do is double-click the WorksWizard you want to use. (You can also click it once and click **OK**.)

Creating an Address Book

The Address Book WorksWizard helps you create a database of names, addresses, and related information. You have some choice in the appearance of the address book and in the information it contains. Once you've learned how to design your own databases, you can modify the address books you create now.

You might want to develop several address books. In general, it's not a good idea to put everyone you know in one address book. Try to think of how you will use an address book to send form letters and print mailing labels. You will naturally separate out groups of people that you address at once—customers, club members, students, donors, and so on. Each group deserves a separate address book so that you can easily print mailing labels, for example, for that group alone.

You'll probably have a miscellaneous set of people left over whom you don't address in any group—Aunt Matilda, your publisher, your Congressional representative, and so on. These people also deserve an address book, even though you won't use it to issue mailing labels or form letters. It comes in handy for addressing individual letters and faxes and for keeping addresses and phone numbers up to date without creating the scratched out mess that most paper address books turn into.

Designing the Address Book

Start by double-clicking **Address Book** in the WorksWizard list box. The Address Book Welcome dialog box shown in Figure 3.2 appears. This screen shows the fields that are automatically included in your database—Date Entered, Mr./Mrs./Ms., First Name, Last Name, and so on. When you have read this screen and are ready to continue, click **Next >**.

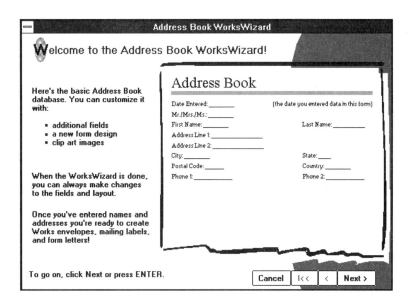

Figure 3.2 *Address Book Welcome dialog box*

The next dialog box, Additional Field Groups, lets you add some optional fields to your database (see Figure 3.3). Each checkbox represents a group of fields. In the figure, the dotted box around **Additional Address** indicates that the focus is on that item; the fields in the display box are the fields that would be added to your address book if you selected **Additional Address**.

Press **Tab** to see what's in the other field groups. Each time you press **Tab**, the focus moves to the next group and the display box shows the fields in that group. (Press **Shift+Tab** to move the focus back to the preceding group.)

To include a group in your address book, click it so that an X appears in the checkbox. If you change your mind, click it again to remove the X from the box. You're not limited to just one extra group of fields; you can select any or all of the checkboxes.

What if you want to include some fields in your address book that the WorksWizard doesn't provide? For example, suppose you're developing a directory of local entertainers and you want to include each person's specialty, fees, and whether they perform for children, teenagers, or adults. The Extra Fields group gives you four miscellaneous fields, called Field 1 through Field 4, that you can use for this purpose.

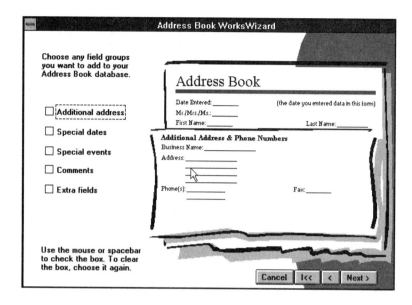

Figure 3.3 *Additional Field Groups dialog box*

Notice at the bottom of the Additional Field Groups dialog box that several buttons are available. The **Next >** button takes you on to the next dialog box when you have selected all the items you want from this one. The < button takes you back to the preceding dialog box. The |<< button takes you to the first dialog box (the Welcome screen) so that you can review and change all your choices; since you're only on the second dialog box right now, it has the same effect as <. But once you reach the third dialog box, |<< and < have different results. The **Cancel** button cancels the entire address book; don't click it unless you want to eliminate all the work that you've done so far. These four buttons are available with almost every dialog box as you develop the address book.

When you press **Next >**, the next dialog box, Style Selection, lets you select a style for your address book (see Figure 3.4). Notice that these items are radio buttons; you must select one and only one item, but you can opt for **No style, thanks**. When the Style Selection dialog box appears, the Professional style is selected and is shown in the display box. Click each style to see what it looks like in the display box. Click **Next >** when you find the style you want.

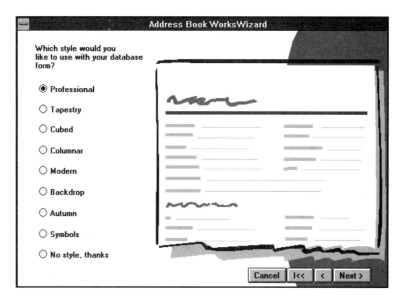

Figure 3.4 *Style Selection dialog box*

By the way, the style controls the appearance of your address book on your monitor screen only; it does not affect the way addresses are printed out on letters, envelopes, mailing labels, and so on. So go ahead and choose a style that appeals to you; you can always change it later.

The next dialog box depends on which style you choose. With some of the styles, you're done designing the address book and are ready to start using it. With others, you have the chance to choose artwork to fit with the style. Figure 3.5 shows the Art dialog box, which appears if you go with the Professional style. You now can choose to include a small drawing on the display.

If you choose to place it on the left or right, the Choose ClipArt dialog box gives you a choice of drawings (see Figure 3.6). The art box on the left shows two clipart drawings. The selected one has a dotted box around it and appears in the display box on the right. There are a lot more drawings. Click the arrowhead icons underneath the box to scroll through the entire library. Click a drawing to see how it looks in the display box. You can continue scrolling and trying out drawings until you find the one you want to use. If you decide that you don't like any of them, click **No Clip Art**. When you have made your choice, click **Next >** to continue.

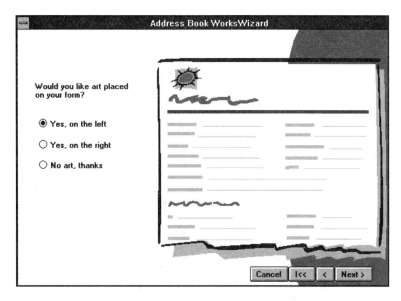

Figure 3.5 *Art dialog box*

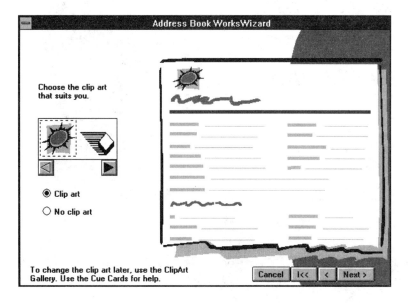

Figure 3.6 *Choose ClipArt dialog box*

N O T E

Other address book styles may have other types of art options. Just follow the directions on the screen to choose an option and continue.

The dialog box shown in Figure 3.7 appears when your design is done. Don't forget that you can review your choices by clicking the < or |<< button. When you click the **Create** button, Works creates your database. You'll see it working, but don't try to interfere; just wait until it's done. A small dialog box keeps you informed of progress. You can click **Cancel** in this dialog box if you change your mind.

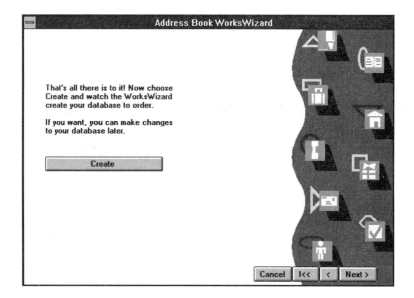

Figure 3.7 *That's All dialog box*

After the database is created, a dialog box tells you that it's ready. Click **OK** to see the first page in your address book. You're now ready to start entering data.

The following procedure summarizes the address book design process.

❖   **To design an address book:**

1.   In the WorksWizards list box, double-click **Address Book**. The Welcome dialog box opens (see Figure 3.2).

2.   Click **Next >**. The Additional Field Groups dialog box appears (see Figure 3.3).

3.   Press **Tab** and **Shift+Tab** to review the additional field groups. Check the ones you want to use in your address book. Then click **Next >**. The Style Selection dialog box appears (see Figure 3.4).

4.   Click the various radio buttons to see what the styles look like. When you find the one you want, click **Next >**. If an Artwork dialog box appears, go on to Step 5. Otherwise, go on to Step 6.

5.   If you are given a choice of artwork, review the artwork options and select the one you want. Then click **Next >**. The Create Database dialog box appears (see Figure 3.7).

6.   Click **Create** to create the address book you have designed. Works creates the database. When it's ready, the Ready dialog box appears.

7.   Click **OK**. WorksWizards closes and the first record of the address book appears on the screen.

Entering Data into the Database

Figure 3.8 shows a sample database using the standard fields and the Professional style. Each entry in a database is called a *record*. It's equivalent to one card in your Rolodex or one line in a telephone book. There are a couple of ways of looking at your database; the one in the figure is called *Form view* because each record is displayed on that form you designed using WorksWizards. You work on one record at a time. Don't forget that you can call up Cue Cards to guide you as you enter data by choosing **Help Cue Cards.**

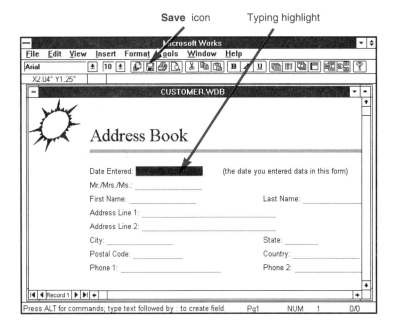

Figure 3.8 *Sample Address Book*

In the figure, the first field is highlighted, waiting for you to type a date. Works recognizes dates in any of these formats:

12/1/93   12/1   Dec 1, 1993   Dec 1

Press **Ctrl+;** (**Ctrl+semicolon**) to enter today's date.

Press **Tab** to move to the next field or click the field where you want to enter data. Keep typing data in fields until you have completed the first record. (You are not required to fill in all the fields.)

If you want to change a field, click it or tab to it to highlight it. Then type the new information to replace the former information.

When you're ready to start the next record, press **Ctrl+PageDown**. (There are other ways to get there, but this is the easiest.) At the bottom of the window is a status bar; at the left end is a box showing the current record number. You can also click on the arrowheads next to that box to move back and forth among the records. The outer arrowheads (with I marks), jump to the first or last record. The inner arrowheads move one record at a time.

You don't have to enter records in alphabetical order (or any other order). You can ask Works to sort your database whenever you like.

N O T E

Be sure to save your address book. Click the **Save** icon (indicated in Figure 3.8) or choose **File Save** to open the Save dialog box shown in Figure 3.9. Type a name for your address book in the **File Name** text box. The name must have eight characters or less, as in CUSTOMER, STUDENTS, PHONEDEX, FAMILY, and so on. Works will add the extension WDB (for "Works DataBase") to this name, so that the full name is CUSTOMER.WDB, STUDENTS.WDB, or whatever.

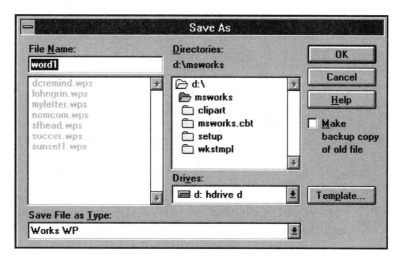

Figure 3.9 *Save dialog box*

Works gives you the option of saving documents in any directory you'd like, and eventually you might want to establish other directories for your documents. But for now, save everything in the Works default directory (MSWORKS) so that you can find them easily. You don't have to do anything special to use the default directory; just type a filename in the **File Name** text box.

When you're done entering records into the database, double-click the **Control Menu** icon to close it. (Be sure to save any unsaved changes.)

Now how do you get back to it later on? The following procedure shows you how.

❖ **To reopen a database:**

1. Return to the Startup dialog box.

2. Click the button labeled **New & Recent Documents**. The dialog box will resemble Figure 3.10.

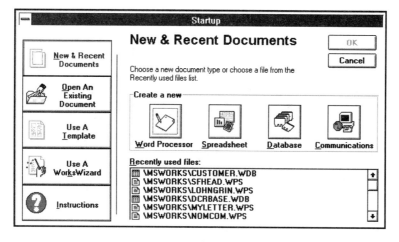

Figure 3.10 *Startup dialog box set up for New & Recent Documents*

3. Double-click the name of the desired database in the **Recently Used Files** list box.

Designing Your Letterhead

Now that you have an address book, you can use it to send a form letter. But first, you might want to design a letterhead. In the WorksWizard list box, double-click **Letterhead**.

Designing your own letterhead is much like designing your address book. In a series of dialog boxes, Works asks you for the information to display on the letterhead (name, address, etc.) and lets you choose from a variety of letterhead styles. The four buttons |<<, <, **Cancel,** and **Next >** appear at the bottom of most dialog boxes.

Figure 3.11 shows the Letterhead Data dialog box in which you supply the name, address, and other information you want on the letterhead. Fill in only the boxes you want to use. For a company letterhead, for example, you might want to omit your name and title. For a personal letterhead, you would not enter a company name or job title.

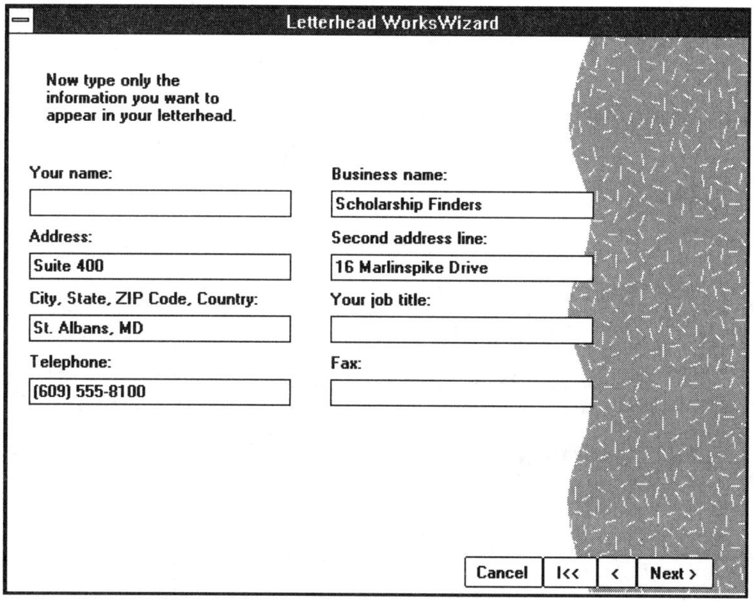

Figure 3.11 *Letterhead Data dialog box*

Figure 3.12 shows the Letterhead Styles dialog box where you select a letterhead style. Click each style and examine the results in the display box. When you see the style you want to use, click **Next >** to go on. You'll then get a chance to add some artwork to your letterhead.

When you have completed the letterhead design, click **Create** to actually create the letterhead. As with an address book, it takes a few seconds, so be patient.

When your new letterhead appears on the screen, it's in a Word Processor window. You can start right in typing a letter on the new stationery, or you can save just the letterhead (with no letter) and use it for many future letters.

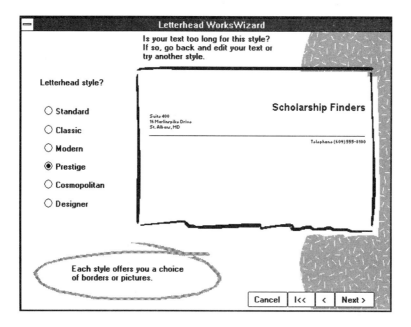

Figure 3.12 *Letterhead Styles dialog box*

To save the blank letterhead, click the **Save** icon or choose **File Save** immediately. Give the document a name such as MYLETTER, LETHEAD, BLANKLET, or some such. Works will add the extension WPS to the file name. Then close the letterhead window.

The following procedure shows you how to use the blank letterhead to create and print a letter.

❖ **To create and print a letter using your new letterhead:**

1. In the Startup dialog box, press the **New & Recent Documents** button. A list box of recently used documents appears (see Figure 3.10).

2. Double-click the name of your blank letterhead document. The letterhead document opens.

3. Type the letter, but don't save it.

4. Find the **Printer** icon (see Figure 3.13). Click it to print the letter.

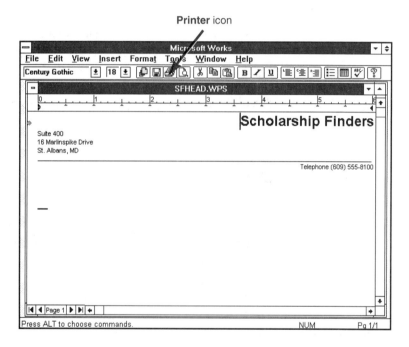

Figure 3.13 *The* ***Printer*** *icon*

A dialog box opens while the letter is printing.

If you want to save a copy of the letter on disk, choose **File Save As** and give the letter a new name. Don't click the **Save** icon or choose **File Save** or you'll overwrite your blank letterhead file with the new letter. But if you do accidentally save the letter in your letterhead file, there's no great harm done. The following procedure resaves both files where they should be. It starts with the assumption that the letter is the active document in your Works window.

❖ **To remove letter text from a letterhead file:**

1. Choose **File Save As** (not **File Save**). The Save As dialog box opens. (See Figure 3.9).

2. Type a new name for the letter file and click **OK**. Works saves the letter under the new file name with the extension WPS.

3. Delete the text of the letter from the open document. (Don't delete the letterhead itself.)

4. Choose **File Save As** to save the blank letterhead in its original file. Works displays the Save As dialog box again so you can specify a name for the file.

Now you have a blank letterhead file and a saved copy of the letter, under two different names.

Sending a Form Letter

Now that you have a database and a letterhead, it's time to send a form letter. From the WorksWizard list box, choose **Form Letter**. When Works asks if you already have a database, choose yes and choose the name of one of your address books. When it asks if you already have a letter, choose yes and choose the name of your blank letterhead.

Next, Works displays the Overview dialog box shown in Figure 3.14. This message overviews what you're going to do in the next window. You don't have to do anything in this dialog box; just read it and press **Next >**.

Now a special window opens (see Figure 3.15). The top half shows all the fields in your address book. The bottom half shows your letterhead, which is blank at this point.

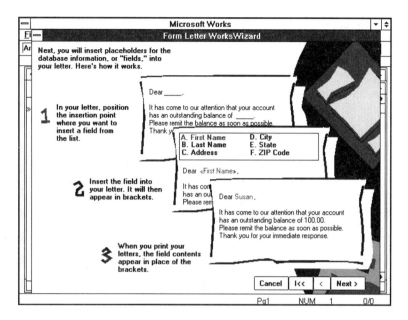

Figure 3.14 *Overview dialog box*

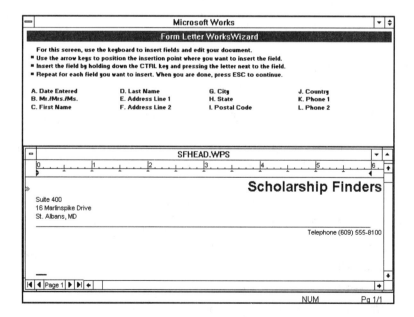

Figure 3.15 *Creating a form letter*

Press the **Down Arrow** key to move the cursor down below the letterhead data and begin preparing your letter. You probably want to type today's date at the top. Then press **Enter** twice to move down a couple of lines. In a casual letter, you probably want to start with a salutation like the following, where <<First Name>> represents the first name of each person in the address book:

```
Dear «First Name»,
```

Type **Dear** followed by a **space** and then insert the placeholder for <<First Name>>. To insert the placeholder, press **Ctrl** plus the letter associated with the field name in the top half of the screen. To insert <<First Name>> from the example in the figure, you would press **Ctrl+C**. Works always inserts a space after a placeholder, and in this case you don't want a space, so you would **backspace** once to delete it and then type a **comma**.

Suppose you're doing a more formal letter and you want to include an address block and salutation for the recipient, like this:

```
«First Name» «Last Name»
«Address Line 1»
«Address Line 2»
«City», «State» «Postal Code»
Dear «Mr./Mrs./Ms.» «Last Name»,
```

The following procedure shows how to set up this address block and salutation using the database shown in Figure 3.15.

❖ **To set up a formal address block and salutation:**

1. Position the cursor where you want the first line of the address block. (You might have to press **Enter** a few times to insert some blank lines before the address block.)

2. Press **Ctrl+C** to insert the <<First Name>> placeholder.

3. Press **Ctrl+D** to insert the <<Last Name>> placeholder.

4. Press **Enter** to start a new line.

5. Press **Ctrl+E** for <<Address Line 1>>.

6. Press **Enter** to start a new line.

7. Press **Ctrl+F** for <<Address Line 2>>.

8. Press **Enter** to start a new line.

9. Press **Ctrl+G** for <<City>>.

10. **Backspace** once to eliminate the space after <<City>> and type a **comma** followed by a **space**.

11. Press **Ctrl+H** to insert <<State>>.

12. Press **Ctrl+I** to insert <<Postal Code>>.

13. Press **Enter** twice to skip a line.

14. Type **Dear** followed by a **space**.

15. Press **Ctrl+B** to insert <<Mr./Mrs./Ms.>>.

16. Press **Ctrl+D** to insert <<Last Name>>.

17. **Backspace** once to eliminate the space after <<Last Name>> and type a **comma**.

18. Press **Enter** twice to position the cursor for the text of the letter.

Now simply type the body of the letter. You can use placeholders within the body to insert information from the database. For example, you might type:

```
We have tried several times to reach you at «Phone 1», but
we have been unsuccessful.
```

When you have finished typing the letter, press **Esc** to finish the WorksWizard. You'll also need to click **Done** on one final dialog box. Then the letter appears in a normal document window and you can review and edit it.

Don't forget to save your form letter. If you want to keep your letterhead file blank, be sure to use **File Save As** to save the form letter under a new name.

It's a good idea to preview it before printing it. Choose **File Print Preview** to see what your letter looks like with real data filled in. Figure 3.16 shows an example of the Print Preview screen. Examining this screen can tell you if the spacing around the placeholders is wrong, for example. Notice that the mouse pointer says ZOOM. If you have trouble reading the text of the letter, click anywhere on the letter to display it in larger print.

Your database must be open before you can print or preview from it. If it's not open, Works asks if you want to open it or use another database.

N O T E

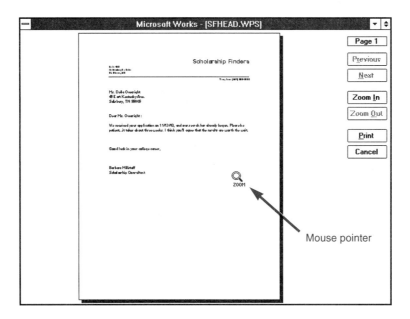

Mouse pointer

Figure 3.16 *Print preview for a form letter*

If your database has more than one record in it, click **Next** to see the next letter and **Previous** to see the previous one.

You can't edit the letter on this screen. Click **Cancel** to return to the document window for editing. When you're ready to print the letter, click the **Print** icon on the toolbar. One copy of the letter will be prepared and printed for each record in your address book.

Printing Mailing Labels and Envelopes

You can use the same address book to print envelopes or mailing labels for your form letter. If your printer can't handle either envelopes or mailing labels, go on to the next section, *Meet Some More WorksWizards*. But if you would like to print envelopes or mailing labels, read on.

Works doesn't include a WorksWizard to create the envelopes or mailing labels. You must do it through the Word Processor. Make sure your form letter document is the active document. Then follow one of the following procedures.

❖ **To print envelopes from the address book:**

1. Choose **Tools Envelopes and Labels**. The Envelopes and Labels dialog box opens (see Figure 3.17).

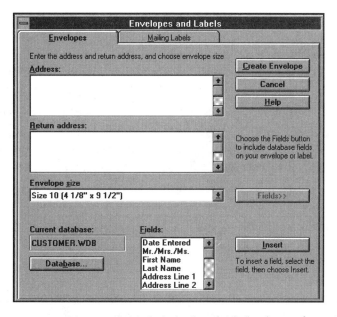

Figure 3.17 *Envelopes and Labels dialog box (with database information)*

2. Click the **Fields>>** button. Database information is added to the bottom of the Envelopes and Labels dialog box as shown in Figure 3.17.

3. Click the **Address** box. The typing cursor appears in the **Address** box.

4. In the **Fields** box, double-click the field(s) that you want on the first address line.

5. Press **Enter** to move the typing cursor to the beginning of the second address line and double-click the field(s) you want on that line.

6. Continue setting up the **Address** box with database fields. Don't forget to adjust spacing and add a comma after the city name.

7. Fill in the **Return Address** box with your name and address. The information in the **Return Address** box will be printed in the upper-left corner of each envelope.

8. Select the correct size in the **Envelope Size** drop-down list.

9. When everything is ready, click **Create Envelope**. The Document window returns with the new envelope displayed at the top.

10. To preview the envelopes with data filled in, click the **Print Preview** icon. Page through the envelopes using **Next** and **Previous** as desired. The Print Preview screen shows you one envelope at a time.

11. If you need to correct the envelopes, return to the document window and choose **Tools Envelopes and Labels** again.

12. When you're ready to print, load envelopes into the printer and click the **Print** icon in the document window.

N O T E

You might also need to choose **File Print Setup** to tell your printer what size envelopes and/or what input tray to use.

Printing on a new kind of paper, especially something as radically different as an envelope, might not always work the first time. You may have to make several adjustments to your printer as well as the Print Setup dialog box. Keep trying until you figure out how to make it work.

❖ **To print mailing labels:**

1. Choose **Tools Envelopes and Labels**. The Envelopes and Labels dialog box opens (see Figure 3.17).

2. Click the **Mailing Labels** tab. The Mailing Labels page appears (see Figure 3.18).

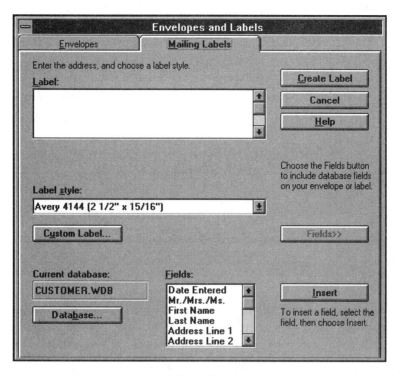

Figure 3.18 *The Mailing Labels page*

3. Click the **Fields>>** button. Database information is added to the bottom of the Mailing Labels dialog box as shown in Figure 3.18.

4. Click the **Label** box. The cursor appears at the beginning of the **Label** box.

5. In the **Fields** box, double-click the fields that you want on the first address line of each label.

6. Press **Enter** to move the cursor to the beginning of the second address line and double-click the field(s) you want on that line.

7. Continue setting up the **Label** box with database fields. Don't forget to adjust spacing and add a comma after the city name.

8. Select the correct label style in the **Label Style** drop-down list.

9. When everything is ready, click **Create Label**. The Document window returns with the new label displayed at the top.

10. To preview the labels with data filled in, choose **File Print Preview**. Page through the labels as desired. The Print Preview screen shows you one page of labels at a time. Make sure the setup on the screen matches the labels that you will be using.

11. If you need to correct the labels, click **Cancel** to return to the Document window and choose **Tools Envelopes and Labels** again.

12. When you're ready to print, load labels into the printer and click the **Print** icon in the Document window.

NOTE

You might also need to choose **File Print Setup** to tell your printer what size labels and/or what input tray to use.

Printing on a new kind of paper, especially something as radically different as a sheet of labels, might not always work the first time. You may have to make several adjustments to your printer as well as the Print Setup dialog box. Keep trying until you figure out how to make it work.

NOTE

If your printer can't handle labels but you have a photocopier that can, you may be able to print the labels on regular paper and photocopy them onto the labels, if you can line everything up correctly.

Meet Some More WorksWizards

You've seen three of the WorksWizards: Address Book, Letterhead, and Form Letter. But what else is available to you? There are several more databases:

Business Contacts   Lists names, addresses, phone numbers, and events.

Business Inventory   Tracks stock numbers, descriptions, locations, and so on.

Customer Profile   Tracks customer names and credit information.

Home Inventory   Tracks your personal possessions.

Membership Tracker	Tracks organizational membership, including such items as date joined, dues paid, and so on.
Quick Database	Provides a general database with up to ten fields.
Student Profile	Tracks classroom and administrative information.

Two other WorksWizards are not databases. **File Organizer** helps you locate missing files in your system. And **Footnote** helps you compose a bibliographical reference in acceptable format by asking you a series of questions. Position the cursor where you want to insert the footnote reference in your document. Then choose **File WorksWizards** and choose **Footnote** to create the footnote.

Summary

In this chapter, you have learned how to use the WorksWizards. You have learned how to start a WorksWizard, create an address book, create a letterhead, create and print a form letter, and print envelopes or mailing labels for your form letter. You have also seen briefly what other WorksWizards are available to you. In Chapter 4, you'll start learning how to use Word Processor.

PART II

Word Processor

Word Processor Basics

I f you created a letter using WorksWizards in Chapter 3, you have already used the Word Processor. It's not just for letters; it helps you prepare any kind of written documents—reports, memos, contracts, newsletters, outlines, books, and so on.

This chapter shows you how to:

- ❖ Create a new Word Processor document
- ❖ Save a document
- ❖ Print a document
- ❖ Set margins and tabs for a document
- ❖ Close a document
- ❖ Open an existing document
- ❖ Set up Works to open the same documents every time

What Can Word Processor Do?

Word Processor helps you prepare a document in your computer's memory, where you can correct and revise it to your heart's content. As you make revisions, Word Processor reworks the paragraphs and pages so that they're always perfectly formatted. You don't print the document until you're satisfied that it's ready. And you also save it on disk so that you can come back and revise it after people have had a chance to review it. In fact, it's becoming increasingly common to let reviewers work on the document on disk, instead of on paper, so that it doesn't get printed until it has been reviewed and approved.

Working electronically instead of on paper saves an enormous amount of time, not to mention paper and ink. Not only that, but making corrections is so easy that most people find they type faster with a word processor because they're not so afraid to make a mistake. In fact, many people who wouldn't dream of doing their own typing 10 years ago now create at the keyboard—they wouldn't dream of writing something in longhand and letting someone else type it.

But that's not Word Processor's only advantage by a long shot. It offers a wealth of features to help you prepare professional-looking documents: a **Spell Checker**, a **Thesaurus**, a **Word Counter**, a clipboard for moving blocks of text around, automatic centering of paragraphs, automatic placement of page numbers and footnotes, a **ClipArt** library, a **Drawing** tool—and that's just the beginning. Word Processor's font capabilities let you select from a variety of typefaces and sizes, and then enhance the text with bold, italics, underlines, strikethrough (for legal documents), superscripts, subscripts, and even color if your monitor and printer can handle it.

And then there's the interface with other Works tools. You've already seen in the preceding chapter how Word Processor integrates with Database to prepare form letters. And, of course, Word Processor also integrates with Spreadsheet to include tables, charts, and graphs in a typed document.

Starting a New Word Processor Document

To start a new Word Processor document from the Startup dialog box, click the **New & Recent Documents** button (see Figure 4.1). Find the box labeled **Create a new** in the middle of the Startup dialog box and click the **Word Processor** button.

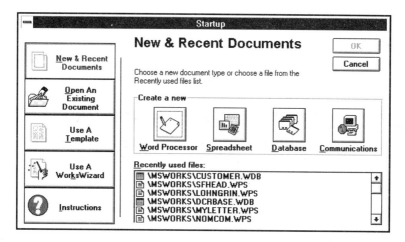

Figure 4.1 *The StartUp dialog box with* **New & Recent Documents** *selected*

If Startup isn't open, choose **File Create New File** to open it.

N O T E

The Word Processor Window

Figure 4.2 shows the Works window with a new Word Processor document open. The title bar identifies the window as belonging to Microsoft Works, which helps when you have several other windows open on your desktop. The menu bar provides the menus for the Word Processor, which are different than the menus for the other tools. The toolbar makes a number of Word Processor features available with a single mouse click. For example, you can save your document on disk by clicking the icon that looks like a floppy disk; you can print your document by clicking the **Printer** icon; you can spell check a document by clicking the tool that says "ABC" with a check mark. All these functions (and more) are also available from Word Processor menus, but they're more convenient on the toolbar. The status bar shows messages, the current page number and total number of pages, and the following status indicators:

NUM Indicates that **NumLock** is on.

CAPS Indicates that **CapsLock** is on.

OVR Indicates that overtype mode is on, insert mode is off.

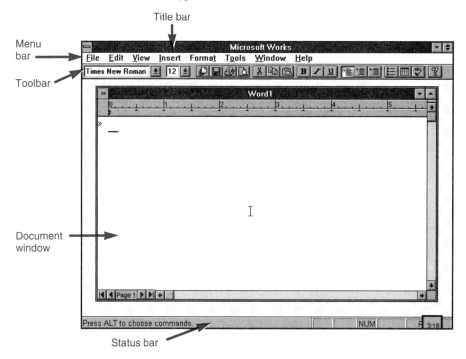

Figure 4.2 *The Word Processor window*

The document window shows the contents of one document, which could be a Word Processor, Spreadsheet, Database, or Communications document. You can have several document windows open at once; they can be all one type or any mixture of types. Only one document is active, and the menu bar and the toolbar in the Works window pertain to that document.

The Document Window

Figure 4.3 shows another view of the Works window; this time the document window has been maximized. Notice that the document window no longer has a border or title bar. The name of the document, "Word1," has been added to the Works window's title bar. The document window's **Control Menu** icon and **Restore** icon appear in the Works window's menu bar. To close the document window, double-click the **Control Menu** icon at the left end of the menu bar. To restore it to its unmaximized size, click the **Restore** icon at the right end of the menu bar.

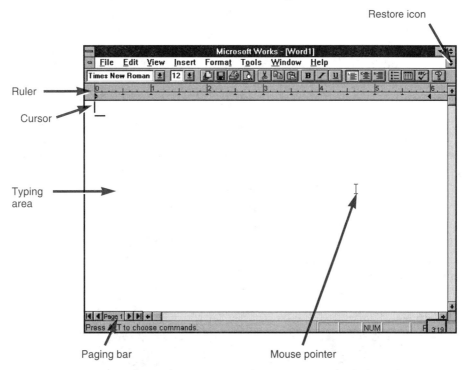

Figure 4.3 *A Maximized Document window*

This document window is a child of the Works window and always stays within its parent's workspace. You can move, size, minimize, and maximize the document window within the limits of the Works window, but you can't move it outside the parent's workspace. When you minimize it, for example, the minimized icon appears in the lower-left corner of the Works window, not the Windows desktop.

The *ruler* provides a guide for locating margins, tabs, indents, spacing between columns, artwork, and so on. Margins and tabs are displayed on the lower half of the ruler. You can even set margins and tabs on the ruler instead of using dialog boxes if you wish; you'll learn how in Chapter 6.

The *vertical* scroll bar (on the right side of the window) lets you use your mouse to scroll up and down in the document, as you have learned to do elsewhere in Windows. The *horizontal* scroll bar lets you scroll sideways when the text is wider than the window.

When the focus is in the typing area, the cursor takes the shape of a flashing vertical bar thin enough to fit between two characters. This cursor indicates where the next character you type will be positioned; in other words, it shows where you are in the document. The page number in the paging bar indicates the page containing the cursor.

The mouse pointer changes shape as you move it around the window. When it is over the typing area, it takes the shape of an "I" bar, as shown in Figure 4.3. The "I" bar is also designed to fit between two characters. One way to reposition the cursor is to click where you want the cursor to be. When the cursor is in other parts of the window, it takes its usual arrow shape. Works includes a feature called **Helpful Mouse Pointers** that pops up small messages as you point at various icons in the toolbar. In Figure 4.4, the mouse is pointing at the **Spelling Checker** icon, and the message Spelling Checker reminds you what this icon does. When you're first working with the toolbar and can't remember what every icon means, the **Helpful Mouse Pointers** come in very handy. Later on, you can turn off this feature.

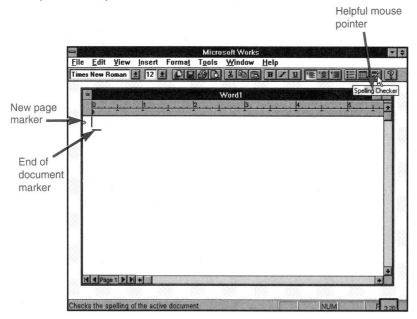

Figure 4.4 *Helpful Mouse Pointer*

There's an intentional delay before the helpful message pops up. That way, you're not annoyed by messages popping up when you don't need them. If you want to find out what an icon does, point to it and wait a couple of seconds.

Figure 4.4 also shows two markers in the typing area. The *new page marker* indicates the top of each page. The *end of document marker* follows the last line in the document. You'll see it move as you add lines to the document.

Creating a New Document

To create a new document, just start typing. If you make a mistake, backspace to erase it and type the correct text. When you're typing narrative paragraphs, you don't have to press **Enter** at the end of every line. Works knows where the right margin is and starts a new line automatically. You should press **Enter** only at the ends of paragraphs. If you're typing some kind of list, you'll want to press **Enter** at the end of every line, of course; Works sees each line in a list as a separate paragraph.

Unless you turn the **Automatic Hyphenation** feature on, Works starts new lines after a space, a hyphen, or some other punctuation mark. It never splits a word in the middle unless that word is longer than the complete line.

If you're like most people, you like to go back and review your work as you go along, making revisions and corrections as needed. You can scroll back and forth in the document by using the scroll bar, or you can move the cursor using the keys shown in Table 4.1 and let the window scroll automatically to keep up with the cursor.

When you scroll using the scroll bar, the cursor maintains its position in the text and you have to click somewhere if you want to make a revision. (If you start typing when the cursor is off the screen, the document automatically scrolls so you can see where you're typing.)

Table 4.1 *Cursor movement keys*

Key	Action
Arrow Keys	Move up or down one line, left or right one character
Ctrl+up arrow	Jumps to the previous paragraph
Ctrl+down arrow	Jumps to the next paragraph
Ctrl+left arrow	Jumps to the previous word
Ctrl+right arrow	Jumps to the next word
Home	Moves to the beginning of the line
End	Moves to the end of the line
Ctrl+Home	Jumps to the beginning of the document
Ctrl+End	Jumps to the end of the document
Page Up	Moves up one window
Page Down	Moves down one window
Ctrl+Page Up	Jumps to the first line in the document window
Ctrl+Page Down	Jumps to the last line in the document window

Saving a Document

As you create or modify a document, your work is stored in the computer's memory, but it isn't saved on a disk until you specifically tell Works to do so. As long as the document exists in memory only, you could lose it if you reboot or turn off the computer, if there's a sudden power outage, or if a program problem freezes up your system (which happens all too often in Windows).

N O T E If one of your Windows applications stops responding, press **Ctrl+Alt+Delete**. Windows will display a message asking you to press **Enter** to terminate the malfunctioning program. Then you should close all open applications, exit Windows, reboot, and start everything up again.

When a document hasn't been saved yet, it has no name. Works assigns it a generic name in the title bar: Word*n*. As long as you see that generic name, you know the document hasn't been saved. As soon as you have spent a few minutes on a new document, you should think about saving it for the first time.

❖ **To save a new document:**

1. Click the **Save** icon in the toolbar (see Figure 4.5). If the document has never been saved before, the Save As dialog box opens.

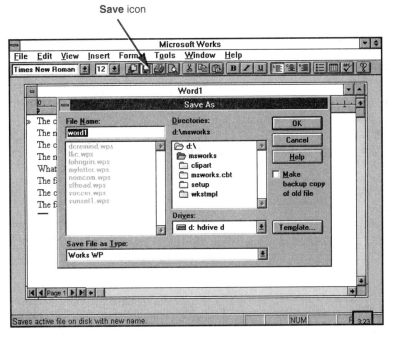

Figure 4.5 *The* **Save** *icon and the Save As dialog box*

2. Type a file name of up to eight characters in the **File Name** text box. Works adds the WPS extension to this file name. By default, the file is saved in the MSWORKS directory.

3. Click **OK**. The file is saved on disk; the Save As dialog box closes; the new file name appears in the title bar of the document window.

Saving a document is like taking a snapshot of its current contents. As you continue creating and modifying the document, the changes once again exist in memory only. The data on disk still represents the last time you saved the file. You could lose your latest changes (but not the saved file) if the computer loses power or reboots. To minimize the amount of work you might lose, save the file often.

After a file has a name, saving it again is easy. Just click the **Save** icon in the toolbar (or choose **File Save**). Works replaces the previously saved version with the current version.

Assigning a New Name to an Old File

Sometimes you don't want to replace the previously saved file with your latest changes. For example, suppose you have a file that contains your blank letterhead. Each time you open it and type a letter, you want to save the letter under a new name, so that the original file contains only the blank letterhead.

❖ **To save a file under a new name:**

1. Choose **File Save As** (instead of **File Save**). The Save As dialog box opens (see Figure 4.5).
2. Type a new name for the file.
3. Click **OK**. Works creates the new file and closes the old file; the Save As dialog box closes; the document title bar shows the new name.

Printing a Document

The easiest way to print the current document is to click the **Print** icon in the toolbar. This prints one copy of the entire document. If you want to print more than one copy, or if you want to print only certain pages, choose **File Print** (**Ctrl+P**) instead. The Print dialog box opens (see Figure 4.6). To print more than one copy, change the 1 in the **Number of copies** box to a higher number.

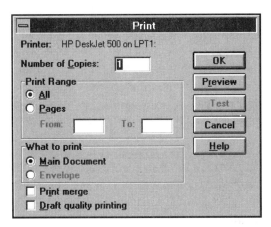

Figure 4.6 *Print dialog box*

❖ **To print a specific page range:**

1. Click **Pages**. The **From** and **To** boxes become available.

2. Click the **From** box and type the first page number.

3. Click the **To** box and type the last page number. (The **To** number can be the same as the **From** number if you want to print only one page.)

4. Click **OK**.

Working with Print Manager

When you print a document, Works sends the print data to a Windows program called Print Manager. Nothing starts to print yet. You'll see a message while Works transfers the data to Print Manager. (You can click **Cancel** in the message box if you change your mind.) When Works finishes transferring the data to Print Manager, the message disappears. Then Print Manager starts printing the document.

Print Manager provides several advantages over printing the document directly from Works. For one thing, Works has to wait only while the data is transferred to Print Manager, a very quick process; then you can go on to work on something else in Works or another program. For another, Print Manager can store up a long list of print jobs, keeping them organized and printing them in order. You don't have to wait for the current job to finish printing before you can order another print job.

 You can open the Print Manager window and pause or cancel print jobs. See Print Manager's Help Library (not Works) to find out how to work with the Print Manager window. Print Manager is located in the Main group.

N O T E

Print Preview

In many cases, you'll save yourself some mistakes, and you'll save paper and ink or toner, if you take a look at what the printed document looks like before you actually print it. Figure 4.7 shows the screen that appears when you click the **Print Preview** icon on the toolbar (it's next to the **Print** icon and looks like a page with a magnifying glass) or choose **File Print Preview**. You can see the text exactly as it will appear on the printed page, including all the inserted material such as headers, footers, footnotes, artwork, database fields, and page numbers.

When the mouse pointer is on the printed page, it takes the shape of a magnifying glass with the word *ZOOM* underneath to remind you of the zoom facility. Clicking anywhere on the page cycles among three distances: far (as shown in the figure), medium, and close. You can also click the **Zoom In** and **Zoom Out** buttons to zoom in or out among the three levels.

Click the **Next** and **Previous** buttons to change pages. The current page number is shown in a box at the top of the button area.

If you decide that the document is ready to print, click **Print** to print it using the default print options. Or click **Cancel** to return to the Document window so that you can use the **File Print** command (to select your own options) or do some more editing before printing. You can't edit on the Print Preview screen; that's why it has no menus or toolbar.

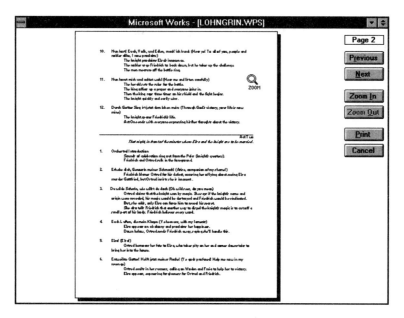

Figure 4.7 *The Print Preview screen*

Margins and Tabs

Works sets default margins for a document at 1 inch on the top and bottom and 1.25 inches on the left and right. The left margin is indicated by 0 on the ruler. Works sets default tab stops every .5 inch from the left margin. Default tab stops are marked by ⊥ symbols on the ruler. You can change the margins and the spacing of the default tabs for a document.

Setting Document Margins

You set margins for an entire document using the **File Page Setup** command. The Page Setup dialog box (see Figure 4.8) has three pages, as indicated by the tabs at the top. Click a tab to see that page. The Margins page is shown in Figure 4.8. Change the document's margins by replacing the values in the text boxes on the left. You can't specify different margins for part of a document, although you can specify indents for individual paragraphs, as you'll learn in Chapter 6.

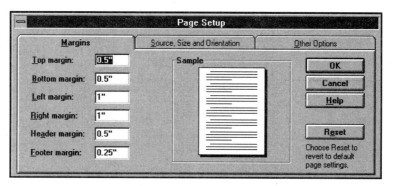

Figure 4.8 *The Page Setup dialog box*

You'll learn how to use header and footer margins in Chapter 6.

N O T E

You don't have to type leading zeros or the " mark for inches. In other words, you can just type **.5** to request a half-inch margin. You can specify margins in centimeters, millimeters, points, or picas instead of inches, if you wish, in which case you must include the unit of measure, as in "2 picas" or "50 millimeters."

Determining the correct margins for your printer sometimes can be tricky. Works assumes that all measurements start from the upper-left corner of the paper. But with tractor-fed printers such as most dot-matrix printers, the starting position might be half an inch or so down from the real top edge of the paper; it could also be inset from the real left edge of the paper, depending on where you set the paper guides. If you want to center the printed area on the paper, you have to compensate for the extra space at the top and left.

Suppose you load your dot-matrix printer so that the print head starts 0.5 inch down from the top and 0.5 inch in from the left. To center the text area with 1-inch margins all around, you would have to define the top margin as 0.5 inch, the left margin as 0.5 inch, the bottom margin as 1.5 inches, and the right margin as 1.5 inches.

Most laser printers (and other types of printers that have cut-sheet paper trays instead of continuous-form tractors) don't have problems with paper alignment, but they often can't print close to the edges of the paper. You should check your printer manual to see if it specifies minimum margins.

Setting Default Tabs

When you don't set specific tab stops for a paragraph, it uses the default tab stops, which are set every 0.5 inch. If you don't like the default spacing of .5 inch, you can change it.

❖ **To set default tab stops:**

1. Choose **Format Tabs**. The Tabs dialog box shown in Figure 4.9 opens.

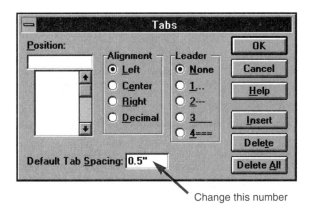

Figure 4.9 *Tabs dialog box*

2. In the **Default Tab Spacing** box, change the number to indicate the spacing you want.

3. Click **OK**. After the Tabs dialog box closes, you'll see the new tab stops on the ruler.

As with margins, these default tab stops affect the entire document. You'll learn how to set specific tab stops for individual paragraphs in Chapter 6.

Word Processor Views

The View menu, in general, controls the way your document is presented to you on your monitor (see Figure 4.10). The second section contains commands that determine the on-screen look of your document.

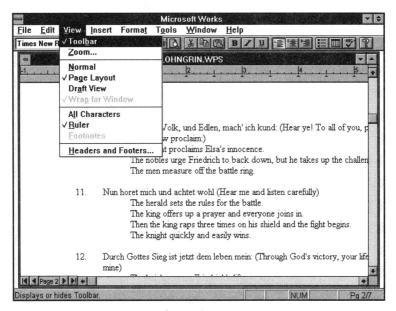

Figure 4.10 *The View menu*

Figure 4.11 shows three views of the same part of a document—the bottom of page 1. (Two of the views include the top of page 2 as well.) **Draft** view is the most efficient; it doesn't show your fonts or artwork—nor does it show page formatting such as headers, footers, page numbers, footnotes, and so on—so it demands less memory space and processor time and you can scroll around in your document faster. But you don't get much of a feel for what your document will actually look like when printed.

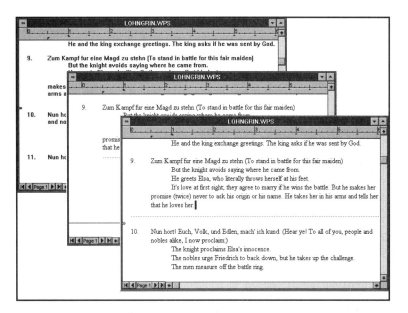

Figure 4.11 *The three document views*

Page Layout view is just the opposite. It shows the page pretty much as it will appear in print. The edges of the page appear as solid lines, and you can see only one page at a time. This view is very close to **Print Preview**, but you can edit the document in this view. (Also unlike **Print Preview**, it doesn't fill in data that is supplied at print time, such as print dates and database fields.) **Page Layout** view is the least efficient view; it demands a lot of memory space for font and artwork information as well as page formatting. It demands more processing time to scroll around in a document because Works has to format every page as you scroll past it. (Works can't figure out what's on page 10 without figuring out what's on pages 1 through 9, even if they're not displayed.) You might notice delays if you scroll long distances, especially if other applications are also demanding processing time.

Normal view is a compromise between the other two views. It shows fonts and artwork but not page formatting (headers, footers, etc.). It keeps track of pages and marks page breaks with a dotted line, but it doesn't present the display as separate pages. **Normal** view is the default view. Most people draft their documents in **Normal** view, then switch to **Page Layout** view to examine and fine-tune the page layout before printing.

Managing Documents

You've already seen how to start a new document and how to save and print your work, but there are some other things that you need to know about managing documents.

Closing a Document

Suppose you are done working with a document and want to close it without exiting Works. Choose **File Close** or double-click the **Control Menu** icon in the document window (not the Works window). If you have made changes to the document that haven't been saved, a dialog box asks if you want to save them. You can click **Yes** to save the changes, **No** to eliminate them, or **Cancel** to cancel the **Close** command and keep the document window open.

What happens after the document window closes depends on several factors. The Startup dialog box might return. Another open document might receive the focus. Or Work's workspace might simply be blank. If you get a blank, you can use the File menu to start your next Works task. **File Create New File**, **File WorksWizards**, and **File Templates** all open the Startup dialog box (with different options selected). **File Open Existing File** opens a different dialog box, as you'll see in the next section.

Opening an Existing Document

After you've created a new document, printed it, saved it, and closed it, you'll probably need to open it again sometime later to make changes to it. When the **New & Recent Documents** button is selected in the Startup dialog box, the list box shows your most recently used files (see Figure 4.1). If you can find the document you want in the list, just double-click it to open it. Otherwise, click the **Open an Existing Document** button to open the dialog box in Figure 4.12.

So far, you have been saving all your documents in Works' default directory, MSWORKS, so you should be able to find any document you want there. Find its name in the **File Name** list box (remember that Works assigns the extension WPS to all Word Processor documents) and double-click it. The file will open in a new document window, and you'll be ready to edit it.

The list of files might also include some databases (extension WDB) and spreadsheets (extension WPS) if you have created those types of documents using Works.

N O T E

You'll learn how to work with other directories in Chapter 7.

N O T E

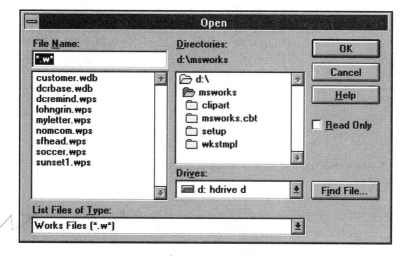

Figure 4.12 *Open dialog box*

Saving the Workspace

If you work with the same set of documents all the time, you might want to open them automatically whenever you start Works. You can set up Works to do that.

Any kind of Works documents can be set up for automatic opening: Word Processor, Spreadsheet, Database, and/or Communications.

N O T E

❖ **To open one or more documents automatically when you start Works:**

1. Set up the workspace exactly as you want it to be when you start up Works. Open all the documents that you want Works to open automatically; close all others. Arrange the open window(s) exactly as you want Works to arrange them. You can even have some minimized documents, if you wish.

2. Choose **File Save Workspace**. Works records the open documents and their window arrangements.

Now you can continue using Works and exit normally when you're done. The next time you start it up, and every time after that, the workspace will be restored to the same condition it was in when you chose **File Save Workspace**. You'll no longer get the Startup dialog box when you start Works, unless it was on the screen when you chose **File Save Workspace**.

You can revise the saved workspace at any time by setting up a new one and choosing **File Save Workspace** again. If you decide that you don't want to start up with the saved workspace anymore, you can turn it off.

❖ **To stop using the saved workspace:**

1. Choose **Tools Options**. The Options dialog box opens. (See Figure 4.13). If you have previously used the **File Save Workspace** command, the **Use Saved Workspace** checkbox will have an *X* in it.

2. Click **Use Saved Workspace** so that the *X* disappears from the checkbox.

3. Click **OK**. From now on, Works will start with the Startup dialog box.

If you change your mind and want to use the saved workspace again, repeat the previous procedure, restoring the X to the **Use Saved Workspace** checkbox.

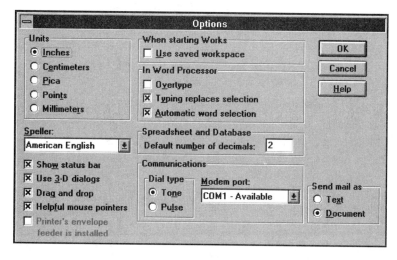

Figure 4.13 *The Options dialog box*

Summary

In this chapter, you have learned how to:

❖ start up Word Processor, create a new document, save it, and print it

❖ set margins and default tab stops for the document

❖ close a document and open it again

❖ save the Works window's workspace so that it will be re-established every time you start up Works.

Now that you have some documents, you probably need to revise them. The next chapter shows you how to do that.

CHAPTER 5

Editing a Document

As soon as you create a new Word Processor document, someone will want you to revise it. Fortunately, revisions are easy. This chapter shows you how to:

- ❖ Select text
- ❖ Delete, insert, and replace text
- ❖ Copy and move text
- ❖ Undo changes
- ❖ Find specific places in a document
- ❖ Create and use bookmarks
- ❖ Count words
- ❖ Set editing options
- ❖ Return to the former (unedited) version of a document

Selecting Text

Many types of changes require you to select text first. You select text by dragging your mouse over it. Position the mouse pointer at one end of the block of text to be selected. Hold down the left button and drag the pointer to the other end. (You don't have to pass over all the text; just go directly from one end to the other.) You'll see an inverse highlight develop as you drag the mouse pointer (see Figure 5.1). The highlight marks the exact text that is selected.

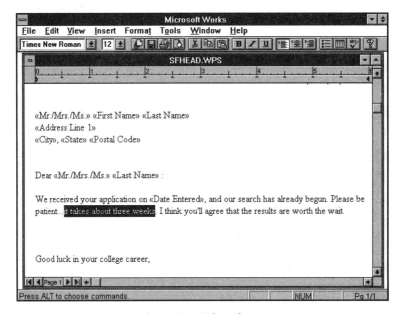

Figure 5.1 *Selected text*

N O T E   There's another way to select a block of text that you might find just as handy. Position the cursor and one end of the block by any means you'd like. You could click one end of the text or use the cursor keys to move the cursor into position. Then hold down Shift and move the cursor to the other end of the block by any means. Again, you could click the other end or use the keyboard to move the cursor to it. You'll see the highlight materialize as you move the cursor while holding down the Shift key.

Works also provides a number of selection shortcuts, as shown in Table 5.1.

Table 5.1 *Text selection shortcuts*

To select	Do this
One word	Double-click the word.
One line	Click the left margin beside the line.
Several lines	Drag the pointer up or down in the left margin.
One sentence	Hold down **Ctrl** and click the sentence.
One paragraph	Double-click the left margin beside the paragraph.
The entire document	Hold down **Ctrl** and click anywhere in the left margin.

Once you have selected a block of text using any of the above techniques, you can adjust the second end of the selection by holding down **Shift** and moving the cursor to a new position. You can't adjust the first end without clearing the selection and starting over.

To clear the selection, move the cursor by any means without **Shift**. You could click somewhere on the screen or press **Home**, **End**, or one of the other cursor keys.

WARNING

When a block is selected, anything you type replaces the entire block. In other words, the selected text is deleted. (You'll learn how to use this feature to your advantage shortly.)

Editing Techniques

Works lets you delete, insert, and replace text, move and copy text, and undo the changes you make in case you decide you don't like them.

Deleting Text

There are a number of ways to delete text:

❖ The **Delete** key deletes one character to the right of the cursor. Hold it down to delete a string of characters to the right.

❖ The **Backspace** key deletes one character to the left of the cursor. Hold it down to delete a string of characters to the left.

❖ If one or more characters are highlighted as a selected block, either **Backspace** or **Delete** deletes the block.

Suppose, for example, you want to delete a paragraph. Double-click the left margin beside the paragraph to select it. Then press **Backspace** or **Delete**. It's as simple as that.

Undoing Changes

Because we all make mistakes, Works lets us undo them. The **Edit Undo** command undoes your last editing sequence. If you delete something, **Undo** restores it. If you replace some text, **Undo** eliminates the new text and restores the original.

Works identifies the beginning of a new editing sequence when you move the cursor or execute a command. When you click a new position or press **Home**, **left arrow**, or one of the other cursor keys, you start a new editing sequence. Choosing a command from a menu or clicking an icon on the toolbar starts a new editing sequence. Everything that comes after that until you move the cursor again or choose another command comprises the sequence. Suppose you move the cursor and type three paragraphs; all three paragraphs would be considered one sequence and **Undo** would remove them all. Suppose you press **Ctrl+Click** to select a sentence, then press **Delete** to delete it. **Undo** would restore the sentence.

If you pull down the Edit menu, the first command says **Undo *action***, where ***action*** is replaced by:

❖ **Typing**—if your last editing sequence added text to the document (or used **Backspace** to delete it)

❖ **Editing**—if the last thing you did was a deletion

❖ **Overtyping**—if you replaced some text

If you're not sure what **Undo** will undo at a particular time, looking at the Edit menu may help. Sometimes it says **Can't Undo**, which means that you haven't done anything undoable since the last time you moved the cursor or chose a command.

To undo your last editing sequence, choose **Edit Undo *action*** or press **Ctrl+Z**. The **Undo** command on the Edit menu immediately changes to **Redo *action***. Choose **Edit Redo *action*** or press **Ctrl+Z** to undo the undo, at which point the command changes to **Undo *action*** again. You can actually sit there and press **Ctrl+Z** repeatedly to pop a text block in and out of your document.

Undo handles more than just typing and deletions. As you'll see later, you can undo the work of the **Spelling Checker**, the **Thesaurus**, the find and replace function, and so on.

Inserting Text

Works offers two basic typing modes: insert and overtype. In insert mode, anything you type is inserted at the cursor position. Any existing text to the right of the cursor is shoved to the right and down as you insert text. In overtype mode, anything you type overtypes (or replaces) the text to the right of the cursor. Most people prefer to work in insert mode, switching to overtype mode only for special tasks. The **Insert** key toggles between insert and overtype mode. When you're in overtype mode, the message *OVR* appears on the status bar. (There is no insert mode message.) If you see that you're in overtype mode and you want to insert some text, press **Insert** once to change back to insert mode.

To insert text in a document, make sure you're in insert mode, position the cursor and start typing. Works reformats the paragraph and the remainder of the document as you type.

Replacing Text

You can overtype text by pressing the **Insert** key to turn on overtype mode, but there's an easier way. Select the text to be replaced and simply type the new text. The first character you type automatically deletes the entire selection. As long as you're in insert mode, not overtype mode, the remaining characters are inserted as normal. The overall effect is to replace the selected text with the new text. The **Undo** command will say **Undo Editing** at this point and will remove the inserted text and restore the deleted text.

Some people don't like automatic text replacement. They make too many accidental replacements by inadvertently pressing a key while a block is highlighted. You can turn off automatic text replacement if you prefer not to use it.

❖ **To turn off automatic text replacement:**

1. Choose **Tools Options**. The Options dialog box opens. (See Figure 4.13.)

2. In the **In Word Processor** section, click **Typing replaces selection**, so that the *X* disappears from the checkbox.

3. Click **OK**. The dialog box closes.

With automatic text replacement turned off, if you start typing when a text block is selected, the block is deselected (that is, the highlight disappears), and the new text is inserted or typed over at the cursor position according to the current insert/overtype mode setting. To resume automatic text replacement, restore the *X* to the **Typing replaces selection** checkbox.

Cutting, Copying, and Pasting

If you need to move or copy a text block, you can do it through Windows' Clipboard facility. The Clipboard is simply a memory area that programs can copy data to and from. You can place a text block in the Clipboard, move the cursor to some other location, and copy the data from the Clipboard again.

There are two ways to place text in the Clipboard: Cut and Copy. *Cutting* deletes the selected text from its original location, whereas *copying* doesn't. You cut text when you want to move it to another location; you copy text when you want to copy it to another location. In either case, you paste the text in the other location.

WARNING

The Clipboard can hold only one thing at a time. When you cut or copy a block of text, it replaces the previous contents of the Clipboard.

The Edit menu contains **Cut, Copy,** and **Paste** commands, but you'll probably prefer the toolbar icons (see Figure 5.2).

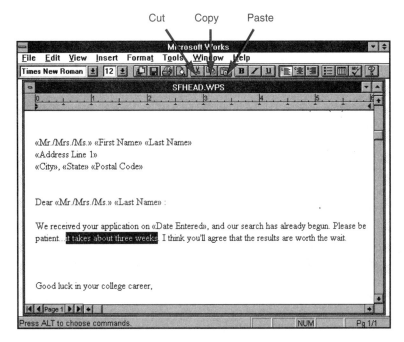

Figure 5.2 *Toolbar icons*

❖ **To move text:**

1. Select the text.

2. Click the **Cut** icon. The selected text is copied to the Clipboard (which you can't see) and deleted from the document.

3. Position the cursor at the desired new location.

4. Click the **Paste** icon. The contents of the Clipboard are inserted at the cursor, whether or not insert mode is selected.

After cutting, **Undo** restores the deleted text, but it doesn't remove it from the Clipboard.

❖ **To copy text:**

1. Select the text.
2. Click the **Copy** icon. The selected text is copied to the Clipboard.
3. Position the cursor at the desired new location.
4. Click the **Paste** icon. The contents of the Clipboard are inserted at the cursor.

Copying a block provides a quick way to create a new item that's only somewhat different from the original. Suppose you had to type the two procedures shown above. You would type the procedure named "To move text" from scratch. Then you could make a copy of it and edit that copy to create "To copy text." That takes much less time (and is less error prone) than typing the second procedure from scratch.

Once text is in the Clipboard, it stays there until some other **Cut** or **Copy** command replaces it. You can continue to paste it wherever and whenever you want. In fact, because the Clipboard is not just a Works feature but a Windows-wide feature, you can paste the contents of the Clipboard into any Windows application that uses the Clipboard. You could, for example, move or copy a block to another Works document, to a Word for Windows document, and to many other documents.

Dragging Text

Another way to move a block is to drag it. Select it, then position the mouse pointer over it. (The message *Drag* pops up on the mouse pointer if you wait long enough.) Hold down the left button and drag the text to the desired new position.

If you want to copy the block instead of move it, hold down **Ctrl** while you drag it. You can also drag information to another document window or non-Works window. But you must hold down **Shift** to move it or **Ctrl** to copy it.

Find and Replace

Sometimes you need to make a repetitive change throughout a document or a section of a document. For example, suppose you need to change "king" to "emperor" everywhere it occurs. You can ask Works to make this change for you. You start by selecting **Edit Replace**. The dialog box in Figure 5.3 opens. You type **king** in the **Find what** box and **emperor** in the **Replace With** box. Then you click one of the command buttons.

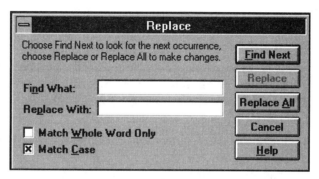

Figure 5.3 *Replace dialog box*

Assume for the moment that you're sure you want to replace all occurrences of "king" with "emperor" throughout the entire document. You could click **Replace All**. The message *Working...* appears in the status bar while Works makes the replacements. When the job is done, Works displays the message *Number of occurrences replaced: nn*. The dialog box stays on the screen so you can set up another replacement if you wish. Click **Cancel** to get rid of it. The **Undo** command now reads **Undo Editing**, and choosing it undoes all *nn* replacements.

Capitalization in Replace Tasks

By default, Works ignores capital letters when searching for text to replace; that is, it replaces "king," "King," and "KING." However, it duplicates the capitalization in the replacement text if it can. That is, it replaces "king" with "emperor," "King" with "Emperor," and "KING" with "EMPEROR." But it can't duplicate the capitalization of "KiNg" and "kiNG;" it considers only the first letter and replaces the former with "Emperor" and the latter with "emperor."

But if you check **Match Case**, Works considers capitalization when searching. If the **Find What** box says "king," Works does not find "King" or "KING" or any other variation on capitalization. It replaces each occurrence of "king" with the exact capitalization shown in the **Replace With** box; it doesn't try to adapt the replacement's capitalization.

Suppose you want to change the capitalization of "king" throughout the document; you want it to start with a capital "K". You would type **king** in the **Find What** box, type **King** in the **Replace With** box, and check **Match Case**.

Replacing Whole Words Only

By default, Works finds and replaces words that are part of longer words. If you ask it to replace "king" with "emperor," it also replaces "kings" with "emperors," "Vikings" with "Vikemperors," "asking" with "asemperor," and so on. If this happens to you, don't forget that you can undo the entire replacement job with **Edit Undo Editing**.

One way to circumvent this problem is to check **Match Whole Word Only**. Then Works finds only those occurrences of "king" that are surrounded by spaces, tabs, punctuation, carriage returns, page breaks, the beginning of the file, and the end of the file. It finds the "king" in "Hail to the king," "(the deposed king)," and "priest-king" but not in "kings" or "Viking" or "asking."

Suppose you want to replace all occurrences of "king" with "emperor" and "kings" with "emperors," but you don't want to modify other words containing "king." You could do two replacement operations. First, replace "king" with "emperor," checking **Match Whole Word Only**. Then, since the dialog box is still on the screen, add an "s" to each box and do a second replacement.

Replacing One Item at a Time

The best way to make sure that every replacement is correct is to walk through them one by one. It's a lot slower, but it produces fewer problems. Instead of starting the job with **Replace All**, click **Find Next**. Works searches forward from the cursor, finds the next matching word, highlights it, scrolls the document so that the highlighted word is in the top line of the window, enables the **Replace** button, and waits for a response. Figure 5.4 shows what the Works window looks like at this point.

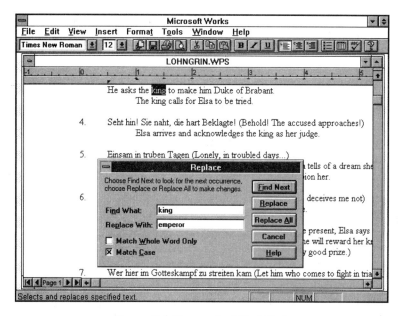

Figure 5.4 *The result of Find Next*

If you decide that you don't want to make the replacement, click **Find Next** to look for the next match. If you do want to replace the highlighted text, click **Replace**. Works replaces the text and searches for the next match. You can also click **Replace All** to make the rest of the replacements automatically or **Cancel** to cancel the entire operation, close the dialog box, and deselect the highlighted text.

In most cases, you're safest with the **Find Next...Replace** procedure. Use **Replace All** only when you're positive that no erroneous replacements will occur.

Replacing Part of the Document

Sometimes you want to make replacements only in one section of a document. Select the section before choosing **Edit Replace**. When a block is selected, Works searches for matching text only within that block.

If you use **Find Next** and the cursor is not at the beginning of the document, when Works reaches the end of the document, it will ask if you want to continue at the beginning of the document. If you say *Yes*, **Find Next** keeps searching until it reaches the place where the cursor was originally. But if you say *No*, it stops at the end of the document and you don't replace any occurrences that preceded the original location of the cursor.

Finding a Particular Location

As a document gets longer, it's sometimes difficult to locate the place where you next want to edit. Several Works features discussed in this section can help you locate a particular place.

Searching for Text

The **Find** feature is very much like the **Replace** feature, but it only finds the text. Figure 5.5 shows the dialog box that opens when you choose **Edit Find**. Fill in the **Find What** box and click **Find Next**. Works searches forward from the current cursor position, locates the next occurrence of the requested text, scrolls it to the top line of the document window, and highlights it. The dialog box remains on the screen so you can press **Find Next** again if you'd like. You could also change the text in the **Find What** box and/or change the selected options before pressing **Find Next**. When you have found the text you're looking for, click **Cancel** to close the box.

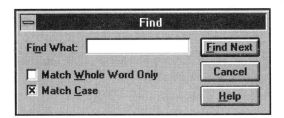

Figure 5.5 *The Find dialog box*

As with the **Replace** function, you can check **Match Whole Word Only** and **Match Case** to limit the text that is found.

If you select a block before starting a search, Works searches only the selected block. If it reaches the end of the document, it asks if you want to continue at the beginning of the document. It also displays a message if it can't find the desired text within the limits of the search.

Going to a Particular Page

When you're working from corrections marked on a printed version of the document, you know what page you want next. Choose **Edit Go To** or press **F5** to open the dialog box shown in Figure 5.6. Type the desired page number in the text box and press **Enter**. Works moves the cursor to the beginning of the specified page.

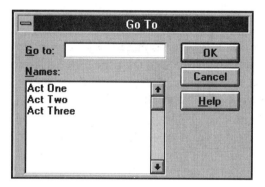

Figure 5.6 *The Go To dialog box*

Using Bookmarks

If you often return to the same locations in a document, you can speed up your search time by using bookmarks, which assign names to specific locations. Works can quickly jump to a bookmark without having to scroll or search the document.

❖ **To create a bookmark:**

1. Position the cursor where you want to insert the bookmark.

2. Choose **Insert Bookmark Name**. The dialog box shown in Figure 5.7 opens.

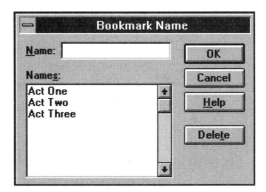

Figure 5.7 *Bookmark Name dialog box*

3. Type a name for the bookmark you want to create. It can have up to 15 characters, including spaces, punctuation, and digits, but it can't consist entirely of digits. Legitimate bookmarks are **Table 3.1**, **Chapter 2**, and **3rd dimension**.

4. Press **Enter** or click **OK**. The dialog box closes. You won't see the bookmark on your screen, but Works knows it's there.

Once you have created one or more bookmarks in your document, you can jump to any one bookmark. To jump from the current cursor position to the next bookmark, press **Shift+F5**. You can keep pressing **Shift+F5** until you reach the one you want. Or you can jump to a specific bookmark by name.

❖ **To jump to a specific bookmark:**

1. Choose **Edit Go To** or press **F5**. The Go To dialog box opens. (See Figure 5.6.)

2. In the **Names** list box, double-click the name of the desired bookmark. (Or type it in the text box and press **Enter**.) The dialog box closes and the cursor jumps to the specified bookmark.

If you want to delete a bookmark, choose **Insert Bookmark Name**, click the name of the bookmark to be deleted, and click **Delete** (see Figure 5.7). To move a bookmark, delete it from its old position and create it again in the new position. To rename a bookmark, create a new bookmark with the desired name in the same position as the old one. Works asks if you want to replace the old name with the new one.

Counting Words

If you've ever been asked to write so-many words on something, you can appreciate how hard it is to count words on your monitor screen. It's somewhat easier to print the document and count on paper, but there's a simpler way. Simply choose **Tools Word Count** to pop up a dialog box like the one shown in Figure 5.8. Click OK when you're done with it.

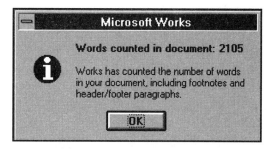

Figure 5.8 *Word Count dialog box*

If no text is selected, Works counts all the words in the document. When text is selected, Works counts only the words in the selection. Works is pretty good at identifying separate words. It understands that expressions such as "2.33," "Ctrl+PageDown," and "multi-processing" should be counted as one word each.

File Management

Don't forget to save your changes. To update the original file, just click the **Save** icon. To save them as a new file, keeping the original file intact, choose **File Save As** and type a new name in the **File Name** box.

If you make a bunch of changes and decide you don't like them, you can fall back to the last version that you saved on disk. Close the document without saving it. Then open the document again. The version that you open will be the last version that you saved. Any revisions that you made after that will be gone.

Summary

In this chapter, you have learned the basics of revising a Word Processor document. You know how to:

- ❖ Open an existing file
- ❖ Make deletions, insertions, and replacements
- ❖ Move and copy text
- ❖ Save the file again
- ❖ Undo any changes that you make

You can find your way around a document using a variety of techniques. You can even count the words in a section or the entire document.

In the next chapter, you'll start formatting your documents with fonts, indents, headers, page numbers, and the like.

CHAPTER **6**

Formatting a Document

Word Processor provides a wealth of formatting features to pep up your documents. This chapter shows you how to:

❖ Format text characters with fonts, bold, italics, and so on

❖ Format paragraphs with alignment, indentation, and so on

❖ Format pages with headers, footers, and so on

❖ Insert special characters such as the date and time

❖ Copy character and paragraph formatting

❖ Use two or more newspaper-style columns

❖ Use some of the AutoStart templates

❖ Create your own templates

A Brief Introduction to Fonts

In personal computers, a font is another word for typeface—a set of characters (letters, numbers, and symbols) that have the same design. Some of the fonts you might have in your system are:

Arial, which looks modern and clean

Courier New, which looks like typewriter type

Times New Roman, which looks like newspaper type

Fonts come in variable sizes, which are measured in points. A point is approximately 1/72 of an inch, so a 12-point font is approximately 12/72 or 1/6 of an inch tall. A font also has a style, which might be normal, **bold**, *italic*, <u>underline</u>, or ~~strike-through~~ (for legal documents). You can also select a color and a position (normal, subscript, or superscript).

Fonts can be monospaced or variable width. In a monospaced font, all the letters have the same width. Courier New is a monospaced font that resembles typewriter output. Many people prefer to use a monospaced font such as Courier New to print letters and memos so that they look typed.

Variable-width fonts adjust the width of each letter so that thin letters, such as "l" and "i", occupy the least amount of space; wide letters, such as "M" and "W", are given the most space. Text printed in a variable-width font takes up less space and looks more sophisticated than the same text printed in a monospaced font. This book is printed in a variable-width font named Adobe Garamond.

A font may or may not have serifs, which are small cross-strokes at the ends of the main strokes, as shown in Figure 6.1. *Sans serif* fonts don't have the cross-strokes. A *Sans serif* font, such as Arial, looks modern and artistic, but some people find it harder to read when it's used for dense text, such as a narrative paragraph.

Most American documents use fonts with serifs for the text that makes up the body of the document. Headings and labels often use *sans serif* fonts for contrast.

A font can be weighted or unweighted (also shown in Figure 6.1). A weighted font mixes thick and thin strokes. With an unweighted font, all the strokes have the same thickness. Fonts that have serifs also tend to be weighted, whereas *sans serif* fonts are usually unweighted, although that's not a hard and fast rule. Many people find weighted fonts easier to read for dense text, such as narrative paragraphs. Unweighted fonts are fine for headings and labels.

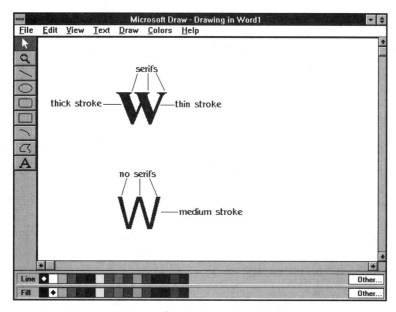

Figure 6.1 *Serifs and weights*

Some fonts don't use the standard set of characters. The Symbols font, for example, contains the Greek alphabet and other symbols (such as ≈) that are needed to type mathematical formulas. The Wingdings font includes graphical characters that come in handy in newsletters, advertisements, headers, and the like. Some Wingdings are shown below:

Windows comes with several standard fonts and allows you to install many more. Personal computers used to have different fonts for monitors and printers, which caused a great deal of confusion because you couldn't always see on your screen how something would look in print. Windows 3.1 provides a solution to this problem with TrueType fonts—including Arial, Courier New, Times New Roman, Symbols, and Wingdings—which look the same in print as they do on the screen. If you want to see exactly what your documents will look like before they print, be sure to select TrueType fonts when you create your documents. TrueType fonts have the TrueType logo next to them in your font list (see Figure 6.2).

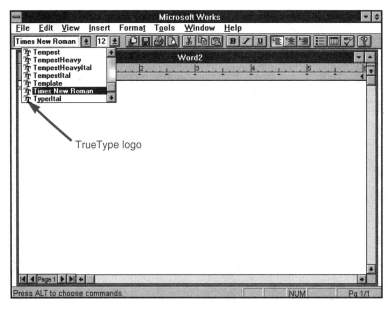

Figure 6.2 *Fontname drop-down list*

Character Formatting

Formatting having to do with fonts is applied on a character-by-character basis. You select some text, then select the font, size, style, color, and position you want that text to have. Or you can set up the font and other text characteristics before you type the text. The toolbar is set up to let you select the text characteristics you'll use most often: font, size, and some of the styles. Color, position, and the other styles are controlled via a dialog box.

Suppose you're typing a new file and you want to set the next four words in Arial. Before you type the words, select Arial. Then type the four words. Then select your regular font and continue typing.

❖ **To select a font:**

1. Click the down-arrow next to the font name on the Toolbar to pull down the Fontname drop-down list (see Figure 6.2). The current font is highlighted in the list.

2. Scroll through the list and click the font you want. The selected font appears in the text box at the top of the list, and the list closes.

When you set character formatting this way, imagine that you insert a hidden code in your text that says "start Arial here." When you select the regular font again, you insert another hidden code that says "start Courier New here" (or whatever your regular font is). Now what happens if you come back and insert more text in that area? It takes on whatever characteristics are already on at that particular position. In other words, if it's between "start Arial" and "start Courier New," it will be in Arial. Of course, you can select another font for it, in which case, more hidden codes are inserted in the text.

The same is true when you change the font size, the style, and the other character formatting characteristics. For each characteristic you select, you insert a hidden code in the text that turns that characteristic on. It stays on until another hidden code supersedes it. When you go back and insert text in any part of a document, its appearance is determined by the characteristics that are currently on at that position. As you move the cursor around in a document, the toolbar changes to show the current font, size, and style.

N O T E If you delete an entire section controlled by a code, you delete the code too.

❖ **To select a font size:**

1. Pull down the Font Size drop-down list (see Figure 6.3).

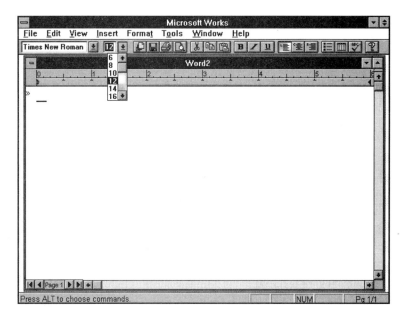

Figure 6.3 *Font Size drop-down list*

The current font size is highlighted in the list, and the sizes are listed in points.

2. Scroll through the list and click the size you want. The selected size appears in the text box at the top of the list. If any text is selected, it changes to the selected size.

❖ **To select bold, italic, or underline:**

Click the desired style icon on the toolbar (see Figure 6.4).

When you're done with the bold, italic, or underline style, click the icon to turn it off again. When you move the cursor into bold, italic, and/or underline text, the appropriate icon(s) appear to be pressed down on the toolbar.

Suppose you want to go back and change the characteristics of some text you have already typed. Select the text, then select the font, size, and/or style. Only the selected text is affected. (Hidden codes are inserted before the first selected character and after the last selected character.)

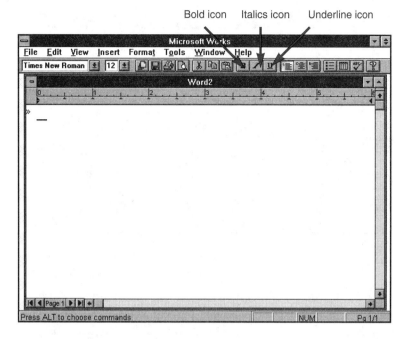

Figure 6.4 *Style icons on the toolbar*

Edit Undo Editing undoes the last formatting action. If you do a whole series of formatting actions in a row—as in changing the font, the size, and the style—it undoes the last one only.

N O T E

Another way to change fonts makes use of the **Format Font and Style** command, which opens the dialog box shown in Figure 6.5. As you can see, you can select a font, a size, and a style (including **Strikethrough**). You can also select a position and a color.

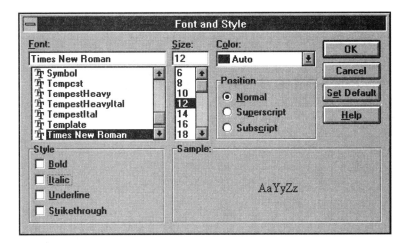

Figure 6.5 *Font and Style dialog box*

Even if you don't have a color printer, colors on the screen can be helpful. For example, if you're creating a document from an outline, you can change the color of each outline section as you finish writing it; you'll be able to see at a glance what you have completed and what's left. If you want to come back later and review a questionable statement, you could turn it red; it will stand out when you're scanning the document.

Copying Character Formatting

Once you've set up some text the way you want it, you might want to copy that formatting to other text. You can do it using the **Paste Special** command.

❖ **To copy character formatting:**

1. Select any portion of the formatted characters.
2. Click the **Copy** icon. Works copies the selected characters and *their formatting characteristics* to the Clipboard.
3. Select the characters to be formatted.
4. Choose **Edit Paste Special**. The Paste Special dialog box opens (see Figure 6.6).

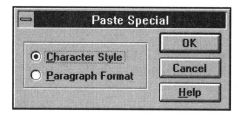

Figure 6.6 *Paste Special dialog box*

7. Click **Character Style**.

8. Click **OK**. Works gives the selected characters the same format as the contents of the Clipboard.

Keyboard Shortcuts for Character Formatting

When you're typing along on the keyboard, you might not want to lift your hand to use the mouse. You can do some character formatting from your keyboard, as shown in Table 6.1. Notice the last line in particular, **Ctrl+Spacebar**, which removes any style and position characteristics. (It doesn't affect the font, however.)

Table 6.1 *Character formatting shortcut keys*

Key Combo	Action
Ctrl+B	Make text **bold**
Ctrl+I	Make text *italic*
Ctrl+U	<u>Underline</u> text
Ctrl+=	Make text subscript
Ctrl+Shift+=	Make text superscript
Ctrl+Spacebar	Give text normal style and normal position

Paragraph Formatting

Not all formatting is done on a character basis. Formatting such as tabs, indentation, and spacing applies to whole paragraphs. You can't set single-spacing for part of a paragraph, for example.

To format a paragraph, place the cursor in the paragraph, then choose the formatting commands, which are explained shortly. If you want to format more than one adjacent paragraph, select them all before choosing the commands.

SHORTCUT

When selecting adjacent paragraphs, you don't have to select the entire first or last paragraph. If any portion is selected, paragraph formatting commands apply to the entire paragraph.

Paragraph formatting is also stored in the document in the form of hidden codes. They are stored with the carriage return at the end of the paragraph. If you delete the carriage return, you also delete the formatting codes, and the paragraph takes on the characteristics of the next paragraph, with which it is combined.

Ordinarily, you can't see the carriage returns at the ends of paragraphs. But sometimes it helps to display them so you can delete one. Choose **View All Characters** to display not only carriage returns but also spaces and tabs (see Figure 6.7). Choose **View All Characters** again to return to the normal view.

When you position the cursor anywhere in a paragraph and press **Enter** to create a new paragraph, the current paragraph's formatting codes are included with the new carriage return. In other words, the new paragraph has the same format as the one it came from. Suppose you want to insert a new paragraph between two paragraphs that have different formatting. If you want the new paragraph to have the same format as the first paragraph, position the cursor at the end of the first paragraph and press **Enter**. But if you want the new paragraph to have the same format as the second paragraph, position the cursor at the beginning of the second paragraph and press **Enter**.

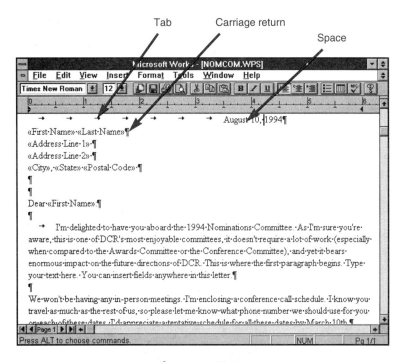

Figure 6.7 *View All Characters*

When you are creating a new document, set up the first paragraph with the formatting you want to use throughout the document. Then, as you complete each paragraph and press **Enter**, the new paragraph will have the same formatting as the previous one and the original paragraph's formatting will carry throughout the document. You can go back afterward and change any paragraphs that should vary from the standard formatting.

Indentation

The indent markers on the ruler depict the current paragraph's indentation (see Figure 6.8). By default, they are located at the document margins to indicate that the paragraph is not indented. On the right side, you can indent the entire paragraph only, but on the left side, you can indent both the first line and the entire paragraph. That's why the left marker has two parts while the right has only one.

Right side

Entire paragraph

First line

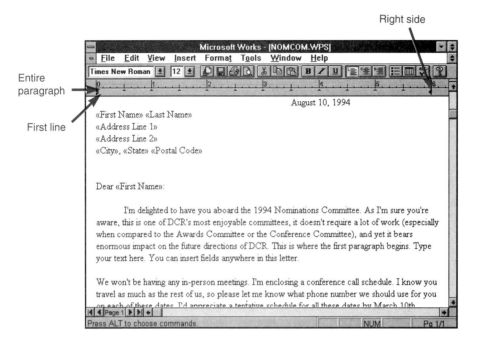

Figure 6.8 *Indent markers*

❖ To indent a paragraph from the right margin:

1. Place the cursor in the paragraph.

If you haven't typed the paragraph yet, place the cursor at the beginning of the first line, where you will start typing.

N O T E

The indent markers indicate the current indentation for the paragraph.

2. Drag the right indent marker to the left or right. Drop it at the point where you want to position the paragraph's right margin. If the paragraph already contains text, Works reformats it for the new indentation.

3. You can continue to adjust the right marker until the indentation is just right.

The left paragraph marker is a little more complicated, of course. You drag the bottom part to indent the entire paragraph, including the first line. When you drag the bottom part, the top part moves with it. You drag the top part to indent just the first line. It moves independently of the bottom part.

Once they are separated, if you move the bottom part, the top part also moves, but it maintains its distance from the bottom part. For example, suppose you set the top part at 1 inch. Then you move the bottom marker to 0.5 inch. The top part moves to 1.5 inch.

Because it's a little hard to indent paragraphs on the left, where most indentation takes place, Works provides a shortcut key to indent the entire paragraph. Each time you press **Ctrl+N**, you add another level of indentation to the current paragraph or to all the selected paragraphs. The amount that **Ctrl+N** indents is equal to the current setting of the default tab stops. If they are set to 0.5 inch (the Works default), each time you press **Ctrl+N**, you indent another 0.5 inch, starting with the paragraph's current indentation. If the paragraph is not indented, then pressing **Ctrl+N** twice would indent to 0.5 inch first and 1 inch next. But if the paragraph is already indented to 0.25 inch, pressing **Ctrl+N** twice indents it first to 0.75 inch, then to 1.25 inch. If the default tab spacing has been set to some other value, then each time you press **Ctrl+N**, you add that much indentation to the current indentation.

Similarly, **Ctrl+M** removes the default amount of indentation. If the default tab stops are set to 0.25 inch, each time you press **Ctrl+M**, you move the paragraph's indentation 0.25 inch to the left. **Ctrl+M** stops at the left margin. It has no effect when the paragraph isn't indented.

You can't move the indentation markers beyond the document margins. That is, you can't position a paragraph to the left of the left margin or to the right of the right margin.

NOTE

You can outdent the first line from the rest of the paragraph to create a *hanging indent*. Figure 6.9 shows an example of paragraphs that use hanging indents. In the sample paragraphs, the first line starts at the left margin, while the rest of the paragraph starts at 0.25 inch, as you can see by the indent markers. This is a perfect setup for bulleted and numbered lists.

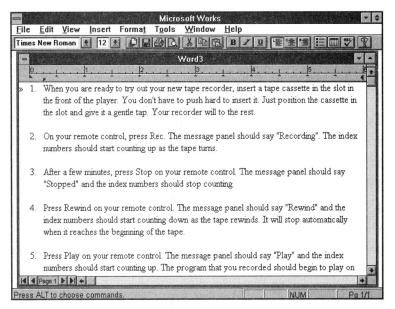

Figure 6.9 *Hanging indents*

You can set up a hanging indent by dragging the indent markers, but Works gives you an easier way. Press **Ctrl+H** once to indent all but the first line of the current paragraph or selected paragraphs. As with **Ctrl+N**, the amount of the indent is equal to the default tab stop spacing. Pressing **Ctrl+H** again does not increase the amount of the hanging indent; it simply indents the entire paragraph, hanging indent and all, just as does pressing **Ctrl+N**. Press **Ctrl+G** to undo the hanging indent.

Once you've set up a hanging indent, how do you use it? Type the text that should be outdented, such as "10." or "(a)," and then press **Tab**. You'll tab to the position of the bottom indent marker. Then continue typing the paragraph.

Alignment

Works offers four types of paragraph alignment, as shown in Figure 6.10. Left alignment lines up the paragraph along the left side at the margins or indents; the right end is ragged. For most documents, left alignment is normal. Center alignment centers each line of the paragraph within the margins or indents. Center alignment is often appropriate for a title, a heading, or a page number. The paragraphs that make up the body of a document are rarely centered.

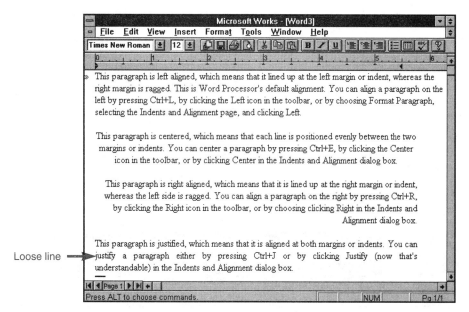

Figure 6.10 *Paragraph alignment examples*

Right alignment lines up the right side of a paragraph at the margin or indent; the left side is ragged. You might use right alignment in a header, a footer, a heading, or for some kind of special effect. Right alignment is used rarely in the body of a document.

Justified alignment lines up a paragraph on both the left and the right sides at the margins or indents, except for the last line, which is aligned on the left only. Many typeset documents are justified, so justification gives your document a professional feel, especially if you use a weighted, variable-spaced font with serifs such as Times New Roman. However, there can be problems. Works must justify a paragraph by adding extra space into each line. It normally can spread the space so evenly that you can't spot it. But occasionally a line is so short that Works must create noticeable gaps. Notice the line labeled *loose line* in Figure 6.10. The reason it's so short is because the word *understandable* at the beginning of the next line is too long to fit at the end of the preceding line. You can often cure a loose line by rewording the sentence.

N O T E   Another way to cure a loose line is to hyphenate the long word so that Works can put part of it at the end of the short line. See your Works user's guide and on-screen help for more information on hyphenation.

The Word Processor toolbar includes icons for left, center, and right alignment (see Figure 6.11). To justify one or more paragraphs, press **Ctrl+J**. The other alignments also have keyboard shortcuts, as shown in Table 6.2.

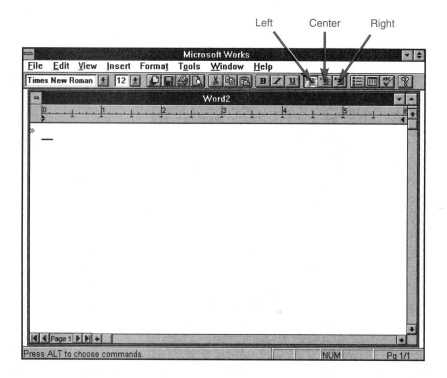

Figure 6.11 *Alignment icons on the toolbar*

Table 6.2 *Alignment Shortcut Keys*

Alignment	*Shortcut*
Left	**Ctrl+L**
Right	**Ctrl+R**
Center	**Ctrl+E**
Justified	**Ctrl+J**

Spacing

The Breaks and Spacing page of the Paragraph dialog box (see Figure 6.12) controls the spacing within and around the paragraph as well as where page breaks are allowed.

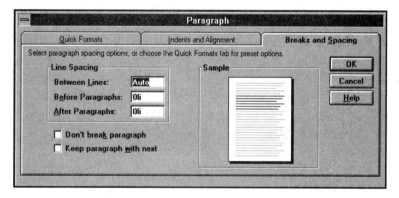

Figure 6.12 *Breaks and Spacing dialog box*

Spacing Between the Lines

The **Between Lines** text box controls single-spacing, double-spacing, and so on. By default, it is set to **Auto**, which means that Works adjusts the spacing of each line to the tallest character on the line. In general, auto spacing gives the appearance of single-spaced paragraphs, but if you change to a larger font for a word, you'll see the difference in the spacing for that line.

You can replace the word "Auto" with a number to indicate a fixed spacing: a 1 requests single spacing, a 2 requests double spacing, and so on. You can use fractional numbers such as 1.5. You can also specify the spacing in terms of **picas**, **points**, **inches**, **millimeters**, or **centimeters** by including the name of the unit of measure in the box. (A pica is approximately 1/6 of an inch, and a point is approximately 1/72 of an inch.) For example, you could set the line spacing to "2 picas," ".1 inch," "14 points," or ".3 centimeters."

If you specify spacing so small that the lines would overlap, Works shows your spacing in the dialog box, but it uses **Auto** spacing.

N O T E

Spacing before and after Paragraphs

When you work at a typewriter, you add spacing between paragraphs by hitting the carriage return a few extra times. Many people also do that when working with a word processor, but you don't have to. You can have Works insert extra lines before and after paragraphs using the **Before Paragraph and After Paragraph** boxes. As with the spacing between lines, you can specify whole lines, fractional lines, points, picas, inches, centimeters, or millimeters.

There are several advantages to letting Works insert the spacing between paragraphs rather than using extra carriage returns. First, if you set up extra spacing when you type the first paragraph in the document, that extra spacing is carried over as you press the **Enter** key to start each subsequent paragraph. You don't have to bother with it any more.

The second advantage appears if you're preparing a document file that will be fed to a typesetting program. Typesetters do all their between-paragraph spacing by adding extra space before and after paragraphs, not by inserting extra carriage returns. If you submit a document file with extra carriage returns, someone has to remove them. If they miss one, the document looks wrong and someone has to fix it.

N O T E

A third advantage relates to controlling breaks, which is discussed in the next section.

When a paragraph with after spacing precedes a paragraph with before spacing, Works adds together both amounts to determine the total space between the paragraphs. The example in Figure 6.13 shows how this works. The first body paragraph (after the title) is formatted to be followed by one blank line. That blank line is added to the blank line that precedes the "Background" heading, creating two blank lines between the paragraphs.

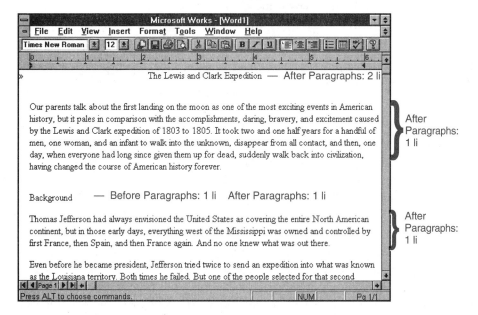

Figure 6.13 *Paragraph spacing example*

In general, your life will be easier if you stick to after-spacing throughout a document. That way, you won't begin a page with a gap before the first paragraph. (Even if the paragraph isn't at the top of a page now, it can be moved there by a revision somewhere else in the document.)

Keyboard Shortcuts for Spacing

Table 6.3 shows the keyboard shortcuts for spacing paragraphs. Also included is a **Ctrl+Q** shortcut, which removes all formatting from a paragraph; this is the only way to unformat a paragraph in one move.

Table 6.3 *Spacing shortcut keys*

Key	Action
Ctrl+1	Single space lines
Ctrl+2	Double space lines
Ctrl+5	Space lines 1.5 lines apart
Ctrl+0	Remove space before paragraph
Ctrl+O	Set spacing to 1 line before paragraph
Ctrl+Q	Remove all paragraph formatting

The **Ctrl+O** key changes the paragraph's before-spacing to 1 line. If the paragraph has no before-spacing, this increases it. But if the paragraph has more than one line of before-spacing, **Ctrl+O** reduces it to one line. **Ctrl+0** (zero) removes any before-spacing. It does not affect any spacing after the preceding paragraph, so there might still be a gap between paragraphs.

Breaks

In the Breaks and Spacing dialog box (Figure 6.12), the two checkboxes at the lower left determine whether or not a page break can interrupt or follow the paragraph. Most body paragraphs can be split over two pages, but some paragraphs should not be split. In a screenplay, for example, dialog should not be split. When you mark a paragraph with **Don't break paragraph**, if it won't fit at the bottom of a page, Works moves the entire paragraph to the top of the next page, leaving a gap at the bottom of the preceding page.

NOTE

Mark paragraphs that shouldn't be split even if they fall at the top or middle of the page when you type them. Later revisions could move them to the bottom of the page and cause them to be split. You don't want to have to inspect the bottom of every page in your document with every revision.

Many paragraphs are not meant to be the last paragraph on the page. Headings, such as "Background" in Figure 6.13, should be followed by at least two lines of body text. In a screenplay, the character's name precedes each dialog paragraph, like this:

```
            DIANNA
      You can forget that.
      I will not sell a product
      that I wouldn't use myself.
```

A page break should not fall between the character's name and the dialog. When you format a paragraph with **Keep paragraph with next**, if it becomes the last paragraph on a page, Works moves it to the top of the next page.

WARNING

If you accidentally format every paragraph in a document with **Keep paragraph with next**, Works can't resolve the paradox and breaks pages where it normally would, ignoring the **Keep with next** instructions.

Now you see the third reason to add spacing before and after paragraphs instead of using extra carriage returns to separate them. When you mark a heading with **Keep paragraph with next**, you don't want the next paragraph to be an empty carriage return. You want it to keep the heading with the next body paragraph.

Borders

Works can draw lines, called *borders*, along any or all sides of a paragraph. It can draw a normal (thin) border, a bold border, or a double border. Figure 6.14 shows some examples.

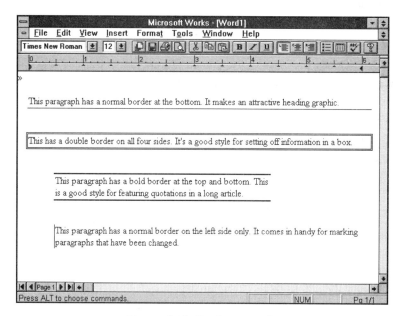

Figure 6.14 *Border examples*

As you can see, Word Processor's borders aren't very fancy—no vines or wooden fences. These plain borders come in handy for setting off information and providing some low-key graphic interest to the page. If you're working on a newsletter and want some fancier borders, you'll have to find them elsewhere.

Borders stretch from the left margin or indent to the right margin or indent, regardless of how much text is on the line. Use indents to position your borders.

If several paragraphs in a row have the same borders, the left and right borders will be continuous lines embracing all the adjacent paragraphs. The effect of the top and bottom borders depends on how you create the paragraphs. If you type the first one and mark it with a top and bottom border, then press **Enter** to start the next paragraph; each paragraph will have its own top and bottom border. The bottom border of the first paragraph will coincide with the top border of the second paragraph, so you'll see only one border between them, but technically, both borders are there. If you want top and bottom borders or a box surrounding several paragraphs with no lines between the paragraphs, type the paragraphs first, select them all, then select the border.

Choose the **Format Border** command to create a border. Figure 6.15 shows the dialog box that lets you select border options. Just click the items you want and click **OK** to draw the border. Notice that you can add color to your border by dropping down the **Color** list box and selecting a different color.

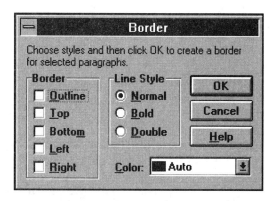

Figure 6.15 *Border dialog box*

The Border dialog box can be a little confusing if you select one or more paragraphs that already have borders. If the cursor is in a single paragraph that has an outline border (that is, a box around it), instead of **Outline** being checked, **Top**, **Bottom**, **Left**, and **Right** are checked. You have to uncheck all four of them to eliminate the border.

If you have selected several paragraphs with borders, the checkboxes have gray squares in them, indicating that they have different values for different paragraphs. When you click an item, an *X* appears in the checkbox, turning on that option for all selected paragraphs. If you click it again, the checkbox clears, turning off that option for all selected paragraphs. Click it again and the gray square returns, which causes all selected paragraphs to retain their current setting for that option.

Tabs

You have seen already how to set the spacing of the default tab stops for a document. You can override the default tab stops for individual paragraphs by setting specific tab stops. You can set tab stops by clicking the ruler, which provides limited functions, or by using the **Format Tabs** command, which provides several more functions.

❖   **To set tab stops on the ruler:**

1. Place the cursor in the paragraph to be changed, or select the paragraphs to be changed.

2. Click the bottom half of the ruler in each position where you want a tab stop to appear. You will see a left tab marker (see Figure 6.16) in each position that you click. All default tab stops preceding that position are removed.

Figure 6.16 *Left tab markers on the ruler*

3. You can adjust the tab stops by dragging the markers left or right.

The tab stops that you set by clicking the ruler are called left tab stops because they align text on the left. Works also offers right, center, and decimal tab stops, which you can see in Figure 6.17.

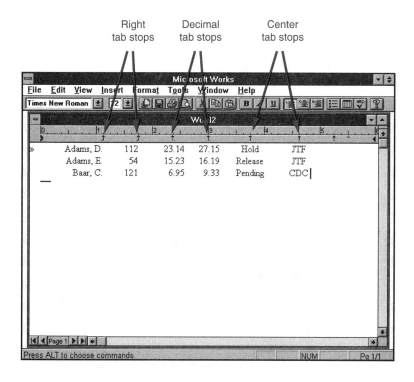

Figure 6.17 *Other types of tab stops*

A right tab stop aligns text on the right. When you tab to a right tab stop and start typing, the cursor holds still and your text moves to the left. It's a weird feeling at first, but you get used to it. (The same thing happens when you align a paragraph on the right.) Right tabs stops are most often used to type columns of numbers that don't contain decimal points, but they can have other uses.

A center tab stop centers text under the tab stop position. The center tab marker is an arrow pointing straight up.

A decimal tab stop aligns text at the decimal point (or period). It's used to type columns of numbers with decimal points. It's difficult to see in the figure, but a decimal tab marker is an up arrow (like the center tab stop) with a decimal point next to it.

Tab stops are used most often to create tables, as in Figures 6.16 and 6.17. With Works, it's often easier to create a table using Spreadsheet and copy it into your Word Processor document. You'll learn how to do that in Part 3 of this book.

Another use of tab stops is to produce tables of contents as shown in Figure 6.18. The page numbers are aligned under a right tab stop. This table of contents also shows how to use *leaders*, the row of dots before the numbers. When you specify a leader for a tab stop, Works inserts dots (or whatever character you select) to fill in the empty space leading up to the aligned text.

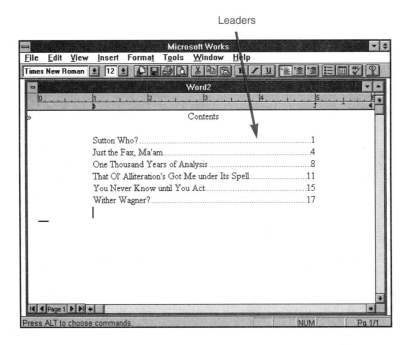

Figure 6.18 *A sample table of contents with leaders*

Figure 6.19 shows the Tabs dialog box, which opens when you choose **Format Tabs**.

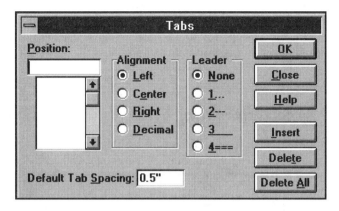

Figure 6.19 *Tabs dialog box*

❖ **To set tab stops for one or more paragraphs:**

1. Place the cursor in the paragraph or select the desired paragraphs.

2. Choose **Format Tabs**. You will see the ruler in the background as you decide where to place the tab stops. If you want, you can move the dialog box so that you can see some text, too.

3. Type a tab stop position in the **Position** text box. (For example, type **2** (for 2 inches), **1.75** (for 1.75 inches), **3 picas**, **1 centimeter**, and so on.)

4. Click the desired option in the **Alignment** group.

5. Click the desired option in the **Leader** group.

6. Click **Insert** to create the tab stop. The tab stop appears in the list box, but the dialog box doesn't close.

7. Repeat Steps 3 through 6 for each tab stop you want to set.

8. Click **OK**. The Tabs dialog box closes, and the tab stops appear on the ruler. Any tabbed text in the selected paragraphs aligns to the new stops.

You don't have to return to the Tabs dialog box to adjust or delete tab stops. Be sure to position the cursor in the paragraph to be changed or, if more than one paragraph is involved, select all the paragraphs you want to adjust. Then drag the tabs stops on the ruler line to adjust them. To delete a tab stop, simply drag it away from the ruler and drop it anywhere.

Quick Paragraph Formatting

Because it might take several steps to set up a paragraph the way you like it, Works offers a number of quick paragraph formatting options (see Figure 6.20). **Normal** removes all indentation, selects left alignment, sets the spacing to **Auto**, and sets before- and after-spacing to **0**. **1st line indent** indents the first line according to the default tab stop spacing; it also selects left alignment, selects **Auto** spacing, and sets before- or after-spacing to **0**.

    Bulleted sets up a hanging indent according to the default tab stop spacing and inserts a bullet and a tab at the beginning of the paragraph; it also selects left alignment, **Auto** spacing, and sets before- and after-spacing to **0**. **Hanging indent** also sets up a hanging indent, but it doesn't insert anything; it selects left alignment, and **Auto** spacing, and sets before- or after-spacing to **0**.

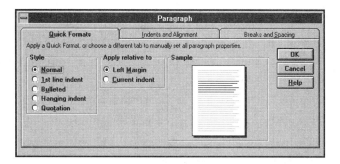

Figure 6.20 *Paragraph dialog box*

Quotation sets up a paragraph in the accepted format for long quotations: It indents both sides by the amount of the default tab stop spacing, and it justifies the paragraph; it also selects **Auto Spacing** and sets before and after spacing to **1** (not 0).

All these formats are affected by the **Left Margin/Current Indent** option. If the paragraph is currently indented and you want to maintain or add to the indentation, be sure to click **Current Indent**. If you want to ignore the current indentation, click **Left Margin**. If you're not sure which settings you want, try them out and watch the changes in the **Sample** box. The paragraph represented by dark solid lines shows the current formatting for the paragraph. You can see it change as you click various options.

Page Formatting

A *header* is one or more paragraphs that appear in the top margin of every page. A *footer* is just like a header except it appears in the bottom margin. People use headers and footers to identify the document, the version, the author, the company, the chapter or section, the print date, and so on. Page numbers are usually included in the header or footer.

Creating Simple Header and Footers

If all you want is a single line in your header or footer, you can set it up fairly easily. Choose **View Headers and Footers** to open the Headers and Footers dialog box shown in Figure 6.21. Type whatever text you want in the **Header** and **Footer** boxes. If you don't want the header or footer to appear on the first page, click **No header on 1st page** and/or **No footer on 1st page**. Then click **OK**. You won't be able to see the header or footer in Normal or Draft view, but you can switch to Page Layout view or Print Preview to see them. You can't edit them in either view. You must reopen the Headers and Footers dialog box to edit them.

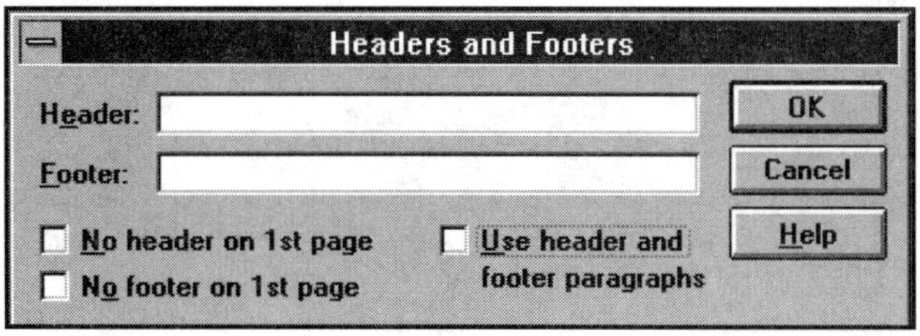

Figure 6.21 *Headers and Footers dialog box*

SHORTCUT

You can reopen the Headers and Footers dialog box by double-clicking the header or the footer in Page Layout view.

Works centers the single-line header and footer by default. Table 6.4 shows some characters you can insert in the header or footer to change the default alignment. Also shown are some special characters you can use to insert system information such as the date and time. You can use more than one of these characters in a line. For example, if you want the text *Quarterly Report* to appear on the left, *First Draft* to appear in the center, and the print date to appear on the right, you would create this line:

&LQuarterly Report&CFirst Draft&R&D

N O T E

You can type the codes in uppercase or lowercase; &c is the same as &C.

Table 6.4 *Header and Footer codes*

Code	Action
&L	Left align the text that follows
&C	Center the text that follows
&R	Right align the text that follows
&P	Print the page number
&D	Print the date in short format (12/1/94)
&N	Print the date in long format (December 1, 1994)
&T	Print the time
&F	Print the filename
&&	Print an ampersand (&)

Since an ampersand is used to signal the special codes, you have to enter a double ampersand (&&) to specify that you want to print an ampersand in the text.

N O T E

Paragraph Headers and Footers

If you want either a header or footer that is longer than one line, you must create header and footer paragraphs. In the Headers and Footers dialog box, click the **Use header and footer paragraphs** checkbox along with any other appropriate checkboxes, but don't fill in the **Header and Footer** text boxes. When you click **OK**, Works creates a blank header paragraph and a footer paragraph that says, "Page - *page*", where *page* represents the page number. You edit these two paragraphs to contain the text and codes you want.

In Normal and Draft views, the header and footer paragraphs appear at the beginning of the document. The header paragraph is marked with an H in the left margin, and the footer paragraph is marked with an F. In Page Layout view, the header and footer paragraphs appear at the top and bottom of every page (except page 1 if you have omitted them from that page). They do not have any special identifiers in the left margin, so remember what they are. (Don't forget that the header paragraph is blank at first.) In all three views, you can edit these paragraphs just like any other paragraphs: You move the cursor to them using either the keyboard or the mouse.

You can format header and footer paragraphs just like any other paragraphs. You can modify the alignment, the spacing, the tabs, the indentation, and so on. And yes, they can have borders. In fact, a bottom border on a header and a top border on a footer create a nice effect.

If you want to format a one-line header or footer with such things as borders and fonts, use the **Header and Footer Paragraphs** feature.

N O T E

Since the header and footer can be one paragraph only, you can't just press **Enter** to start a new line; pressing **Shift+Enter** starts a new line without starting a new paragraph. In the following example, the ↵ symbol shows where **Shift+Enter** was pressed:

Just Passing By.↵
by Carmel Degela.↵
Room 24

By default, the header and footer paragraphs have a center tab stop in the middle and a right tab stop at the right margin. These tab stops are set up so that you can have some information on the left, some in the middle, and some on the right. But you can move the tab stops, delete them, add more, or do whatever you want.

You can't use the special codes from Table 6.4 in header and footer paragraphs. But you can insert the special characters from the dialog box shown in Figure 6.22. These special characters aren't limited to headers and footers; you can insert them anywhere in your document. They are explained as follows (except for the hyphenation characters, which are beyond the scope of this *teach yourself...* book):

Special Character	Action
End-of-line mark	This starts a new line without starting a new paragraph; it's the same as pressing **Shift+Enter**.
Print page number	Inserts a *page* placeholder in the document. Works replaces the placeholder with the page number each time you print or preview the document.
Print filename	Inserts a *filename* placeholder at the cursor. Works replaces the placeholder with the filename each time you print or preview the document.
Print date	Inserts a *date* placeholder at the cursor. Works replaces the placeholder with the short date (as in 12/1/94) each time you print or preview the document.
Print long date	Inserts a *longdate* placeholder at the cursor. Works replaces the placeholder with the long date (as in December 1, 1994) each time you print or preview the document.
Print time	Inserts a *time* placeholder at the cursor. Works replaces the placeholder with the time whenever you print or preview the document.
Current date	Inserts the current date in the document. (The date is not replaced when you print or preview the document.)

Current time   Inserts the current time in the document. (The time is not replaced when you print or preview the document.)

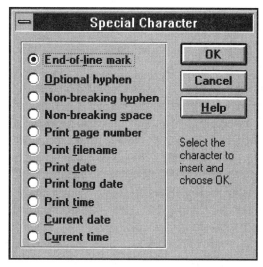

Figure 6.22 *Special Character dialog box*

Notice that the date special characters come in handy when preparing letters or memos. Rather than type the date yourself, for example, you could insert the *longdate* placeholder and Works will insert the current date when the letter is printed. These special characters, along with the time special characters, are helpful when creating forms, newsletters, contracts, and other dated and time-stamped documents.

❖ **To insert a special character:**

1. Position the cursor where you want the special character to appear.

2. Choose **Insert Special Character**. The Special Character dialog box opens.

3. Click the character you want to insert and click **OK**. The dialog box closes, and the designated text or placeholder is inserted at the cursor.

If you insert a placeholder, you can see what the actual text will look like in print preview mode.

Spacing for Headers and Footers

The header and footer are printed in the top and bottom margin. You must make sure there is room for them in the margins. If your bottom margin is only 0.25 inch, for example, a footer would be squeezed in between the bottom of the regular text and the bottom edge of the paper. A 1-inch margin, or greater, is a better choice when you're using a header or footer. (If it has multiple lines, use an even larger margin.)

You can control the placement of headers and footers in the margin with the **File Page Setup** command. Choose the **Margins** dialog box (see Figure 6.23). The default header margin of 0.5 inch means that the header will be printed 0.5 inch from the top edge of the paper. (Don't forget to adjust all these measurements if your printer doesn't align perfectly with the top of the paper.) If it's a multiple line header, the margin designates the position of the first line. If you use a three-line header in a normal 10- to 12-point font, you should probably use a 1.5-inch top margin and place the first line of the header at 0.5 inch. This leaves approximately 0.5 inch above and below the header. If you use a single-line header, a 1-inch margin and a 0.5-inch header margin look fine.

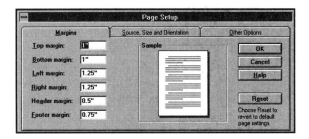

Figure 6.23 *Margins dialog box*

Similarly, the footer margin designates the position of the first or only line of the footer. If the footer has multiple lines, be sure to make the footer margin wide enough to hold the entire footer and still leave some room at the bottom of the page. For a single-line footer, the default 1-inch margin and 0.75-inch footer margin are adequate. For multiple-line footers, you'll probably need to increase both the bottom margin and the footer margin.

The header and footer margins must not be wider than the top and bottom margins, respectively. If you make them too large, Works adjusts them to the same size as the top and bottom margins. If you make them too small and

Works doesn't have room to print the header or the footer, an error message at print time says **Header (or footer) too tall**. You can choose to print or preview the document anyway, but the header or footer won't be printed.

Columns

If you're preparing a newsletter, a brochure or program to be folded in half or in thirds, or a booklet, you probably want to use several columns on the page. Choose **Format Columns** to open the Columns dialog box shown in Figure 6.24. All you have to do is enter the number of columns you want in the **Number of columns** box. By default, Works puts a half inch of space between the columns and draws a line down the middle of the space. You can specify a different spacing in **Space between**. If you don't want a line down the center, click **Line Between** to remove the *X* from the checkbox. When you click **OK**, if you're not in Page Layout view, Works asks if you want to switch to it because it's much easier to see the column layout in that view.

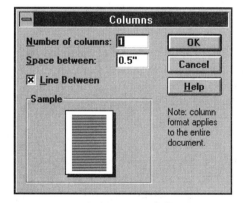

Figure 6.24 *Columns dialog box*

All the columns have the same width, and if there are more than two, they all have the same space between them. There's no way to make some columns or spaces wider than others. There's also no way to have columns for just part of a document; the entire document is affected by the columns setting.

You can run a heading across two or more columns by inserting it as WordArt or a drawing. The next chapter shows you how to do that.

N O T E

The **Format Columns** command creates "newspaper" or "snaking" columns. When the first column fills up first, you go to the top of the second column and continue. The indent markers in the ruler show the margins of the current column.

If you justify paragraphs in two or more columns, you'll end up with many loose lines unless you use hyphenation.

N O T E

AutoStart Templates

Until you have gained some experience at formatting, your documents probably won't be very sophisticated. In the meantime, you can use WorksWizards and AutoStart templates to take advantage of some professional designs provided by Microsoft. You have already seen the WorkWizards letterhead designs in Chapter 3. This section shows you the AutoStart templates for Word Processor documents.

An AutoStart template is a previously designed document in which you can replace generic data with your personal data. The difference between an AutoStart template and a WorksWizard is primarily that the templates don't use dialog boxes to collect the information. When you open the template, the document appears on your screen, and you replace the generic text with your own.

Most of the AutoStart templates are Spreadsheet documents, but there are a few Word Processor documents: a resumé, a newsletter, an overdue account letter, and several types of tests (for classroom teachers). This section shows you how to use the resumé and the newsletter. Once you know how to use them, you'll quickly figure out the others.

Opening an AutoStart Template

Choose **File Templates** or press the **Use a Template** button in the Startup dialog box to display template information (see Figure 6.25). The templates fall into several groups, and each group has several categories. Drop down the group list to pick a group. Then choose a category. And finally, choose a template. In the Template list, each template has an icon indicating whether it is a Spreadsheet document (as with Sales Invoice, Service Invoice, and Account Statement in the figure), a Word Processor document (Past Due Statement in the figure), or a Database (Accounts Receivable). Double-click the template you want to open.

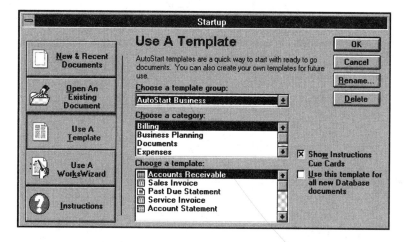

Figure 6.25 *Startup dialog box set up for AutoStart templates*

The Resumé Template

The Resumé template is in the AutoStart Personal group, the Documents category. (It's also in the AutoStart Education group, the Productivity category.) Figure 6.26 shows what it looks like when you first open it.

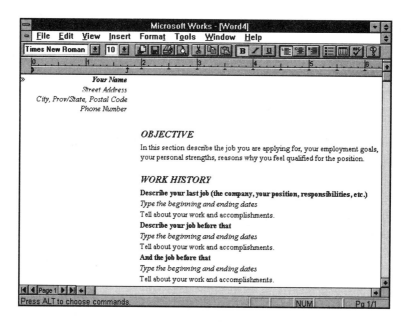

Figure 6.26 *Resumé template*

 If you leave **Show Instructions Cue Cards** checked in the Startup dialog box, a Cue Card appears on the screen with instructions to replace the generic data with your own. The Cue Card has been
N O T E eliminated from Figure 6.26.

All you have to do is replace data. On a color monitor, all the data to be replaced appears in dark red. Headings such as *Objective* and *Work History* appear in black because they should not be replaced.)

As you can see from looking at the figure, the template provides you with an attractive format, but it doesn't really write your resumé for you. You still have to write your objective, organize your work history, and so on. Delete from the template any sections that you don't want to use. And, of course, feel free to add sections, being careful to maintain the format.

When you're done with the resumé, save it and print it as normal. When you save it, you'll have to provide a name for it, just like any other new document. Your personal data will be saved in the new file; it will not affect the

AutoStart template. If you decide to open the template again, it will look like Figure 6.26.

When you replace the dark red text in the template, your replacement text also appears in dark red. If you print on a black and white printer, it will come out black and no one will be the wiser. But if you have a color printer, you might want to change it to black before printing.

The Newsletter Template

The Three-Column Newsletter template is also in the AutoStart Business group, the Documents category, as well as other locations. Figure 6.27 shows what the Newsletter looks like, using Print Preview so you can see the whole first page.

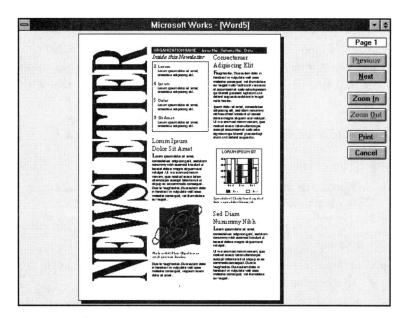

Figure 6.27 *Three-Column Newsletter template in Print Preview*

Again, what you have is a professional-looking format. It's up to you to fill in the name of the organization, the issue number, volume number, the date, and, of course, the articles (which are in Latin in the template). You might want to replace the huge "Newsletter" banner with the name of your organization's newsletter.

NOTE Unfortunately, you can't just replace the word "Newsletter" with your own text because the banner was created by WordArt. You have to completely edit the WordArt. You'll learn how to do that in the next chapter. You'll also learn how to replace, move, or delete graphics such as those on the first page.

The Three-Column Newsletter template has a second page, containing more "articles" and graphics. If you need additional pages, all you have to do is make copies of the second page and continue replacing generic articles with real ones.

As with all templates, saving your new newsletter creates a new file and does not change the template in any way.

Creating Your Own Templates

As you can see, templates can come in handy, so you might want to create a few of your own. For example, if you made your blank letterhead into a template, you could use it repeatedly to create letters, and the template would always be blank.

❖ **To create a template:**

1. Open or create the document that you want to turn into a template.

2. Choose **File Save As**. The Save As dialog box opens. (Refer back to Figure 4.5 on page 91).

3. Click the **Templates** button. The Save As Template dialog box opens.

4. Type a name for the template, such as "My Letterhead" or "Membership Form."

5. Click **OK**. Works makes the current document into a template in the Custom group, the Custom category.

Summary

In this chapter, you have learned how to make your documents much more attractive and professional looking. You now know how to:

❖ Change the font, size, style, position, and even the color of a block of text

❖ Control alignment, indentation, tabs, borders, spacing, and breaks of paragraphs

❖ Add headers, footers, and page numbers to your document, as well as work with columns.

❖ Use some of the AutoStart templates

❖ Create your own templates

Your document is starting to look pretty good now. But what about some of the bells and whistles, like footnotes and graphics? And when do you check spelling? These features, and more, are covered in the next chapter.

CHAPTER 7

Word Processor Special Features

Typing and formatting a document is just the beginning with Works. Word Processor provides a number of special features to polish your documents as well as to manage your document files. This chapter shows you how to:

- ❖ Use the Spelling Checker
- ❖ Look up words in the Thesaurus
- ❖ Open and work with multiple documents
- ❖ Split a document window
- ❖ Insert footnotes in a document
- ❖ Attach Note-Its to a document
- ❖ Insert ClipArt in a document

❖ Create and use WordArt

❖ Work with documents in other directories

❖ Convert text to and from other formats

❖ Save backup versions of a document

Checking Spelling

Works includes a Spelling Checker that can find and correct typographical errors in your document. You can check the entire document or a selected block. If you're not sure how to spell a word, for example, type it as best you can and let Works correct the spelling.

❖ **To find out how to spell a word:**

1. Type the word as best you can.

2. Double-click the word to select it.

3. Click the **Spelling Check** icon. Works checks the highlighted word. If it's correct, you'll see a message that the spelling check is finished. If it's wrong, the Spelling dialog box appears (see Figure 7.1).

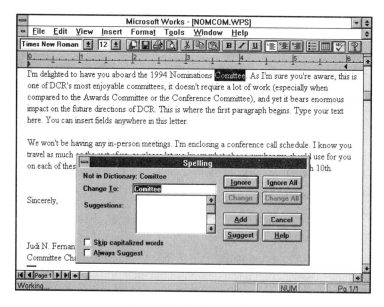

Figure 7.1 *Spelling dialog box*

4. If the Spelling dialog box appears, click **Suggest** to see a list of suggested spellings. For "Comittee", Works suggests "Committee" and "Comity." It's fairly easy to figure out which one you want.

5. Double-click the correct spelling. Works replaces the highlighted word with the word you choose in the list.

If you add a new paragraph to a document that has already been proofed, you can select and check only that paragraph. Or, if you don't select any text, Spelling Checker starts at the cursor, works forward to the end of the document, and then asks if you want to continue at the beginning of the document (if it didn't start at the beginning).

Works checks spelling by comparing words to its spelling dictionary. If a word isn't in the dictionary, Works reports it as a possible misspelling. If you ask for suggestions, Works lists one or more words from the dictionary that come close to it.

Spelling Checker often doesn't recognize technical jargon, proper names, acronyms such as NAFTA or YWCA, and other uncommon combinations of letters. You can tell it to ignore such words or add them to its dictionary.

In Figure 7.1, notice that the unidentified word is highlighted and displayed on the top line, so that you can see it in context. It is also repeated in the **Change To** box where you can correct the spelling if you wish.

The command buttons are explained as follows:

❖ **Ignore** If you know that the highlighted word is correct, click **Ignore** to tell Spelling Checker to leave the word alone and continue checking.

❖ **Ignore All** If the highlighted word is correct and appears several times in the document, click **Ignore All** to tell Spelling Checker to ignore all occurrences of the word during this spelling check. (**Ignore All** does not affect future spelling checks.)

❖ **Change** If you type something in the **Change To** box, the **Change** button becomes available. Click it to replace the highlighted word with the text in the **Change To** box.

❖ **Change All** Click **Change All** to replace all occurrences of the highlighted word with the text in the **Change To** box for the duration of this spelling check.

❖ **Add** If the highlighted word is correct and you use it often, click **Add** to add it to Spelling Checker's dictionary. Spelling Checker will recognize it as correct in all future spelling checks.

The larger the spelling dictionary becomes, the longer your spelling checks might take.

N O T E

❖ **Suggest** If the word is incorrect and you don't know how to correct it, click **Suggest** to force Spelling Checker to suggest some alternative words from its dictionary.

You can ask Spelling Checker to suggest alternatives every time by clicking **Always Suggest,** (which slows it down). This command stays selected for the remainder of this spelling check and all future checks until you uncheck it again. Figure 7.2 shows what the Spelling dialog box looks like when Spelling Checker suggests some alternatives. It lists them in the list box and places the most likely one in the **Change To** box. If the word in the **Change To** box is correct, all you have to do is click **Change** or **Change All**. If another word is correct, click it once to place it in the **Change To** box, then click **Change** or **Change All**. If none of the suggestions are correct, type the correct spelling in the **Change To** box and click **Change** or **Change All**.

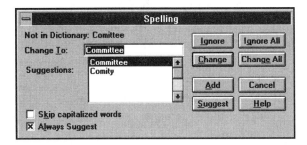

Figure 7.2 *Suggested spellings in the Spelling dialog box*

If you use a lot of acronyms, you might want to check **Skip capitalized words**. Spelling Checker will no longer check any words composed of all capital letters.

Spelling Checker automatically skips words containing digits, such as F114 or A1.

N O T E

Spelling Checker also catches repeated words, as shown in Figure 7.3. The repeated word is highlighted in the document, so you can see it in context. You can choose to ignore the repeated word, delete it by clicking **Change** with an empty **Change To** box, or replace it by typing something in the **Change To** box before clicking **Change**.

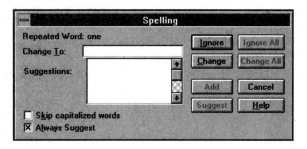

Figure 7.3 *Repeated word in the Spelling dialog box*

The following procedure summarizes the steps for checking spelling.

❖ **To check spelling in a selected section or the entire document:**

1. Position the cursor where you want to start the spelling check, or select the block of text to be checked.
2. Click the **Spelling Check** icon.
3. Decide how to handle each word that is displayed.
4. When Spelling Checker displays its *Spelling check finished* message, click **OK**.

Immediately after a spelling check, you can undo all the changes that were made by choosing **Undo Editing** or pressing **Ctrl+Z**.

Editing the Custom Dictionary

Every time you press **Add**, you add a word to your personal dictionary, not Spelling Checker's main dictionary. You can edit your personal dictionary to delete words you don't need any more or to correct misspellings that you entered into it.

WARNING

The order of words in the spelling dictionary is very important. Do not insert words or move them around. Add words to the dictionary only by the **Add** button in the Spelling dialog box.

❖ **To edit your spelling dictionary:**

1. Choose **File Open Existing File**. The Open dialog box appears (see Figure 4.12 on page 101).

2. In the **File Name** text box, type

    `C:\WINDOWS\MSAPPS\PROOF\CUSTOM.DIC.`

N O T E

If Windows is not installed on drive C, replace the first letter of this expression with the correct drive name for Windows.

The CUSTOM.DIC file should open. If not, you may be using a different custom dictionary (or Windows is not located on the drive you designated).

3. Find the words you want and change or delete them.

4. Click the **Save** icon to save the edited dictionary.

5. Double-click the document window's **Control Menu** icon to close the dictionary.

Using Thesaurus

Thesaurus helps you find synonyms for words. Used with an ounce of common sense, it can help you to find an alternate word, to figure out a very general definition of a word, and even to choose between homophones such as "principal/principle" and "capital/capitol." For example, suppose you want to wax poetic about someone's dark eyes, but you think "dark eyes" is a little commonplace and "black eyes" makes it sound as if he or she has lost a fight. Figure 7.4 shows what happens if you type the word **black** and choose **Tools Thesaurus**.

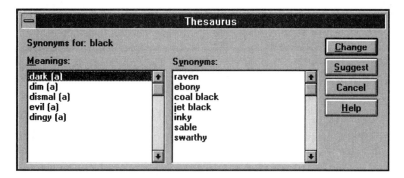

Figure 7.4 *Thesaurus dialog box for black*

On the left, you can see that "black" can have several meanings. The first meaning, "dark," is the one that's selected right now, and that's probably the one you want. (The others would hardly curry favor with the object of your affection.) On the right, you can see a list of synonyms for "black" that pertain to the "dark" meaning.

Now here's where you have to apply some common sense. It's dangerous to select a synonym that you've never heard of. These words are not perfectly synonymous, and you might select a word with unintentional connotations or usages. For example, "swarthy" usually applies to complexion or character, not eyes. Thesaurus can point out a new word, but if you're smart, you'll look it up in a good dictionary before you use it.

You must also exercise caution if you try to use Thesaurus to find out what a word means. Figure 7.5 shows how Thesaurus handles "intone." It's clear that "intone" is related more to talking out loud than to, say, repairing a car or designing wallpaper, but its exact meaning cannot be determined from the information presented here. Also, it's possible that the word has other meanings that Thesaurus doesn't address. In general, a dictionary is a better resource for defining words. But for a quick check without leaving your computer, Thesaurus can be a handy feature.

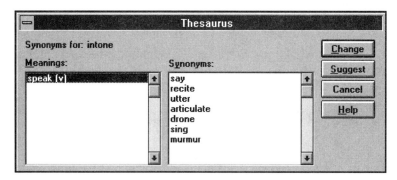

Figure 7.5 *Thesaurus dialog box for intone*

Now suppose you want to say something about the head of the local grade school, and you're not sure whether the correct word is "principle" or "principal." Figure 7.6 shows how Thesaurus responds to the word "principle." Clearly, this is not the word you want. A quick check of "principal" reveals that it's the right word. In this case, Thesaurus is the only reference you need.

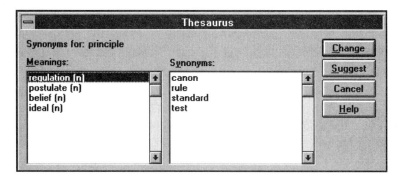

Figure 7.6 *Thesaurus dialog box for principle*

Once the Thesaurus dialog box is open, you can explore other meanings and related words. You can click any word in the **Meanings** box to see the list of synonyms related to that meaning. You can also abandon your original word and look up any word in either list box; click the word, and click **Suggest**. If you find a word in either list that you want to use in place of the original word, double-click it; Thesaurus replaces the word in your document. If you can't find a replacement word, click **Cancel** to close the dialog box.

If the **Meanings** column contains the entry *Similar words*, your word is a spelling variation of a Thesaurus word. For example, the word "awards" results in *Similar words* under **Meanings** and *award* under **Synonyms**. Click **Suggest** to look up "award."

Thesaurus contains nearly 200,000 words, but that might not be enough. It contains "church" but not "chapel" or "cathedral," for example. It contains "naval" but not "navel," it contains "pill" but not "lozenge," and it contains "red" and "blue" but not "orange" or "purple." The only meaning it recognizes for "maroon" is "color". In many cases when you need a thesaurus, you need a more extensive one than this.

❖ **To look up a word in Thesaurus:**

1. Type the word, or, if it's already typed, position the cursor in it.
2. Choose **Tools Thesaurus**. Either the Thesaurus dialog box appears or a message tells you that the word was not found.
3. If the Thesaurus dialog box opens, click each word in the **Meanings** box to explore all the meanings of the word.
4. If you want to look up one of the meanings or synonyms, click it and click **Suggest**.
5. If you find a word you want to use in your document, double-click it. Thesaurus replaces the original word with the selected word.
6. If you don't find a word to use, click **Cancel** to close the dialog box.

Splitting Windows

Sometimes it's handy to look at two parts of a document at once. For example, you might want to see what you said in the introduction to a report as you write the summary. Works won't let you open the same document in two different windows, but you can split a document window in two panes and view a different part of the document in each pane. You can even drag text from one pane to the other.

❖ **To split a document window:**

1. Position the cursor in the text that you want the bottom pane to display.

2. Double-click the **Split** box (see Figure 7.7).

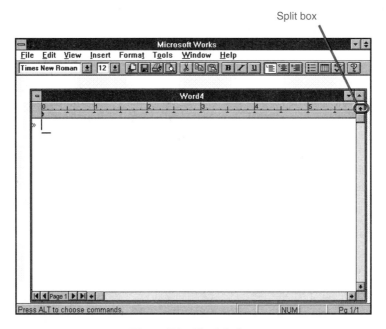

Figure 7.7 *The Split box*

The window splits into two equal panes (see Figure 7.8). Each pane has its own ruler. The top pane shows the beginning of the document, and the bottom pane shows the location of the cursor.

3. Drag the split bar (marked in Figure 7.8) up or down to adjust the sizes of the panes. When the mouse pointer is over the split bar, it takes the shape shown in Figure 7.8.

4. Scroll the top pane to show the desired part of the document.

Now that the window is split, each pane scrolls independently. The cursor can be in only one pane; the active pane shows tabs and indents on the ruler. However, you're still editing only one copy of the document. If you make a change in the top pane and then look at that same part of the document in the bottom pane, you will see the change.

To remove the split, double-click the split bar.

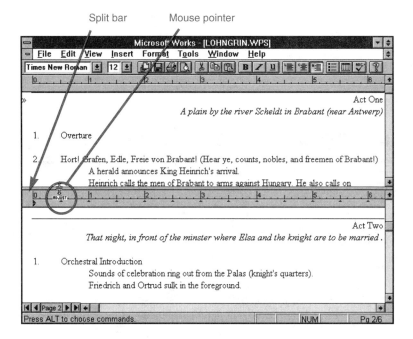

Figure 7.8 *Document window panes*

Working with Multiple Documents

It's also handy to work with two or more documents at one time. You might want to refer to your outline while writing a report, for example. Or you might want to move something from Chapter 1 to Chapter 2. There's no trick to opening multiple documents; just open each one normally. You can have up to eight documents open at once. You can open existing documents as well as new ones.

SHORTCUT

When one document is already open, you can click the **Startup Dialog** icon on the toolbar (the first icon on the toolbar) to open the Startup dialog box.

There are several ways to arrange multiple document windows within the Works workspace. You can just drag them around and resize them until they suit you. The **Window Tile** command fits them all in like a jigsaw puzzle. Figure 7.9 shows how it tiles four document windows.

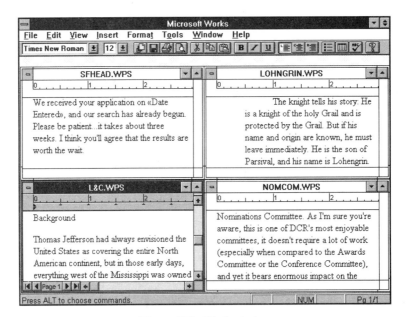

Figure 7.9 *Tiled windows*

Only one window at a time can be active. The window with the highlighted title bar (L&C.WPS in the figure) and a scroll bar is the active one. Click a window to activate it.

The **Window Cascade** command arranges all the open, unminimized windows in step fashion so you can see each title bar, but you can read only the top one, which is always the active one. Figure 7.10 shows what four cascaded windows look like. Click another window to activate it. Activating it brings it to the top, which spoils the neat cascading, but you can always choose **Window Cascade** again to straighten up the windows.

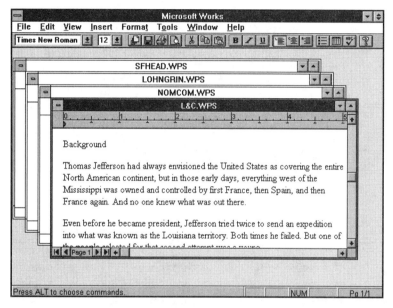

Figure 7.10 *Cascaded windows*

If you maximize one window, you maximize them all. Then you can switch among them by repeatedly pressing **Ctrl+F6**, which cycles through all the open windows, even the minimized ones. If you have so many windows open that it takes too long to find the one you want, pull down the Window menu instead (see Figure 7.11). The bottom section of this menu lists all the open windows, minimized or not. Just click the one you want.

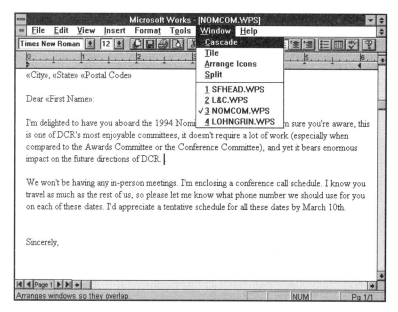

Figure 7.11 *The Window menu*

To copy a block from one window to another, simply drag it to the other window. You don't have to be able to see the entire destination window when you start to drag, but you do have to be able to see some of it. If you drag the block over any part of the destination window and pause for a moment, that window pops to the top and you can find the location where you want to insert the block.

You may find it easier to select the block in the source window, choose the **Edit Copy** command to copy it to the Clipboard, then position the cursor in the destination window, and choose **Edit Paste**.

N O T E

Moving text from one window to another is just like copying it, but you have to hold down the **Shift** key while you drag it.

N O T E   When you're over the destination window, the mouse pointer says *Move* or *Copy* to indicate which action will be taken when you release the mouse button. If it says *Copy*, you can press **Shift** to make it say *Move*.

Footnotes

Footnotes used to be the bane of the typist, but Word Processor makes them easy to manage. Word Processor automatically numbers the footnote and positions it perfectly at the bottom of the page, drawing a partial line above it to separate it from the body of the page. Or, if you prefer, you can use symbols such as * and # instead of reference numbers, and you can print all your footnotes at the end of the document.

Inserting a Footnote

❖   **To insert a footnote:**

1.   Position the cursor where you want the reference to appear.

2.   Choose **Insert Footnote**. The Footnote dialog box opens (see Figure 7.12).

3.   Click **Numbered** if you want Word Processor to number the footnote, or click **Character mark** if you want to use a character such as * or # to refer to the footnote. If you clicked **Character mark**, the **Mark** box becomes available. Type the desired character in the box.

4.   Click **OK**. Word Processor inserts the reference number or mark at the cursor position, as a superscript (see Figure 7.13). In Draft or Normal view, the window splits into two panes; the bottom pane is the footnote pane (also shown in Figure 7.13). In Page Layout view, Word Processor prepares the bottom of the page for the footnote. In all views, Word Processor inserts the reference number or mark in the footnote and positions the cursor so that you can type the text.

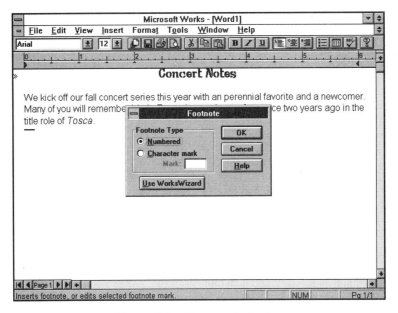

Figure 7.12 *Footnote dialog box*

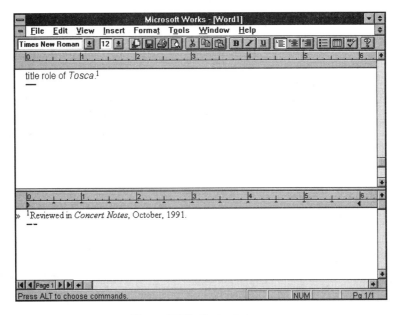

Figure 7.13 *Footnote pane*

5. Type the footnote.

6. In Page Layout view, return the cursor to the regular text and continue working. In Draft or Normal view, double-click the Split bar to close the footnote pane. Then continue working.

You can see what your footnotes will look like in print by examining Print Preview. In Figure 7.14, you may not be able to read the footnote, but you can see how it is positioned on the page.

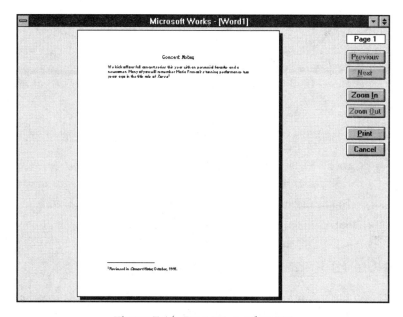

Figure 7.14 *Previewing a footnote*

You can format a footnote just like any other text. You can change the font, the indentation, and so on.

N O T E

Managing Footnotes

Word Processor tracks footnote numbers for you. If you insert or delete a footnote, Word Processor renumbers the others as needed. If several footnotes fall on one page, Word Processor expands the size of the footnote area to accommodate them all. It also carries a footnote correctly over to the next page as needed. If you modify a document so that the reference to a footnote changes pages, Word Processor moves the footnote automatically to keep it on the same page as its reference.

You delete a footnote by deleting its reference number or mark. You can move a footnote by dragging the reference number or mark to another position. For longer distances, you might prefer to cut and paste it. To edit the text of the footnote in Page Layout view, scroll to the bottom of the page and edit it just like any other text. In the other views, you have to open the footnote pane again.

❖ **To edit the text of a footnote in Draft or Normal view:**

1. Choose **View Footnote**. The footnote pane opens. (All the document's footnotes are in one pane, no matter what pages they fall on.)

2. Scroll to find the footnote you want and edit it as normal.

3. Double-click the Split bar to close the footnote pane.

Using the Footnote WorksWizard

Of course, typing a footnote is only half the battle. Writing it is the other half, and if it's a bibliographic reference, many people lose the war right there. If you have to do a bibliographic reference and you're not sure of the correct format, you can let WorksWizard format it for you. Start the footnote as before. But when the Footnote dialog box opens, click the **Use WorksWizard** button. The Welcome dialog box opens (see Figure 7.15). As you can see, you can choose from a number of reference sources.

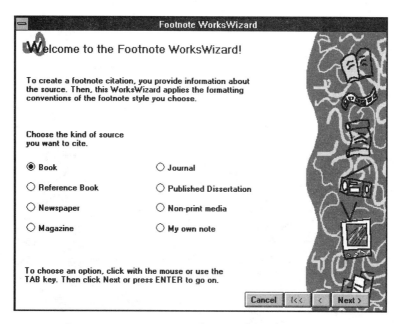

Figure 7.15 *Footnotes WorksWizard—Welcome screen*

If you choose **Book** and press **Next >**, the Footnote Data dialog box shown in Figure 7.16 appears. All you have to do in this dialog box is fill in the data in the text boxes. Click **More Information** if you want to include some additional information in the footnote. Click **Footnote Style** to see how WorksWizard will format the footnote. You have a choice of two styles as defined by the *Modern Language Association* (the default) or the *Chicago Manual of Style*. When you're ready, click **Done** to complete the footnote.

WorksWizard footnotes for the other types of sources, such as newspapers and magazines, are developed the same way. You fill in several text boxes with the information, click **Footnote Style** to select from the two styles, if desired, then click **Done** to create the footnote.

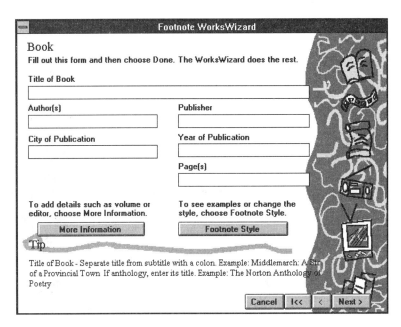

Figure 7.16 *Footnotes WorksWizard—Footnote Data screen*

Note-It

When you review something on paper, do you write directly on it, or do you attach sticky notes to it? Either way, Works simulate the process, letting you attach notes to a document that don't become part of the text. Note-Its, as they are called, are actually graphics that you embed in the document.

Figure 7.17 shows a document with several Note-Its attached. As you can see, they really stand out on the page. On a color monitor, the graphic is bright yellow, like a sticky note. The short message under the graphic is just a caption. You can read the longer message by double-clicking the Note-It.

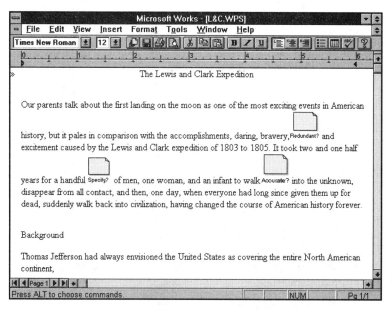

Figure 7.17 *Using Note-Its*

❖ **To attach a Note-It:**

1. Position the cursor where you want the Note-It to appear.

2. Choose **Insert Note-It**. The Note-It dialog box opens (see Figure 7.18).

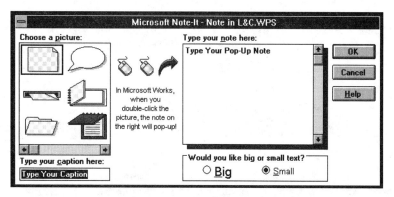

Figure 7.18 *Microsoft Note-It dialog box*

3. Scroll through the **Graphics** box and select a graphic. There are more than 50 graphics to choose from.

4. Replace the generic caption (*Type Your Caption*) with the caption you want to use.

5. Replace the generic note (*Type Your Pop-Up Note*) with the note you want to use.

6. Select big or small text for the caption and note. (If you shrink the note in Step 8, you'll probably need big text.)

7. Click **OK**. The dialog box closes and the Note-It is embedded at the cursor position. It's about twice as large as those shown in Figure 7.17. The line spacing is adjusted to accommodate the graphic.

8. If you want to shrink the Note-It to a more reasonable size, follow these steps:

   a   Click the Note-It to select it. A dotted box appears around the Note-It with eight small squares (called *handles*) at the corners and sides (see Figure 7.19).

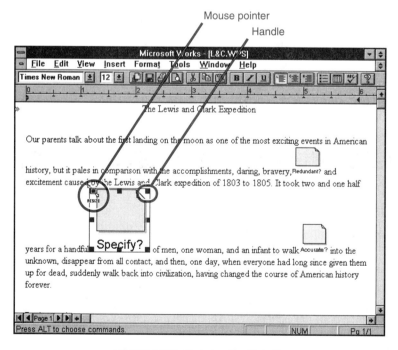

Figure 7.19 *Resizing the Note-It*

b. Position the mouse pointer over a corner handle. The mouse pointer turns into a **Resize** icon (shown in Figure 7.19).

c. Drag the corner toward the center of the graphic to shrink it. When it reaches the size you want, release it.

Double-click a Note-It to read it. A Note box pops up on the screen (see Figure 7.20). The open Note-It is shaded. Click anywhere to close the Note box.

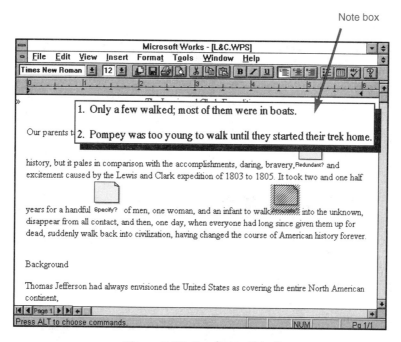

Figure 7.20 *Reading a Note-It*

You can delete a Note-It by deleting the graphic. Just click it and press **Delete**. To move it, click it and drag it. Be careful to drag the note itself, not the handle; the mouse pointer should say *Drag* and then *Move*, not *Resize*.

You can edit a Note-It by using the Edit menu.

❖ **To edit a Note-It:**

1. Click the Note-It. A dotted box with handles appears around the graphic.

2. Choose **Edit Microsoft Note-It Object**. A submenu appears (see Figure 7.21).

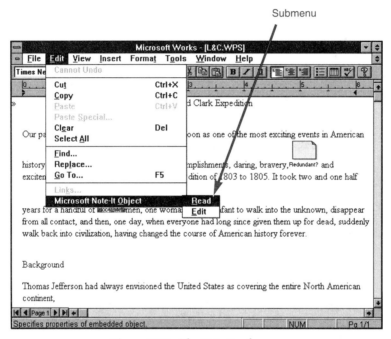

Figure 7.21 *The Note-It submenu*

3. Choose **Edit** on the submenu. The Note-It dialog box opens showing the settings and text for the selected Note-It. (It's just like Figure 7.18.) You can change anything in this dialog box.

ClipArt

Using ClipArt is a lot like using Note-Its, except you don't add any notes to the drawings. You insert and manage the drawings in much the same way.

Inserting a ClipArt Drawing

❖   **To insert a ClipArt drawing:**

1.   Position the cursor where you want to insert the drawing.

2.   Choose **Insert ClipArt**. The ClipArt dialog box opens (see Figure 7.22).

Figure 7.22 *ClipArt dialog box*

3.   Scroll through the pictures until you find the one you want.

4.   Double-click the drawing. The dialog box closes, and the drawing is inserted at the cursor position.

5.   Follow these steps to resize the drawing:

a. Click the ClipArt to select it. A dotted box with handles appears around the drawing.

b. Position the mouse pointer over a corner handle. The mouse pointer turns into a **Resize** icon.

c. Drag the corner in or out to stretch or shrink the ClipArt. When it reaches the size you want, release the handle.

N O T E

This procedure uses corner handles to resize a drawing. You can use the side handles, but you'll distort the proportions of the drawing if you do. By dragging one of the side handles, you can make a drawing tall and skinny or short and fat, if you wish.

Each drawing in the ClipArt gallery belongs to a category, such as Animals or Food. By default, Works displays all the categories. If you select a specific category, Works displays drawings from that category only. The categories supplied by Works have fewer than 12 drawings each, so you don't have to scroll to see them all unless you add more drawings to them.

N O T E

If you insert a ClipArt in the header or footer, it appears on every page of the document.

Positioning ClipArt and Note-Its

By default, a ClipArt or a Note-It is embedded in the text and is part of the text, behaving something like an unusually large character. If you revise the document so that the text moves on the page, the embedded object moves with it, maintaining its relationship to the characters before and after it. You can move the embedded object to another position, just like any other character, and it will maintain its new position in the text.

However, you can also position a Note-It or ClipArt in a fixed position on the page. No matter how much you revise the text, the ClipArt maintains its fixed position. You can position it anywhere on the page, including areas that have no text, like the margins. If you place it in the header or footer margin, it appears on every page in that position.

❖ **To position an embedded object on the page:**

1. Insert the object anywhere in the text, as usual.

2. Select the object and choose **Format Picture/Object**. The Picture/Object dialog box opens (see Figure 7.23).

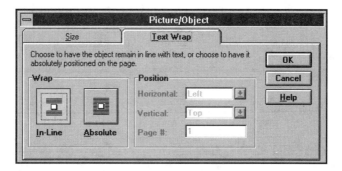

Figure 7.23 *Picture/Object dialog box*

3. Click **Absolute**. The boxes in the **Position** group become available.

4. You don't need to specify the position. Click **OK** to close the dialog box. The selected object moves to the default position on the page.

You need to be in Page Layout view to see and work with the new positioning. If you are in some other view, Works asks if you want to switch to Page Layout view. Click **Yes** to continue.

NOTE

5. Drag the object to whatever position you wish. If the object is in a text area, the text moves aside to accommodate the object. You can't cover text with an embedded object.

Managing a ClipArt Object

You can manage a ClipArt just like a Note-It. You can move it, resize it, copy it, and delete it. If you want to replace it with another picture, double-click it to reopen the ClipArt dialog box.

WordArt

Works' WordArt tool lets you create your own logo out of your company name or slogan. You can also create dramatic headings, titles, newsletter banners, advertising copy, and so on. Figure 7.24 shows an example of a logo created out of the phrase *Sunset Tours*. You embed WordArt in documents in much the same manner that you embed Note-Its or ClipArt.

Figure 7.24 *Logo created by WordArt*

Start creating a WordArt logo by positioning the cursor and choosing **Insert WordArt**. The WordArt program takes over the screen (see Figure 7.25). You can still see your document in the background, but the toolbar and menu bar belong to WordArt, not Word Processor. You create the logo in the shaded box that says *Your Text Here* at the start. Feel free to experiment with the WordArt special effects; you'll see the result in this box.

When WordArt first appears, the text *Your Text Here* appears in the dialog box and is selected. Type the text that you want to work with. It appears in this dialog box as well as the shaded box. Then you can start using the WordArt special effects on it.

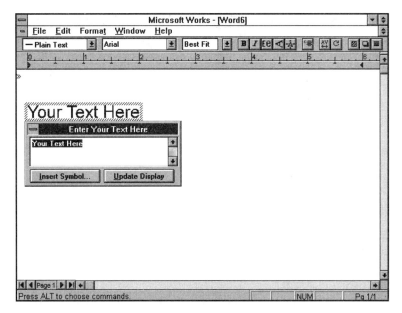

Figure 7.25 *The WordArt screen*

The shaded box marks a frame. It shows the size of the WordArt that will be embedded in the document when you close the WordArt program. You can't resize the frame directly, but it might change size and shape as you manipulate the text inside it. After you close WordArt and the graphic is embedded in your document, you can resize it just like any other embedded object.

Toolbar Features

You use the toolbar to manipulate the text in the frame. From left the right, the features on the toolbar are:

❖ **Shape** Drop down this list to select a shape for the text (see Figure 7.26). The Sunset Tours example uses the shape called **Deflate**, which is convex on both the top and the bottom.

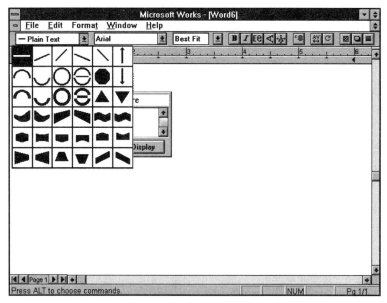

Figure 7.26 *Shape drop-down list*

❖ **Font** Drop down this list to select a font for the text.

❖ **Size** Dropdown this list to select a size for the font. The default **Best Fit** setting selects the best font size for the frame; resizing the object changes the size of the font. If you choose a specific font size, your text will stay that size regardless of how you resize the object later on.

❖ **Bold** Click the **Bold** icon to make the font **bold**.

❖ **Italic** Click the **Italic** icon to make the font *italic*.

❖ **Even Height** Click the **Even Height** icon to make all the letters the same height, even though some are capital and some are lowercase.

❖ **Flip** Click the **Flip** icon to turn each letter on its side; that is, each letter rotates 90 degrees to the left.

❖ **Stretch** Click the **Stretch** icon to stretch the text to fill the frame regardless of how much it becomes distorted.

❖ **Align** Click the **Align** icon to pop up a menu of alignment choices. The text is centered in the frame by default. You can choose **left**, **right**, **center**, **stretch justify** (letters are stretched to justify the text), **word justify** (space is added between words to justify the text), or **letter**

justify (space is added between letters and between words to justify the text).

❖ **Spacing between Characters** Click this icon to pop up a dialog box where you can make the spacing between characters very tight, very loose, or something in between.

❖ **Rotation** Click the **Rotation** icon to rotate the entire WordArt.

❖ **Shading** Click the **Shading** icon to open the shading dialog box where you can select a shading pattern and colors for your WordArt. The Sunset Tours logo uses a horizontal striped pattern with dark red and gray stripes. (Unfortunately, these stripes appear in black and white in Figure 7.24.)

❖ **Shadow** Click the **Shadow** icon to open the shadow dialog box where you can add a shadow to your WordArt (see Figure 7.27).

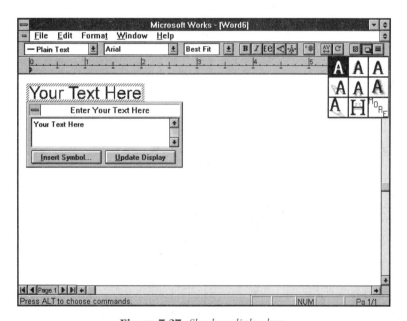

Figure 7.27 *Shadow dialog box*

If a shadow is unreadable when you create it, making the frame larger after you leave WordArt can help.

NOTE

❖ **Border** In WordArt, text can have a border and an interior, both of which can be different colors. By default, it has no border. Click the **Border** icon to select the thickness and color of the border. (Shading affects the interior only.)

Embedding the WordArt in Your Document

When you're done designing your WordArt, click anywhere in your document (not in the WordArt areas) to close the WordArt program and return to Word Processor. Then you can select and manipulate the new logo like any other embedded object. You can move it, resize it, position on the page instead of in the text, and delete it. You can also copy it to other documents.

Unfortunately, there's no way to save a WordArt logo as ClipArt or as a separate drawing. If you want to use it on several documents, you must copy it from one to the other.

NOTE

More on Managing Word Processor Documents

You've already learned how to create a new document, save it, print it, close it, and reopen it. This section shows you some more things you can do.

Using Other Directories

You might want to set up a variety of directories to store the documents you create with Works. For example, you might store all your Word Processor documents in one directory, all your Spreadsheet documents in another directory, and so on. Or you might set up your directories according to projects; one directory for financial management, another for marketing, and so on.

So far, you've been using the Works directory (MSWORKS) to save all your files, but if you continue doing so, it could become so full that you'll have trouble finding the file you want. You can't create new directories through Works. You have to use Windows or DOS. The following procedure shows you how to do it in Windows.

❖ **To create a new directory in Windows:**

1. In the Program Manager window, double-click the **Main** group icon. The Main group window opens.

2. In the Main group window, double-click the **File Manager** icon. The File Manager window opens (see Figure 7.28).

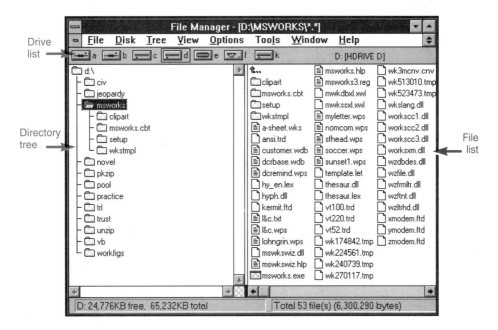

Figure 7.28 *File Manager window*

3. In the Drive list, click the drive name where you want to create the new directory.

You don't have to do this if the desired drive is already selected; the selected drive has a box around it.

N O T E

The directory structure of the selected drive is displayed in the window.

4. In the directory tree, click the directory that should be the parent of the new directory.

You don't have to do this if the desired directory is already selected; you can identify the selected directory by the highlight in the directory tree.

N O T E

5. Choose **File Create Directory**. The Create Directory dialog box opens.

6. Type a name for the new directory in the **Name** box. It can have up to eight characters plus an extension of up to three characters.

7. Click **OK**. The dialog box closes and the new directory appears in the directory tree.

After you have created all the directories you need, you might want to move some of the files you have already created to them. The following procedure shows you how to move files in Windows.

❖ **To move a one or more files in Windows:**

1. If File Manager is not open, follow Steps 1 and 2 in the previous procedure.

2. In the Drive list, click the drive containing the files you want to move. For example, if you want to move files from your MSWORKS directory on drive C, click drive C. (You don't have to do this if the desired drive is already selected.) The directory structure of the selected drive is displayed in the window.

3. In the directory tree, click the directory that contains the files to be moved. For example, if you want to move files from the default Works directory, click **MSWORKS**. (You don't have to do this if the desired directory is already selected.) The File list displays the contents of the selected directory.

4. In the File list, click the name of one file to be moved to another directory. The file name is highlighted.

5. If you want to move more than one file to the same destination directory, hold down **Ctrl** and click the name of each additional file to be moved. Each selected file name is highlighted.

6. Release the **Ctrl** key. Drag any one selected file to the directory tree and drop it on the name of the directory where you want to move all the files. A **Document** icon attaches itself to the mouse pointer as you drag the file(s). When the mouse pointer is in the directory tree, you can tell which directory you are over by the box that surrounds the directory name. When you drop the files, a confirmation dialog box opens.

7. Read the confirmation box carefully. Does it say *move* not *copy?* Does it identify the correct destination directory? If not, click *No* and start over. When the confirmation box shows the correct operation, click *Yes.* File Manager moves the selected files to the destination directory.

You can repeat this procedure as many times as necessary to move files to the new directories you have set up. From now on, when you create a new file, you should save it in the appropriate directory if you don't want to save it in MSWORKS. The following procedures show you how to save a file in another directory and how to open a file in another directory.

❖   **To save a file in a directory other than MSWORKS:**

1. When you're ready to save a file for the first time, click the **Save** icon, as usual. The Save As dialog box opens (see Figure 7.29).

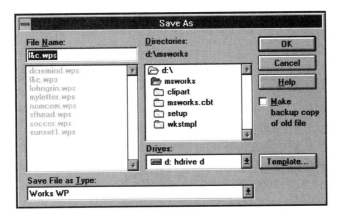

Figure 7.29 *Save As dialog box*

2. Drop down the Drives list and click the drive you want to use. (You don't have to do this if the desired drive is already selected.)

3. In the directory tree, double-click the name of the directory you want to use.

The directory tree in this Save As dialog box doesn't show all the directories on the drive. It shows only the path from the root directory to the currently selected directory (which is identified by an open file folder icon) and all the selected directory's children. If you can't see the directory you want to use, you should double-click the root directory to select it, then follow the path to your directory. For example, if you want to use C:\MYAPPS\RESEARCH, you would double-click **C:** (the root directory); MYAPPS will be included in its children. Double-click **MYAPPS** to select it; RESEARCH will be included in its children. Double-click **RESEARCH** to select it.

4. Once the desired directory is open, type the name of the new document file in the **File Name** box and click **OK**. Works adds the appropriate extension to the file name and stores the document in the specified file in the currently selected directory.

❖ **To open a file in a nondefault directory:**

1. Choose **File Open Existing File**. The Open dialog box opens. (It's nearly identical to the Save As dialog box in Figure 7.29.)

2. Drop down the Drives list and click the drive containing the file. (You don't have to do this if the desired drive is already selected.)

3. In the directory tree, double-click the name of the directory containing the file. As with the Save As dialog box, you might have to start at the root directory and trace the path to the directory you want.

4. Once the desired directory is open, you should be able to see the desired file name. Double-click it. Works opens the requested file.

Sharing Files with Other Word Processors

Sometimes you need to exchange files with a friend who uses another word processor. Most word processors store document files in their own, proprietary format, and unfortunately, they're not compatible with other word processors. Therefore, you can't directly open a document created by another word processor. You have to convert it to Works format.

To open a "foreign" file, you need to know its extension, such as *DOC* for Microsoft Word or *WRI* for Windows Write. Choose **File Open Existing File** and, in the Open File dialog box, drop down the List Files of Type list (see Figure 7.30). Select the name of the word processor that prepared the file. This limits the file list to files that have the extension used by that word processor. If the extension is TXT, choose **Text**. If the word processor is not in the list, or if the file has no extension, choose **All files** to list all the files in the selected directory.

The list is your clue to what word processors, spreadsheets, and databases Works can convert. If the "foreign" word processor isn't in the list, Works probably can't handle its proprietary format. Ask your colleague to store the file in plain text format, which is often called ASCII text or DOS text format, with extension TXT. In the File Type list, click **Text** or **Text (DOS)**.

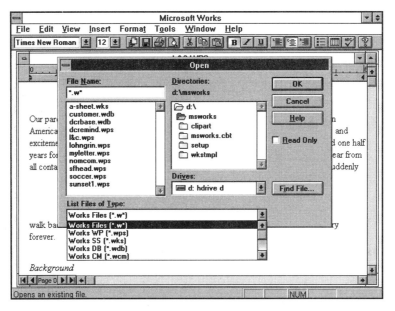

Figure 7.30 *Open File dialog box showing the File Type list*

If the file is not in the default directory, follow the procedure described previously to open a file in another directory. When you find and double-click the name of the non-Works file, Works converts it to its own format. This takes a little while. You'll see a progress message in the status bar while it works.

Choosing a word processor in the List Files of Type list merely controls what extension Works displays in the File list. Works uses information in the file itself to decide what format it is in.

N O T E

If the file is a text file, Works asks if you want to open it in DOS or Windows text format. Try Windows first; if the results aren't satisfactory, try DOS.

N O T E

If you edit the file and click the **Save** icon or choose **File Save**, Works asks if you want to save it in Works 3.0 format. If you say No, Works doesn't save the file. If you say Yes, Works saves the file under its old name, which means the file will have the wrong extension for a Works document. Use **File Save As** instead, and give the file a new name so that Works will assign it the WPS extension.

If you want to save the file, or any file, in a "foreign" format, choose the name of the "foreign" word processor in the File Type list in the Save As dialog box. Then give the file a name but not an extension. If you want to use the generic text type, choose **Text** to save it in Windows text format. If your friend's system has trouble reading that format, try again using **Text (DOS)**. By the way, in either of these formats, you'll lose all formatting information such as fonts, font styles, indentation, and spacing. You'll also lose all embedded objects. All you get is the text, but that's often better than not being able to share the file at all.

Saving Backup Versions

When you save a file that already has a name, Works replaces the previously saved version with the new version. Some people prefer to keep the previous version as a safety measure in case they want to eliminate the current changes to the file. If you would like to keep the previous version of a file, use **File Save As** to save it and check **Make backup copy of old file** in the dialog box. From then on, each time you save the file, Works saves the previous version in a file with the extension BPS.

N O T E   Notice that only one level of backup is saved. If you open a file and save it four times while editing, the WPS file contains the fourth version and the BPS file contains the third version. The version that you opened originally is gone.

If you decide to fall back to the BPS version, select **All files** in the Open dialog box to list files with all extensions. Then find and open the BPS file. Use **File Save As** and replace the BPS extension in the text box with WPS. (You can give it an entirely new name if you want to keep both versions.)

If you decide not to keep backup versions, open the file, choose **File Save As**, and uncheck the **Make backup copy of old file** option.

Summary

This chapter has shown you how to:

- ❖ Use the Spelling Checker and Thesaurus
- ❖ Split the Word Processor window as well as work with multiple documents
- ❖ Use Note-Its, ClipArt, WordArt, and footnotes
- ❖ Save your documents in other directories
- ❖ Share files with other word processors
- ❖ Save backup versions of your documents

Works includes one more graphics feature, in which you can create a drawing from scratch and embed it in your document. Chapter 8 shows you how to use Microsoft Draw.

CHAPTER **8**

Drawing Basics

Microsoft Draw gives you the capability to add line drawings to your documents. Even if you can't draw very well with paper and pencil, you'll be able to create fairly sophisticated looking drawings constructed out of basic geometric shapes. This chapter shows you how to:

- ❖ Draw lines and shapes
- ❖ Draw freehand
- ❖ Select line styles, colors, and shading
- ❖ Add text to drawings
- ❖ Undo drawing actions
- ❖ Modify drawings
- ❖ Embed a drawing in a Word Processor document

Getting Started

You can't start Microsoft Draw as a separate Works tool; you must embed a drawing in a Word Processor or Database document, just as you do with ClipArt and WordArt.

❖ **To start Microsoft Draw:**

1. Position the cursor where you want to embed the drawing. (Remember that you can always move it later.)

2. Choose **Insert Drawing**. The Microsoft Draw window opens (see Figure 8.1).

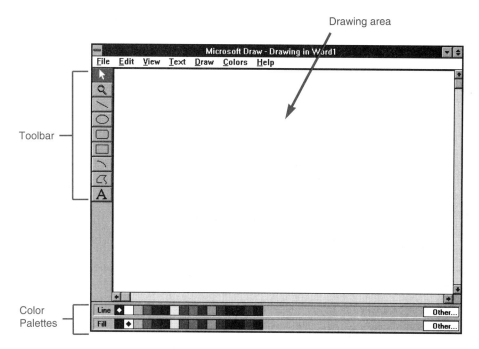

Figure 8.1 *Microsoft Draw window*

NOTE

You'll probably want to maximize the Draw window, as shown in Figure 8.1.

Many of this window's elements should look familiar to you: the title bar, scroll bars, menu bar, and so on. The toolbar runs down the left side of the work area and consists of nine drawing tools. The color palettes let you select colors for your drawing tools.

The Drawing Tools

Figure 8.2 identifies the drawing tools. Six of these tools are used for drawing lines and shapes—from the Line tool to the Freeform tool. Whenever you click one of these tools and move the mouse pointer into the drawing area, the mouse pointer turns into cross-hairs. The intersection of the cross-hairs locates the point of the drawing tool, somewhat like a pencil point. The other three tools have special mouse pointers and special purposes, as you'll see shortly.

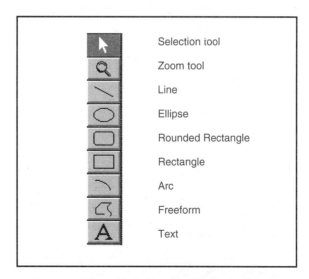

Figure 8.2 *The drawing tools*

Edit Undo removes the last thing you drew or restores the last thing you erased.

N O T E

Your current drawing tool stays selected until you click somewhere. So if you choose the *Line tool*, for example, you can draw several lines without having to reselect the tool each time. Click anywhere to deselect the current tool. When the mouse pointer turns back into an arrow, the drawing tool is no longer selected.

The Line tool draws a straight line. Position the cross-hairs where you want the line to start. Then press and hold down the mouse button and drag the cross-hairs to the end of the line. You can go in any direction, and if you change directions while you draw, the line swings around to the new direction. When you release the mouse button, the new line is fixed on the page. Handles appear at each end of the line because it is selected (see Figure 8.3). They make the line look like it has square ends, but they go away when you do something else.

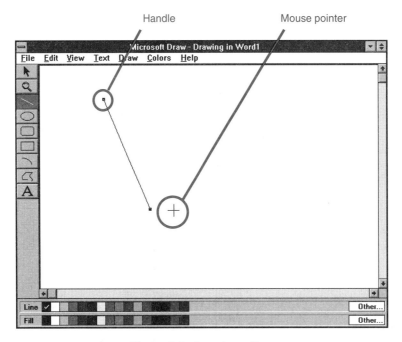

Figure 8.3 *Drawing a line*

To draw the line from the center outward instead of from end to end, press **Ctrl** while you draw it. To force the line to be perfectly vertical, perfectly horizontal, or a perfect 45 degree angle, press **Shift** while you draw it. For example, to draw a perfectly vertical line, hold down **Shift** while you drag in a roughly vertical direction. You can combine **Ctrl** and **Shift** to draw a perfectly angled line from the center.

The *Rounded Rectangle tool* draws rectangles and squares with rounded corners, whereas the *Rectangle tool* draws rectangles and squares with square corners. Figure 8.4 shows examples of each. Position the cross-hairs in one corner of the desired rectangle or square. Then drag the cross-hairs to the opposite corner. You will see the rectangle grow as you drag the cross-hairs, and you can move the pointer around until you get the right shape. When you release the mouse button, the rectangle or square appears on the page. As always, you can undo it with **Ctrl+Z**.

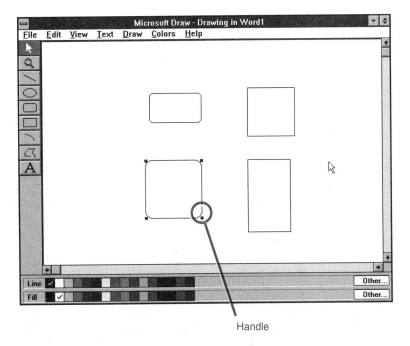

Handle

Figure 8.4 *Drawing rectangles*

N O T E

To start the rectangle from the center instead of one corner, press **Ctrl** while you draw it. To force the rectangle to be a perfect square, press **Shift** while you draw it. You can combine **Ctrl** and **Shift** to draw a perfect square from the center.

The *Ellipse tool* draws ellipses and circles (see Figure 8.5). You use the tool exactly like the Rectangle tools, but you draw an ellipse or circle that is inscribed inside an imaginary rectangle or square.

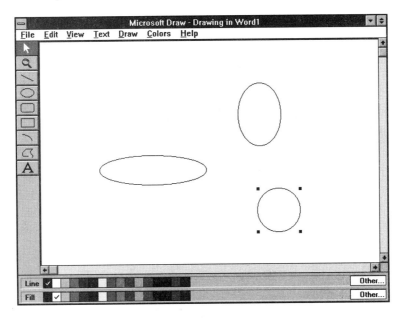

Figure 8.5 *Drawing ellipses*

N O T E

To start the ellipse from the center instead of one corner, press **Ctrl** while you draw it. To force the ellipse to be a perfect circle, press **Shift** while you draw it. You can combine **Ctrl** and **Shift** to draw a perfect circle from the center.

The *Arc tool* draws an arc; actually, it draws one-fourth of an ellipse or circle. Whether you draw the northwest, northeast, southwest, or southeast quadrant of the ellipse depends on which direction you drag the cross-hairs. You can use **Ctrl** and **Shift**, just as you do in drawing an ellipse.

The Draw menu contains a command named **Filled** that affects the Arc tool. If **Filled** is selected when you draw the arc, the entire quadrant is drawn; it looks like a wedge (see Figure 8.6). If **Filled** is not selected, only the outer line of the quadrant is drawn.

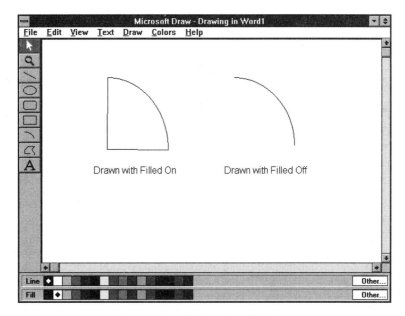

Figure 8.6 *Filled and unfilled arcs*

❖ **To turn the Filled option on and off:**

1. Click somewhere to make sure that no objects are selected.

2. Pull down the **Draw** menu. A diamond appears next to **Filled** if it is selected. If no diamond appears, **Filled** is currently turned off.

3. Click **Filled** to reverse its current status. If you don't want to reverse its status, click **Draw** again to close the menu.

After you have set up **Filled** the way you want it, click the drawing tool you want to use next.

The *Freeform tool* lets you draw freehand. Drawing with a mouse isn't very accurate, so don't expect to reproduce the Mona Lisa. When you move the cross-hairs into the drawing area and click the first time, you can either drag the pointer or move it without dragging. If you drag, the pointer changes into a pencil, and you use it just like a pencil. Move in any direction, scribble, or whatever, the pointer goes with you. When you move the pointer without dragging, a straight line follows the pointer. Click wherever you want to fix the end of the current line segment and start off in another direction. You can alternate dragging and straight-lining. Figure 8.7 shows an example of a freeform drawing made up of line segments.

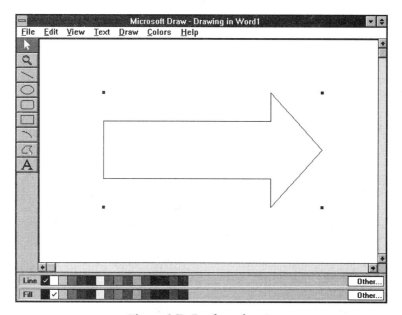

Figure 8.7 *Freeform drawing*

The way that you end a freeform drawing depends on whether or not you want to form a closed figure. To form a closed figure, make your final click as close as possible to the beginning of the figure. Draw will draw a straight line connecting both ends. To leave your figure open, when you reach the end, press **Enter** or **Esc**, double-click anywhere, or click outside the drawing area.

The *Text tool* lets you add labels and other text to your drawing. Before you click it, use the Text menu to select the font, size, style, and so forth. Then click the Text tool and click the position where you want the first letter to be placed. A typing cursor appears. Type the text and press **Enter** or **Esc** or click anywhere to complete the job. Figure 8.8 shows text added to the arrow from Figure 8.7.

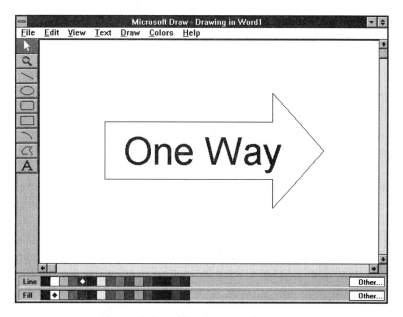

Figure 8.8 *Adding text to a drawing*

If you forget to set the text style before you create the text, you can always change it afterward. Click the text to select it, then use the **Text** menu to set the font, style, size, and so on.

The *Zoom tool* lets you zoom in and out of your drawing so you can examine details or see about half the page at once. The zoom levels are 25%, 50%, 75%, 100% (the actual print size), 200%, 400%, and 800%. To zoom in on an area, click the Zoom tool and click the area you want to examine. Each click increases the level of magnification until you reach the maximum 800%. To zoom out, press **Shift** while you click. You can draw at any level.

The *Selection tool* lets you select objects in the drawing for editing purposes. This is the default tool, and its mouse pointer is shaped like the normal Windows arrow. To select a single object, click it so that handles appear around it. A line has two handles. Every other type of object has four, which form a rectangle, so if it's an ellipse, an arc, text, or a freeform figure, the handles surround it without actually touching it.

An object is a figure that you drew in one action—a single line, a rectangle or ellipse, an arc, or a freeform drawing. Each text label is a single object. You can never select part of an object.

N O T E

You can select more than one object. Click the first one. Then hold down **Shift** while you click each of the others. Or if they are all in one area, you can draw an imaginary rectangle around the area. To draw the rectangle, position the Selection pointer in any corner of the desired area, press the mouse button, and drag the pointer to the diagonal corner. A dotted box (called a *marquee*) shows you where the rectangle is. When you release the mouse button, all objects that are completely inside the marquee are selected. (The marquee then disappears.) Any editing actions apply to all selected objects.

The Color Palettes

Draw includes two color palettes. The top one controls the color of the line that forms an object. The bottom one controls the interior color of filled objects. A diamond marks the default color in both palettes. The default colors affect all new objects. If you want to change the default colors, click the Selection tool to clear all selections and all tools. Then click the colors you want to use. You'll see the new default colors marked by diamonds. (If they're marked by check marks, you didn't clear all selections before changing colors.)

While you are drawing, the line always appears black and the fill always appears white. When you complete the object and release the mouse button, the default colors appear.

You can also change the color of objects after they are drawn. Select one or more objects and click the desired line and fill colors. Only the selected objects are affected. The selected colors in the palette are marked by check marks, not diamonds, to show that these colors pertain to the selected objects only. When you select something else, the palette shows the colors of that object. When nothing is selected, the palette shows the default colors.

Drawing Options

So far, you've been drawing with only one line style and a solid fill color. But there are several drawing options to provide some variety to your objects.

Filled Objects

Any closed object can be filled or unfilled. If it's unfilled, the interior is clear and any objects that are behind it show through. If it's filled, objects behind it are hidden. The fill color in the color palette affects only filled objects.

Figure 8.9 shows the difference between filled and unfilled objects. On the left, the objects are unfilled and appear transparent; you don't get any feeling for layers. On the right, the objects are filled, and the layers are obvious.

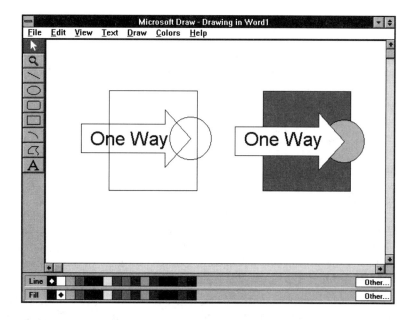

Figure 8.9 *Filled and unfilled objects*

N O T E

Objects that do not form a closed figure cannot be filled. This includes text, open freeform drawings, and arcs that consist of the curved line only.

If you want an object to hide the objects that are behind it but not to have a fill color, fill it with white, like the arrow in Figure 8.9.

You saw earlier how to set up the default **Filled** option for all new objects. You can tell if an object is filled by selecting it. If a check mark appears in the Fill palette, the object if filled. If no color is checked, the object is unfilled. Choose **Draw Filled** to change the status of the currently selected object. When multiple objects are selected, you can't always tell if all of them are filled or not. But you can fill or unfill them all by selecting **Draw Filled**.

SHORTCUT

You can fill an unfilled object simply by clicking a fill color for it, as long as it's a closed object.

When you fill one or more objects, they are filled with the default fill color. Click another color in the Fill palette to change the fill color of the selected objects.

Overlapping Objects

Objects can overlap each other, and you can control which ones are on top of which. If all the objects are drawn with the same line color and are unfilled, their order isn't apparent. But if different line colors are used, or if some are filled, then the order can make a difference.

You can send any object to the front or back of a pile of overlapping objects. Select the object and choose **Edit Bring to Front** or **Edit Send to Back**. If you're trying to arrange the order of several overlapping objects, keep sending objects to the front and back until you reach the right order.

If an object is completely hidden behind another object, you won't be able to select it. Send the covering object to the back so that you can select the hidden object.

N O T E

Four objects are shown in Figure 8.10. The rectangle is filled with dark gray and is at the back. The circle is filled with light gray and is on top of the rectangle. The arrow is filled with white and is on top of the circle. The label is in the front.

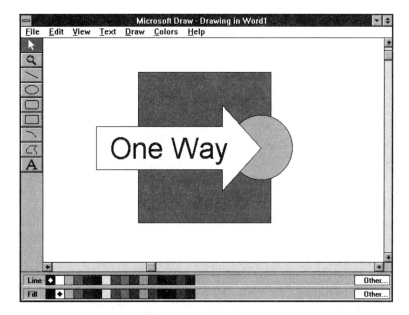

Figure 8.10 *Example of overlapping objects*

Fill Patterns

So far, you've seen only a solid fill pattern, but **Draw** offers several other patterns. Figure 8.11 shows the submenu that appears when you choose **Draw Pattern**. You can select from any of these patterns. The drawing in the figure uses the diagonally striped pattern in the shadow boxes. That pattern has been set up as the default in the figure, although normally the first pattern in the menu (with no lines) is the default.

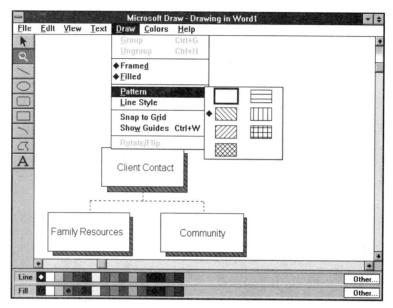

Figure 8.11 *Fill patterns*

❖ **To change the default fill pattern:**

1. Click the Selection tool to clear all selections.

2. Choose **Draw Pattern** and click the pattern you want to use as a default. A diamond appears next to the default pattern in the sub-menu.

❖ **To change the fill pattern of one or more objects:**

1. Select the objects.

2. Choose **Draw Pattern** and click the desired pattern in the sub-menu. The fill pattern of the selected objects change. A check mark indicates their pattern in the submenu.

An object must be filled in order to use a pattern. The fill color determines the background of the pattern, while the line color determines the color of the cross-hatching in the pattern.

Line Styles

Draw also offers a number of line styles in addition to the thin, solid line that you've seen so far. Figure 8.12 shows the submenu that appears when you choose **Draw Line Style**. As you can see, you can select a broken line in any of four patterns (dotted, dashed, etc.), or you can select a solid line in a variety of widths. Clicking **Other** opens a dialog box where you can specify your own width, as in 5 points. In the figure, the default line style is the dotted line, which you can see in the connecting lines in the sample drawing.

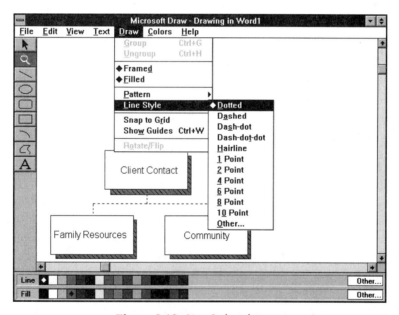

Figure 8.12 *Line Style submenu*

❖ **To change the default line style:**

1. Click the Selection tool to clear all selections.

2. Choose **Draw Line Style** and click the line style you want to use as a default. A diamond appears next the default line style in the submenu.

❖ **To change the line style of one or more objects:**

1. Select the objects.

2. Choose **Draw Line Style** and click the desired line style in the submenu. The line style of the selected objects changes. A check mark indicates their line style in the submenu.

Framing

The line outlining a closed object is called a *frame*, and you can eliminate it if you want to show just the filling without a frame. If you eliminate the frame of an unfilled object, there's nothing left; the object disappears.

The **Draw Framed** command controls the framing of an object in the same way that **Draw Filled** controls the filling. You can set the default value for all future objects (indicated by a diamond in the menu), and you can change the framing of selected objects (indicated by a check mark in the menu).

Working with the Grid

Draw maintains an invisible grid on the drawing surface. There are 12 grid lines to the inch in each direction. By default, everything you draw or move snaps to this grid. You'll notice as you draw that the beginning of an object doesn't quite start where you placed the cross-hairs, and the object grows in small jumps instead of a smooth progression. That's because it's snapping to the grid as you draw. The grid helps you line up objects exactly, make lines meet perfectly at corners, and draw two or more objects that are exactly the same size.

But sometimes the grid gets in the way. When you're trying to center some text perfectly in a box or draw a line in an exact position, it's annoying when it keeps jumping slightly out of position. You can turn the grid off in these cases. Choose **Draw Snap to Grid** to turn it off. It's a toggle option, so choose it again to turn it back on. When you turn it on, you affect all future drawings and moves, but the position of existing items is not affected.

Using the Guides

You might also find guides handy for lining up objects. Figure 8.13 shows what the drawing area looks like when you choose **Draw Show Guides**. You can drag either guide to any position in the drawing area, then use one or both to align new or moved objects. As you drag, your mouse pointer reports the distance in inches from the top of the paper for the horizontal guide, or from the left edge of the paper for the vertical guide. (If **Snap to Grid** is on, the guides snap to the grid as you drag them.) Your drawings will snap to the guides if you come close to them, even if **Snap to Grid** is disabled.

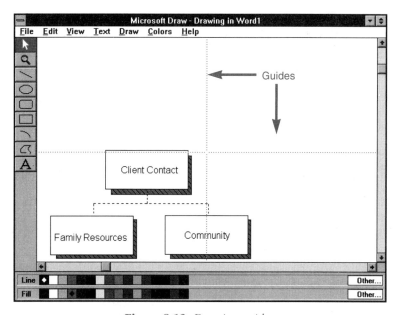

Figure 8.13 *Drawing guides*

Show Guides is a toggle. Choose it again to turn off the guides.

N O T E

Copying Objects

It's often faster and handier to copy an object rather than draw another one. In the organization chart in Figure 8.13, for example, you have to draw only one rectangle. You make a copy slightly to the left and down and change its fill color to make the **Shadow** box. (You'll have to send the **Shadow** box to the back.) Then you select both objects and copy them to create all the other boxes on the chart.

❖ **To copy one or more objects:**

1. Select the object(s) to be copied.

2. Choose **Edit Copy** or press **Ctrl+C**. Draw copies the object to the Clipboard.

3. Choose **Edit Paste** or press **Ctrl+V**. Draw pastes the contents of the Clipboard near the original. The pasted objects are selected.

4. Drag the pasted objects to whatever position you want.

Changing Objects

You've already learned quite a bit about changing objects, but there's a lot more you can do. You can, for example, resize, rotate, and flip an object. And, of course, you can delete objects.

Resizing Objects

❖ **To resize an object:**

1. Select the object or objects. Handles appear around the selected object.

2. Grab a handle and drag it in any direction to make the object larger or smaller. A marquee moves with the mouse pointer. When you release the mouse button, the object adjusts to fit the marquee.

By default, you can distort the proportions of an object as you resize it. You can adjust both the vertical and horizontal dimensions in one move, depending on how you drag the handle. If the object is a line, you can also change the angle of the line. The **Shift** key gives you some control over how much distortion and shifting take place. If you hold down **Shift** while you drag a handle:

❖ If you drag it vertically, you change the height of the object, but the width remains fixed.

❖ If you drag it horizontally, you change the width of the object, but the height remains fixed.

❖ If you drag it diagonally, you change both the width and height, keeping the original proportions.

❖ If you drag a line, you change its length without changing its angle.

The **Ctrl** key can also be used when resizing. Normally, the corner opposite the dragged handle remains fixed in position while the other three handles move according to how you drag the one. Press **Ctrl** if you prefer to resize the object around its center point, so that all handles move as you drag the one.

You can combine the **Shift** and **Ctrl** keys while you drag.

If you're trying to draw lines to connect objects, you might have trouble getting them to touch exactly the objects the first time you draw them. Use the Zoom tool to focus in on an intersection. Then select the line, hold down **Shift** so that it doesn't change direction, and drag the handle in or out until the line exactly meets the desired object. Do the same thing at the other end of the line, and your line will be perfect. Once you have one perfect line, don't forget that you can copy it to create other lines of the exact same size.

Rotating and Flipping

You can rotate an object 90 degrees to the right or left, and you can flip an object horizontally or vertically. Figure 8.14 shows some examples of rotated objects. The top triangle was drawn using the Freeform tool. Then three copies were made. One copy was rotated 90 degrees to the left, one was rotated 90 degrees to the right, and one was flipped vertically. Then all four triangles were moved into position (using the drawing guides to mark the center point) and then filled.

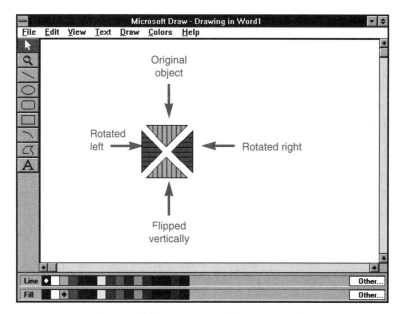

Figure 8.14 *Rotating and flipping an object*

Figure 8.15 shows the submenu that opens when you choose **Draw Rotate/Flip**. Select an object and choose one of the four options. If you rotate or flip in the wrong direction, you can rotate or flip it again to correct it. For example, if you rotate it left instead of right, flip it horizontally and it will be perfect.

You can't rotate a text object. (Use WordArt to rotate and flip text.) A rotated or flipped square or circle doesn't look any different from the original.

NOTE

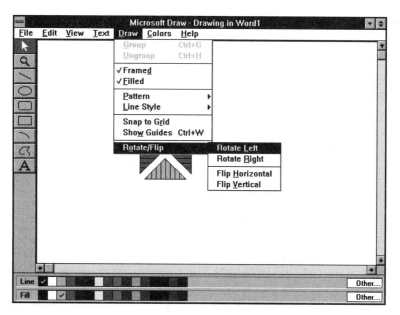

Figure 8.15 *Rotate/Flip submenu*

Updating the Document

Since you can't create a separate drawing file with Microsoft Draw, there is no **Save** command. The **File Update** command updates the host document with the current drawing, and you should do this occasionally to save a copy of the current drawing.

N O T E

Until you save the host document, the drawing is not saved on disk and could be lost if the power goes out.

If you decide to fall back to the last version you saved in the document, exit Draw without updating the document, then reopen the drawing for editing. Both these tasks are explained in the following sections.

Exiting Draw

When your drawing is finished, choose **File Exit and Return to** *filename* to close the Draw window and return to the Word Processor document. A dialog box asks if you want to update the document. Choose **Yes** if you want to update the drawing in the document. Choose **No** if you want to abandon any changes you made to the drawing since the last time you updated the host document. (If you have never updated the host document since starting the drawing, the entire drawing will be abandoned if you choose **No**.)

Managing the Embedded Drawing

Once you return to the document, the drawing is embedded in the text in the same way that Note-It, ClipArt, and WordArt objects are. You can select it, move it, resize it, delete it, copy it, and position it on the page (instead of in the text) just as you can with these other objects. If you have created a logo that you want to appear on every page, position it in the header or footer area.

You can reopen the drawing and edit it. Just double-click it to reopen the drawing in the Microsoft Draw window.

Importing Drawings into Microsoft Draw

You don't always have to draw objects from scratch. You can import drawings from other facilities into Microsoft Draw and edit them or include them as is in your drawing. You can import drawings created by Windows Paintbrush, ClipArt, and other types of drawing files. There are some types of artwork that you can't import, such as TIFF files (created by scanners).

To import a drawing, choose **File Import Picture**. The resulting dialog box looks a lot like Works Open dialog box, but it lists only drawings that can be imported. Change the drive and directory as needed to locate the drawing you want to import. (The ClipArt files are located in the C:\MSWORKS\CLIPART directory.) Double-click the name of the file to import it.

When the drawing appears, it is selected. If Draw can break it down into separate objects, it selects all the objects. For example, if you import the ClipArt cat, the cat's body is one object, and each whisker is a separate object. You can go on to manipulate the objects just as you do the ones you draw yourself.

N O T E Some objects, notably bitmapped drawings such as BMP drawings created by Windows Paintbrush, are treated as one object no matter how complex they are. Bitmapped objects can't be rotated or flipped, filled, or otherwise modified. But they can be moved, copied, and resized. And you can overlap other objects with them.

You can also paste the contents of the Clipboard into the drawing. This means you can import artwork from any Windows facility that can copy artwork to the Clipboard. To paste from the Clipboard, just choose **Edit Paste** or press **Ctrl+V.**

N O T E To copy a picture of the current screen to the Clipboard, press **PrintScreen**. To copy a picture of the active window to the Clipboard, press **Alt+PrintScreen**.

You can embed a picture from the Clipboard directly into your Word Processor document with the **Edit Paste** command, or you can paste it into a Microsoft Draw drawing where you can add other objects to it (such as labels). You can't modify the picture itself, however.

Summary

This chapter has shown you how to use Microsoft Draw to:

- ❖ Draw objects and embed them in a document
- ❖ Use the drawing tools to draw the basic shapes and add text to the drawing
- ❖ Control color, line style, and fill patterns
- ❖ Overlap objects as well as rotate and flip objects
- ❖ Use some of Draw's drawing aids like guides and the grid.

Once the object is embedded in a document, you know how to resize it, move it, copy it, edit it, and so on.

You now have a pretty good handle on Word Processor. It has some advanced features that you'll want to explore later on, but you know enough now to create some pretty polished documents. The next section shows you how to use Spreadsheet.

PART III

Spreadsheet

CHAPTER 9

Spreadsheet Basics

Works for Windows' Spreadsheet helps you develop tables of numeric and text data that you can use to track performance, control finances, control inventories, and many other applications. This chapter introduces Spreadsheet. You will learn how to:

- ❖ Create a new spreadsheet
- ❖ Enter data into cells
- ❖ Locate specific cells
- ❖ Save a spreadsheet
- ❖ Print a spreadsheet
- ❖ Close and reopen a spreadsheet

Why Spreadsheet?

Spreadsheet is a program that helps you develop tables of information called *spreadsheets*. It is designed to line up text and numbers in columns with very little effort on your part. And you can easily add borders, shading, and color to highlight areas. There are two basic types of spreadsheets that you'll develop with Spreadsheet: *textual* and *numeric*.

A textual spreadsheet creates columns of narrative information, as shown in Figure 9.1. Generally, you can create better tables in Spreadsheet than in Word Processor, and it's a simple matter to embed a spreadsheet in a Word Processor document.

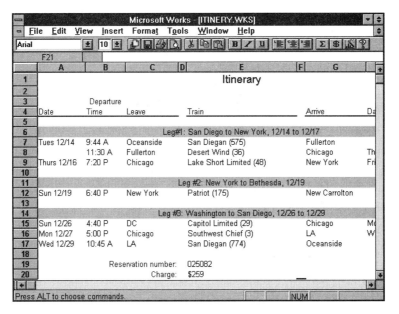

Figure 9.1 *Sample textual spreadsheet*

To assist in developing textual spreadsheets, Spreadsheet includes many of the same text facilities that you have already learned to use in Word Processor such as character formatting, paragraph alignment, and spell checking.

A numeric spreadsheet contains primarily numeric data, such as a monthly budget or a payroll report. Figure 9.2 shows an example of the type of numeric spreadsheet that you can develop with Spreadsheet. It contains text data, but usually in the form of titles and annotations for the numeric data. Spreadsheet includes several features that help you develop a numeric spreadsheet:

	A	B	C	D	E	F	G
		January	February	March	April	May	June
1							
2							
3	Income	$1,245.00	$1,245.00	$1,245.00	$1,245.00	$1,245.00	$1,245.00
4	Outgo	$1,279.69	$1,172.99	$1,292.07	$1,082.41	$1,160.96	$1,066.52
5	Savings	($34.69)	$72.01	($47.07)	$162.59	$84.04	$178.48
6							
7							
8	Totals	$1,279.69	$1,172.99	$1,292.07	$1,082.41	$1,160.96	$1,066.52
9							
10	Household	$649.31	$690.90	$654.92	$635.82	$709.67	$680.73
11	Car	$256.13	$269.45	$340.23	$256.22	$283.91	$259.92
12	Other	$374.25	$212.64	$296.92	$190.37	$167.38	$125.87
13							
14							
15							
16	Household	$649.31	$690.90	$654.92	$635.82	$709.67	$680.73
17							
18	Rent	$425.00	$425.00	$425.00	$425.00	$425.00	$425.00
19	Utilities	$63.15	$95.77	$58.32	$45.25	$32.16	$32.16
20	Telephone	$20.00	$16.95	$32.33	$16.95	$33.25	$28.10

Figure 9.2 *Sample numeric spreadsheet*

❖ You can enter a formula in a cell instead of text or a number. A formula might direct Spreadsheet to sum a column of cells or find an average of a range of cells. When you update a spreadsheet, Spreadsheet recalculates all the formulas. In the example in Figure 9.2, rows 4, 5, 8, 10, 11, 12, and 16 are all calculated from formulas.

❖ Spreadsheet formats numbers automatically so that they are consistent. This saves you typing time. In the figure, Spreadsheet has converted entries like **1245**, **425**, and **20** into **$1,245.00, $425.00,** and **$20.00**.

❖ Spreadsheet will fill a range of cells with a specified value or formula. In the Income row in Figure 9.2, the value 1245 was typed only in the first column; the rest of the columns were filled from the first column.

❖ Spreadsheet includes a variety of preprogrammed numeric functions so that you don't have to create your own formulas for common (and often quite complex) algebraic, trigonometric, and financial functions.

❖ Spreadsheet includes a Charting tool to develop professional-looking charts based on numeric data. Figure 9.3 shows an example of a bar chart developed by Works from spreadsheet data. Spreadsheet can develop pie charts, line charts, and other types of charts in addition to bar charts. It's a simple matter to embed a chart developed by Spreadsheet into a Word Processor document. You can also import a chart into Microsoft Draw and adapt it as desired.

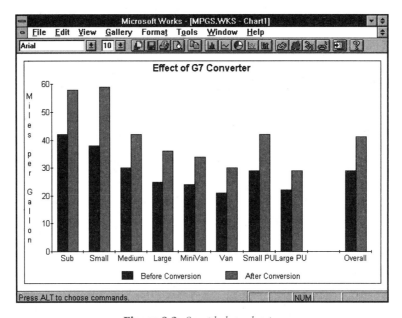

Figure 9.3 *Sample bar chart*

One of the most popular features of a spreadsheet is the capability to try out hypothetical data. You can examine the results of various scenarios. What if I get a 10% raise? What if our sales decline 15% next year? What if the population in our area expands by 20,000? As you change numbers in the spreadsheet, Works automatically recalculates all the formulas to show the effects of the changed numbers.

Creating a New Spreadsheet

If the Startup dialog box isn't open, choose **File Create New** or click the **Startup** icon. Then click the **Spreadsheet** button in the **Create a New** section. Figure 9.4 shows what the Spreadsheet window looks like with a new document open.

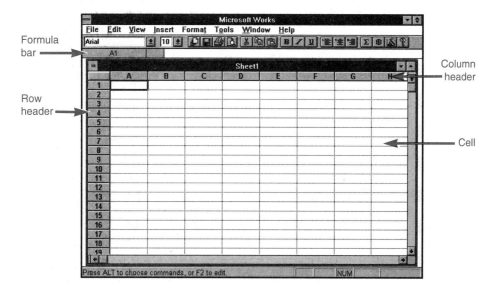

Figure 9.4 *Spreadsheet window*

You can see that the title bar and status bar are the same as they are for Word Processor. The menu bar looks the same, but in fact, many of the menus contain different commands from those in Word Processor. The toolbar also looks the same except for the group of tools at the right, which are unique to Spreadsheet (except for the **Learning Works** icon).

Underneath the toolbar is another bar called the *formula bar*. At the left is the name of the cell that is currently selected, which is A1 in the example. Cells are identified by their column and row labels, so A1 refers to column A, row 1. You can see the highlight surrounding this cell in the work area.

The main portion of the formula bar shows the contents of the currently selected cell. This is where you type and edit values or formulas for a cell. When a cell contains a formula, the cell itself shows the result of the formula while the formula bar shows the formula.

The document window contains a blank spreadsheet, which is evenly divided into rows and columns, creating cells. The row and column headers identify the cells. As you scroll through the spreadsheet, these headers change to identify the cells being shown, but the headers themselves never scroll off the screen.

Entering Column and Row Titles

When you create a new spreadsheet, you'll probably start by setting up the columns and rows you want to use with titles in row A and column 1. Figure 9.5 shows the beginnings of the setup for the Miles per Gallon spreadsheet that eventually resulted in the bar chart in Figure 9.3.

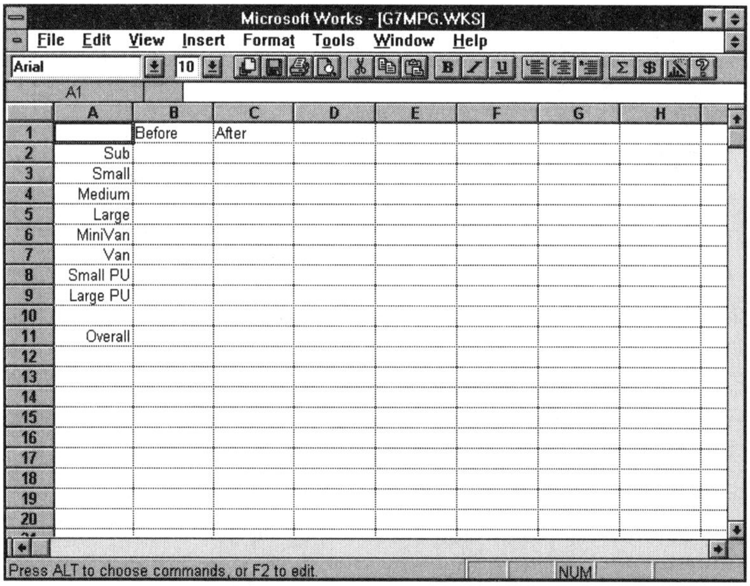

Figure 9.5 *Setting up a spreadsheet with column and row titles*

❖ **To enter text data in a cell:**

1. Click the cell. Works selects the cell. The highlight surrounds it, and its name appears in the cell reference area.

2. Type the text. Whatever you type appears in the cell and in the formula bar.

3. Press **Enter** or select another cell. Pressing **Enter** records the value in the cell but leaves the cell selected. Selecting another cell records the value, moves the highlight, and displays the contents of the newly selected cell in the formula bar.

As soon as you start typing something in a cell, two icons appear in the formula bar, **Cancel** and **Enter**, as shown in Figure 9.6. The focus is now on the formula bar instead of the cell. Click **Cancel** to cancel the current entry and return the focus to the cell. Click **Enter** to complete the current entry, store it in the cell, and return the focus to the cell. The message in the message bar reminds you that the **Esc** and **Enter** keys have the same effect as the **Cancel** and **Enter** icons. When you return the focus to the cell, the icons disappear again.

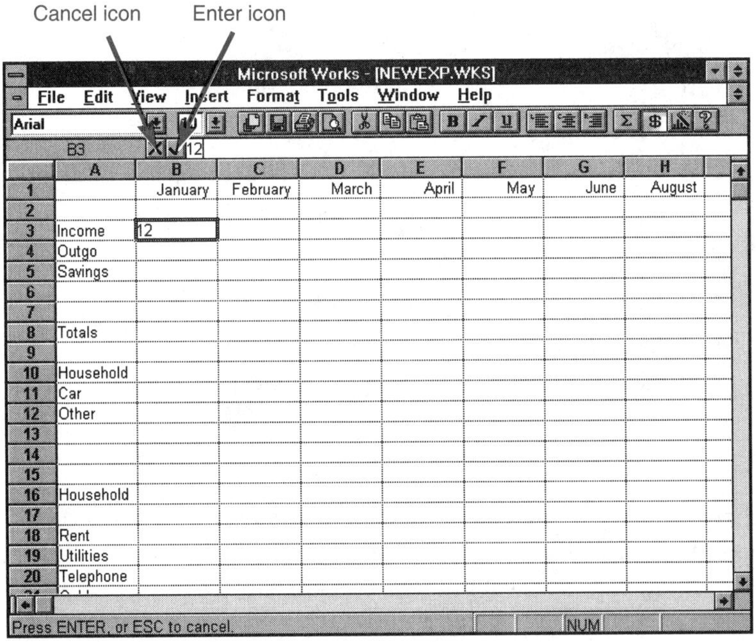

Figure 9.6 *Cancel and Enter icons*

Several more actions record data in the cell and return the focus to the cell area, although to a different cell. You can click another cell, press any one of the cursor movement keys, or press **Tab** or **Shift+Tab**. Table 9.1 shows what the cursor movement and **Tab** keys do.

Table 9.1 *Keys to move the cursor from cell to cell*

Key	Action
Up arrow	Up one cell
Down arrow	Down one cell
Left arrow	Left one cell
Right arrow	Right one cell
Tab	Right one cell
Shift+Tab	Left one cell
Home	To the first cell in the row
End	To the last cell in the row
PageUp	Up one window
PageDown	Down one window
Ctrl+PageUp	Left one window
Ctrl+PageDown	Right one window
Ctrl+Home	To the beginning of the spreadsheet
Ctrl+End	To the end of the spreadsheet
Ctrl+up arrow	Up one block
Ctrl+down arrow	Down one block
Ctrl+left arrow	Left one block
Ctrl+right arrow	Right one block

Spreadsheet size is determined by the data that you have entered so far. If you have entered up through column J and through row 7, then the spreadsheet currently has 10 columns and seven rows. The **End** key jumps to column J of the current row, even if that cell is empty, and **Ctrl+End** jumps to cell J7.

A block is delimited by empty rows and columns. In the example in Figure 9.6, Column A contains several blocks: from Income to Savings, Totals (by itself), from Household (row 10) to Other, and Household (row 16). There's another block that starts with Rent, but you can't see the end of it. Row 1 contains one block, starting with January. Pressing **Ctrl** plus an arrow key jumps the cursor to the beginning or end of the next block. If there is no block, it jumps to the first or last cell in the work area.

Entering Data into Cells

When you type a title, you're usually entering text data into a cell. You can also enter numeric data, formulas, dates, times, and logical values (true and false). Spreadsheet recognizes all these data types and treats them differently. Numeric data can have a variety of formats, such as currency ($25.30) and percentage (25.3%).

Text Data

To enter text data, just start typing it. When you press **Enter** to record the data, Works inserts a quotation mark (") as the first character in the formula bar. This is a Works signal that the data is text. You won't see the quotation mark unless you select the cell. You don't have to type the quotation mark unless you want to force Spreadsheet to treat something as text data that would otherwise be interpreted as one of the other types.

If the text is too long to fit in the cell, it lops over into the next cell if that cell is empty. If the neighboring cell also contains data, the long text is cut off, although the entire value is still recorded and appears in the formula bar when the cell is selected.

 You'll learn how to make cells wider later in this chapter.

N O T E

Numeric Data

Like text data, you enter numeric data by simply typing it. You can use dollar signs, commas, and decimal points. You can indicate a negative value by typing a minus sign before it or by enclosing it in parentheses, as in **-23** or **(15.2)**. You can also enter a number in scientific notation, as in **2.3E-7**, which represents **.00000023**. You can omit nonsignificant zeros; Works inserts them according to the numeric format of the cell. In fact, Works removes the non significant zeros that you type if the numeric format doesn't call for them.

A nonsignificant zero is a leading zero, as in 025, or a trailing zero after a decimal point, as in 25.30.

N O T E

If you try to enter a fraction such as **1/3**, Works will think it's a date. You must enter **0 1/3** to make Works recognize it as a fraction.

When you record the value in the cell, Works formats it according to the format of the cell. By default, it uses General format, which right justifies the number in the cell and suppresses nonsignificant zeros.

In typing the budget spreadsheet in the example, all the values should be formatted as currency, with dollar signs, commas, and two decimal places. Works gives you an easy way to request this format. With the cell selected (whether or not you have typed the value yet) click the **Currency** icon on the toolbar; it's in the last group and has a dollar sign on it.

You can't click the **Currency** icon while the focus is in the formula bar. Either click the **Currency** icon before you start typing the value in the cell or record the value and then click the icon.

N O T E

If the value is too large to fit in the cell, the result depends on the cell format. In General format, Works converts the number to scientific notation; in all other formats, including Currency format, Works displays the value as #####. In either case, the real value appears in the formula bar.

You'll learn how to select and use other formats in Chapter 11.

NOTE

Date and Time Values

You can type a date in any of these formats:

12/1   12/1/94   12/94

December 1   December 1, 1994   December, 1994   December

Works recognizes a date and formats it accordingly. Works can perform calculations on dates. For example, Works can determine the number of days between 1/16/45 and 12/22/94.

You can abbreviate the name of the month to three or more characters. For example, December can be abbreviated as Dec, Decem, and so on.

NOTE

If you want to type a date in a month/year format and the year is before 1932, as in 12/31, works will interpret the value as a month/day date (December 31). Use the month/day/year format instead.

You can type a time in any of these formats:

2:15 PM   14:15   2:15:23 PM   14:15:23

The **PM** can be uppercase or lowercase and you don't have to type a space before it. You can type **AM** too, but it's never required. Trailing zeros are not necessary as long as you type enough information so that Works knows that a time is intended. For example, if you type **2:0**, Works knows that 2:00 AM is intended; you could also type **2 AM**. But if you just type **2**, Works formats it as a General number, not a time, unless you specifically select the Time format.

By the way, Works interpreted those month titles in row 1 of the sample spreadsheet in Figure 9.6 as dates, not text. Notice that they are right justified, as opposed to the category titles in column A, which are in Text format and therefore left justified. Also, if you click a month name so that its value appears in the formula bar, the value doesn't start with a quotation mark. You could force Works to treat the values as text, as you'll learn in Chapter 11, but we'll leave them alone for now.

Logical Values

Type a logical value as **true** or **false**, using upper-case or lower-case. Works converts it to upper-case and right justifies it in the cell. Works can use logical values in formulas. See the Works Help library for information on working with logical values.

Formulas

Enter a formula into a cell when you want Works to calculate the value in that cell. For example, you can ask Works to find the total and average of a column or row.

Start a formula by typing an equal sign **(=)**. You can use numbers, cell references, and arithmetic operators in a formula. For example, if you wanted the current cell to show the sum of cells C5 and C6, you would type this formula:

=C5+C6

 You can include spaces in the formula if you find that easier to read. Works removes the spaces when you record the formula in the cell. All letters can be in upper-case or lower-case; Works converts them to upper-case.

NOTE

If you include more than one type of operator in the cell, Works does not particularly solve the formula from left to right. Instead, it solves the formula according to its order of evaluation. For example, the division operator (/) is evaluated before the addition operator (+). Therefore, the formula =8+4/2 is solved this way:

4 is divided by 2; the result is 2

8 is added to 2; the result is 10

If the formula was evaluated from left to right, the result would be 6, not 10.

Table 9.2 shows the operators in the order of evaluation.

Table 9.2 *Arithmetic operators*

Operator	Action
- and +	Makes a value negative or positive, as in -C4 to negate the value in C4
^	Exponentiates a value, as in C4^2 to square the value in cell C4
* and /	Multiplies or divides, as in C4*2 to double the value in C4
+ and -	Adds or subtracts, as in C4+5 to add 5 to the value in C4

When you record a formula in a cell, Works evaluates it immediately and shows the results in the cell. As you're developing the spreadsheet, you'll probably get a lot of erroneous results and *ERR* (error) messages from formulas that refer to blank cells. The results will become more accurate, of course, as you continue to enter data in cells.

If you forget to type the equal sign at the beginning of a formula, Works treats it as text. Use the following procedure to turn it into a formula.

❖ **To convert text into a formula:**

1. Click the cell.
2. Click the formula bar. A typing cursor appears on the formula bar.
3. Press **Home**. The typing cursor jumps to the beginning of the bar.
4. Type an equal sign (=).
5. Press **Delete**. The quotation mark is deleted.
6. Press **Enter**. The formula is recorded in the cell.

Using Functions

Works includes a long list of *functions* so that you don't have to create formulas for difficult operations. If you need to go beyond simple addition, subtraction, multiplication, and division, look up the functions in the Works Help library or in the *User's Guide* Appendix. Works provides functions to do things such as find the absolute value of a number, find a sine or some other trigonometric function, depreciate an amount using the double-declining balance method, and figure out the monthly payment for a loan.

Two functions that you'll probably use right from the start are *SUM* and *AVG*. **SUM** finds the sum of a set of cells, while **AVG** finds the average.

To use the **SUM** function, type the word SUM followed by a list of the cells in parentheses, as in **SUM(C4,C5,C6,C8,C9,C12)**. If cells are adjacent, you can express them as a range using the format *first-cell:last-cell*. For example, to sum cells C4 through C8, you could type **SUM(C4:C8)**. You can mix ranges and individual cells, as in **SUM(C4:C8,C10,C12,D3:D6)**.

You can also include numbers in the parentheses. The function **SUM(C4:C8,C10,15)** adds cells C4 through C8 and C10, then adds 15 to the total. The function **SUM(C4:C8,C10,-15)** adds the same cells but subtracts 15 from the total.

A range doesn't have to be a column. It can be a row, as in **SUM(C4:G4)**. Or it can be two corners of a rectangle of cells, as in **SUM(C4:E8)**, which sums C4 through C8, D4 through D8, and E4 through E8. You can use any two diagonal corners of the rectangle; **(C8:E4)**, **(E4:C8)**, and **(E8:C4)** are all equivalent to **(C4:E8)**.

You can include a **SUM** function in a longer formula. For example, the following formula divides the sum of C4 through E8 by 6:

=SUM(C4:E8)/6

The **AVG** function finds the mean average of a set of cells. You identify the cells the same way you do for **SUM**, and you can include numbers along with the cell references. For example, the following formula finds the average of cells C4 through E8, E10, E12, and the number 25, then divides the average by 2:

=AVG(C4:C8,E10,E12,25)/2

For both **SUM** and **AVG**, if you have some blank cells in the middle of your spreadsheet for formatting purposes, you don't have to skip around them in your range references. Both **SUM** and **AVG** ignore blank cells in a range. However, a text cell is treated as a 0, which doesn't make any difference in **SUM**, but it does in **AVG**. If you use a specific reference to a blank cell, as in C4, both **SUM** and **AVG** treat it as 0. Again, this makes a difference in **AVG**, but not in **SUM**.

The Easy Way to Enter SUM Functions

Sums are so common in a spreadsheet that Works includes a **Sum** icon on the toolbar; it's in the last group and is labeled with the mathematical symbol for summation (Σ). Click the **SUM** icon to place **=SUM( )** in the formula bar. The cursor appears inside the parentheses so that you can start typing cell references.

But you don't even have to type cell references. While the cursor is in the parentheses, click a cell to include its reference in the function or drag the mouse pointer over a range of cells to include a range reference. You can only do one reference or one range at a time. If you want to add to the list of references, you have to click the formula bar, position the cursor, and type a comma to continue. Then you could highlight another cell or range to insert in the formula.

Resizing Rows and Columns

Figure 9.7 shows what the budget spreadsheet looks like after entering all the income and expenses information for January through August. It would help to widen some of these columns, not only to show complete values (as in **Miscellaneous** in row 19), but also to provide more separation between columns of values.

❖ **To resize a column:**

1. In the row of column headers (A, B, C, etc.), position the mouse pointer over the line that separates that column from the next one to the right. The mouse pointer turns into an **Adjust** pointer (see Figure 9.7).

2. Drag the column separator left or right to make the column narrower or wider. Works adjusts the entire spreadsheet to accommodate the new column size.

You can resize rows in the same manner. Drag the separator at the bottom of the row that you want to adjust.

Adjust pointer

	A	B	C	D	E	F	G	H
		January	February	March	April	May	June	August
1								
2								
3	Income	$1,245.00	$1,245.00	$1,245.00	$1,245.00	$1,245.00	$1,245.00	$1,245.00
4	Total	$1,279.69	$1,172.99	$1,292.07	$1,160.89	$1,160.93	$1,127.98	$1,124.41
5	Savings	($34.69)	$72.01	($47.07)	$84.11	$84.07	$117.02	$120.59
6								
7	Totals	$1,279.69	$1,172.99	$1,292.07	$1,160.89	$1,160.93	$1,127.98	$1,124.41
8								
9	Household	$649.31	$690.90	$654.92	$667.51	$638.63	$655.51	$677.35
10	Car	$256.13	$269.45	$340.23	$265.10	$264.00	$292.21	$319.24
11	Other	$374.25	$212.64	$296.92	$228.28	$258.30	$180.26	$127.82
12								
13	Household	$649.31	$690.90	$654.92	$667.51	$638.63	$655.51	$677.35
14								
15	Rent	$425.00	$425.00	$425.00	$425.00	$425.00	$425.00	$425.00
16	Utilities	$63.15	$95.77	$58.32	$45.25	$32.16	$32.16	$35.10
17	Telephone	$20.00	$16.95	$32.33	$16.95	$33.25	$28.10	$33.81
18	Cable	$16.00	$16.00	$16.00	$16.00	$16.00	$16.00	$16.00
19	Miscellaneo	$22.50	$31.95	$13.00	$43.19	$23.21	$62.09	$62.12
20	Groceries	$102.66	$105.23	$110.27	$121.12	$109.01	$92.16	$105.32

Microsoft Works - [EXPENSES.WKS]

File   Edit   View   Insert   Format   Tools   Window   Help

Arial

A1

Press ALT to choose commands, or F2 to edit.   NUM

Figure 9.7 *Resizing a column*

Managing Your Spreadsheet Files

Shortly after you start developing your spreadsheet, you should save it for the first time so that it has a file name and you won't lose your work in a power outage. Saving a new spreadsheet is just like saving a Word Processor document. Click the **Save** icon to open the Save As dialog box. Works adds the extension WKS to the name you supply. After the first time, clicking the **Save** icon saves it under the same name.

If you want to save a named spreadsheet under a new name so that you don't replace the last version you saved, choose **File Save As**.

N O T E

Print the spreadsheet by clicking the **Print** icon or preview it by clicking the **Print Preview** icon. Close the spreadsheet by double-clicking its control menu icon. If you have made changes since the last time you saved it, Works asks if you want to save the changes. Reopen it from the recent documents list or choose **File Open Existing File**.

Summary

This chapter has shown you how to:

- ❖ Create a new spreadsheet
- ❖ Set up the row and column labels and enter data in the cells
- ❖ Create a formula so that Works will calculate the value of a cell for you
- ❖ Use the SUM and AVG functions
- ❖ Print, save, close, and re-open a spreadsheet.

In the next chapter, you'll see how to come back and modify the spreadsheet. You'll also learn some time-savers, like copying values and formulas from one cell to another.

CHAPTER 10

Editing a Spreadsheet

You'll probably spend more time updating your spreadsheets and trying out hypothetical data than you spent in developing them in the first place. This chapter shows you how to modify your spreadsheets. You will learn how to:

❖ Locate and select cells

❖ Change values and recalculate formulas

❖ Configure the Spreadsheet window

❖ Delete and insert rows and columns

❖ Move and copy cells

❖ Fill cells

❖ Freeze and unfreeze rows and columns

❖ Lock cells so they can't be changed

❖ Create and use ranges

❖ Sort rows

❖ Work with a split window

❖ Work with multiple spreadsheets

Locating Cells

If your spreadsheet fits in the window, you won't have much trouble locating the cells you want to work with. But how can you quickly find a particular cell or range when your spreadsheet is huge?

If you know the name of the cell, choose **Edit Go To** or press **F5** to open the Go To dialog box. Type the **cell reference** and press **Enter**. Works scrolls the spreadsheet as necessary and highlights the desired cell.

N O T E

Notice that **F5** is the same shortcut key you press to go to a page number in a Word Processor document.

If you don't know the name but you do know the value, you can search for that. For example, suppose you want to find the column titled December. You could search for "December."

❖ **To search for a value:**

1. Choose **Edit Find**. The Find dialog box opens. (See Figure 10.1.)

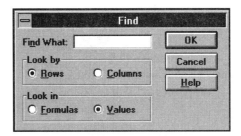

Figure 10.1 *Find dialog box*

2. Type the value you want to find.

3. Click **Rows** to search across rows or click **Columns** to search down columns (explained in the following paragraphs).

4. Click **Formulas** to examine formulas only or click **Values** to examine values only (including values calculated by formulas).

5. Click **OK**. Spreadsheet searches for the specified data and, if found, selects the cell.

6. To repeat the search, press **F7**.

The **Rows/Columns** option controls the direction of the search. Figure 10.2 illustrates the difference. When you choose **Rows**, Spreadsheet searches across the rows (starting from the cursor position) until it finds a matching value. When you choose **Columns**, it searches down the columns. Since it stops at the first match it comes to, the two methods could produce different results. You're not likely to notice any time difference, but you might care about the different results. If you don't care or you're not sure, pick either option and keep pressing **F7** until you find the cell you're looking for.

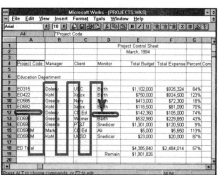

Figure 10.2 *Searching by rows or columns*

As another search example, suppose you want to check the formulas of all cells that reference E4. Enter **E4** in the **Find What** box and click **Formulas**. After checking each formula, press **F7** to find the next one.

Notice that **F7** is the same shortcut key you press to repeat a search in Word Processor.

N O T E

Selecting Cells

Many operations require you to select cells. You already know how to select an individual cell; just click it. The highlighted cell is the selected one, and its content appears in the formula bar.

Selecting a Range

You can select a range of cells by dragging the mouse pointer over them. The selected range is marked by an inverse highlight (see Figure 10.3) and is surrounded by a box. The first cell is still white; that cell contains the cursor and its content is displayed in the formula bar.

		Microsoft Works - [TRIALS.WKS]						

File Edit View Insert Format Tools Window Help

Arial ▼ 10 ▼

B4:D13 | 23

	A	B	C	D	E	F	G	H	
1									
2									
3	Group A	9:00 AM	10:00 AM	11:00 AM	12:00 PM	1:00 PM	2:00 PM	3:00 PM	4
4	S1	23	23	24	23	24	25	25	
5	S2	12	13	12	13	14	22	14	
6	S3	14	14	14	12	12	10	12	
7	S4	9	9	9	10	9	10	12	
8	S5	12	12	15	15	16	16	15	
9	S6	18	18	16	14	14	16	16	
10	S7	23	23	24	25	24	26	26	
11	S8	20	19	18	18	15	15	17	
12	S9	22	22	21	22	22	23	25	
13	S10	14	14	13	14	13	16	17	
14									
15	Average	17	17	17	17	16	18	18	
16									
17									
18	Group B	9:00 AM	10:00 AM	11:00 AM	12:00 PM	1:00 PM	2:00 PM	3:00 PM	4
19	S1	12	14	14	15	14	16	17	
20	S2	23	23	24	26	27	26	25	
21	S3	9	8	10	14	16	15	18	

Press ALT to choose commands, or F2 to edit | | NUM |

Figure 10.3 *Selected range*

To select a range that covers several rows and columns, as shown in the figure, imagine the area as a rectangle. Drag the pointer from any one corner to the diagonal corner of the rectangle. Remember that the corner you start with will contain the cursor, so most of the time you'll want to start with the upper-left corner.

When a range is selected, if you press a cursor key, you deselect the range and select the cell where the cursor lands. The same is true if you click a cell. However, there are some keys you can press to move the cursor within the range without deselecting the range. Press **Enter** to move the cursor to the next cell in the range or **Shift+Enter** to move to the previous cell. Movement is by columns, not rows. So if the cursor is in cell B4, pressing **Enter** would move it to B5 (if B5 is included in the range).

SHORTCUT

If you want to enter data in a specific range of cells, select the range first. As you complete each value and press **Enter** to record it, the **Enter** key moves the cursor to the next cell in the range. If you want to work across rows, select one row at a time.

There are some special places to click to highlight an entire row, an entire column, or the entire spreadsheet, but you should be cautious in using them. If you click a column header, as in A or B, you select the entire column. But you don't just select the cells that you have used, you select all the way down through row 16,384. The same is true if you click a row header; you select through column IV. If you click the blank box in the upper-left corner of the headers, you select the entire work area, from cell A1 through cell IV16384. It's rare when you want to select that much of the work area.

You can also select cells by holding down **Shift** while you move the cursor by using the keyboard or by clicking the mouse. This comes in handy particularly when working with blocks. Remember that **Ctrl** plus an arrow key jumps to the beginning or end of a block. Add in **Shift** along with **Ctrl** and you select from the current cursor position to the beginning or end of the block. You can continue to hold down **Shift** and **Ctrl** and jump in the perpendicular direction to extend the selection to the entire block. For example, if there's a block from C3 to F8 and the cursor is currently in C3, press **Shift+Ctrl+Right Arrow** to select C3 through F3, then press **Shift+Ctrl+Down Arrow** to extend the selection to include the entire block.

Searching a Range

You saw earlier how to search for a value or formula. You can limit the search area by selecting a range before starting the search. If a range is selected, Works searches only within the range.

Changing Values and Recalculating

To change the value in a cell, move the cursor to it. It can be the only selected cell, or it can be in a range. When the cursor is in it, its value appears in the formula bar.

Deleting Cells

If only one cell is selected, you can delete its contents by pressing **Delete**. But be warned that, if a range is selected, pressing **Delete** deletes the entire range. That can be advantageous, but if you want to delete only the cell containing the cursor, you'll have to do it some other way. **Edit Undo** restores all the deleted values.

Replacing Values

If you type a new value, it replaces the former value of the cell containing the cursor. Even when a range is selected, only one cell is affected. When you type the first character of a new value, the entire former value is replaced. Press **Esc** to restore the former value while the cursor is still in the formula bar. **Edit Undo** also restores the former value, but it isn't available until you record the new value in the cell.

Editing Values

You can edit the existing value in a cell rather than completely replace it. To do this, you must go into edit mode by clicking the formula bar or by pressing **F2**. A typing cursor appears in the formula bar, the **Cancel** and **Enter** icons appear, and the word *EDIT* appears on the status bar. The behavior of the **Left** and **Right Arrow** keys changes—they now move the typing cursor instead of changing cells. The **Ctrl+Left Arrow** and **Ctrl+Right Arrow** jump the cursor to the beginning and end of the value or formula, as do **Home** and **End**. **Backspace** and **Delete** erase characters in the formula bar instead of deleting the entire cell. But **Tab**, **Shift+Tab**, **PageUp**, **PageDown**, **Up Arrow** and **Down Arrow** retain their former functions. In fact, they record the new value in the cell and end edit mode, as do **Enter** and the **Enter** icon. If you change your mind about editing the cell, press **Esc** or click the **Cancel** icon to restore the former value and end edit mode. If you record the new value and then change your mind, **Edit Undo** restores the former value; it's not available while you're in edit mode.

Recalculating Automatically or Manually

As you change values, any formulas that refer to those cells are recalculated on the spot. You'll see the effect of your changes as you work. If you're working on a large, complex spreadsheet, recalculation could take time and slow you down. You might want to turn off automatic calculation, especially if you're editing a set of cells that affects the same formula(s). You can ask Spreadsheet to recalculate when you have completed the entire set of changes.

To turn off automatic calculation, choose **Tools Manual Calculation**. This is a toggle command. When it's on, a check mark appears next to it in the Tools menu. This means that Spreadsheet will not recalculate any formulas until you tell it to. To ask Spreadsheet to recalculate all formulas, press **F9** or choose **Tools Calculate Now**. To resume automatic calculation, choose **Tools Manual Calculation** again.

Protecting Cells

Some cells shouldn't be changed. For example, when you have entered the actual mileage data in the MPG spreadsheet (Figure 9.5 on page 234), you don't want anyone to change it. You can protect cells to prevent any further changes to them.

You have two types of cells: *locked* and *unlocked*. When you turn on cell protection, all your locked cells are protected, but your unlocked cells are not. When you turn off protection, you make changes to both types of cells. Notice that it takes two steps to protect a cell: first you must lock it, then you must turn on protection.

NOTE

You can't protect just some of your locked cells. When you turn on protection, all the locked cells in your spreadsheet are protected.

All your cells are locked by default, but you can unlock the ones that don't need protection. For example, you might want to unlock your titles. If you add to your spreadsheet every week or month, you might want to unlock the areas that haven't been used yet so you protect your locked cells and still add new data to the spreadsheet.

To unlock cells, choose the range and choose **Format Protection**. In the Protection dialog box, click **Locked** to remove the *X* from the checkbox. This unlocks the selected range. Repeat this procedure, returning the *X* to the checkbox, to lock cells that have been unlocked.

To protect all the locked cells in your spreadsheet, choose **Format Protection** and click **Protect Data** to place an *X* in the checkbox. Repeat this procedure to remove the *X* from the checkbox.

Configuring the Spreadsheet Window

There are three changes that you can make to the Spreadsheet window that might make your work easier. You can turn off the gridlines, display formulas instead of values in cells, and freeze the rows and columns containing your data headings.

Turning off Gridlines

The gridlines help you see empty cells, but once the spreadsheet is filled with data, you might find it more legible with the gridlines turned off. Turning off the gridlines also gives you a more accurate picture of what the spreadsheet will look like when you print it or import it into a Word Processor document. Figure 10.4 shows what the completed MPG spreadsheet looks like with the gridlines turned off. As you can see, it has a much cleaner appearance.

To turn off the gridlines, choose **View Gridlines**. This command is a toggle, so choose it again to turn them on. When they are on, a check mark appears next to the command in the View menu.

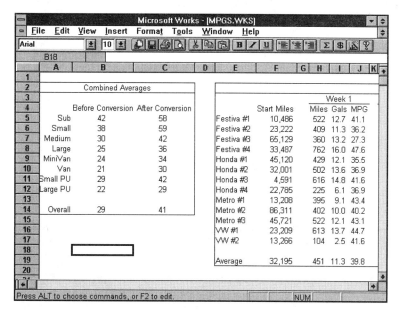

Figure 10.4 *Turning off the gridlines*

You can print the gridlines if you wish. The following procedure shows you how.

❖ **To print gridlines:**

1. Choose **File Page Setup**. The Page Setup dialog box opens.

2. Click the **Other Options** tab. The Other Options page appears.

3. Click **Print Gridlines**. An X appears in the checkbox.

4. Click **OK**. The Page Setup dialog box closes. From now on, whenever you print the spreadsheet, the gridlines will be printed.

Repeat this procedure to turn off gridline printing again.

The **Print Gridlines** option and the **View Gridlines** command have no effect on each other. One can be on while the other is off.

N O T E

Printing Row and Column Headers

While you're in the Other Options dialog box, you can also check **Print row and column headers**. This option causes the row headers (1, 2, 3, etc.) and the column headers (A, B, C, etc.) to be printed whenever you print the spreadsheet. When it's checked, the headers print. When it's unchecked, they don't. It's unchecked by default.

Displaying and Printing Formulas

Normally, Spreadsheet displays formulas in the formula bar only. Formula results are displayed in the cells and printed. But when you're developing the spreadsheet, it sometimes helps to display the formulas in the cells instead of the results. Choose **View Formulas** to display the formulas; they will also be printed if you print the spreadsheet while the command is turned on. This is a toggle command, so choose it again to revert to displaying and printing the results.

N O T E

Spreadsheet widens automatically the columns when **View Formulas** is turned on to accommodate the formulas in the cells. The columns return to their former size when you turn off **View Formulas**.

Freezing Titles

If your spreadsheet is very large, you have to scroll to see it all. But when you scroll, your column and row titles (such as *January* and *Income*) scroll off the screen. You might not be able to identify what data you're looking at. To circumvent this problem, Spreadsheet lets you freeze the titles so they don't scroll.

Figure 10.5 shows an example. You can see the solid lines after row 4 and column A. (They're even more obvious when gridlines are off.) These lines mark the frozen rows and columns. In the example, the spreadsheet has been scrolled to examine the range from F22 through L37, but you can still see the row and column titles for this data.

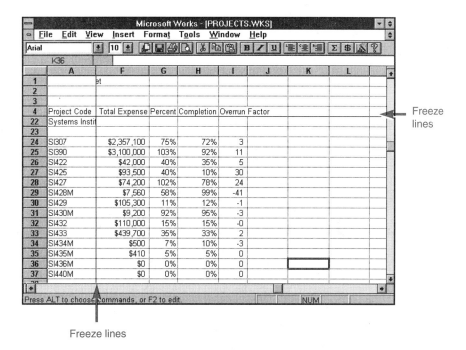

Freeze lines

Freeze lines

Figure 10.5 *Freezing titles*

N O T E Notice that the frozen row and column do scroll. Row 1 scrolls left and right so that the columns are correctly titled, but it doesn't scroll up or down. Similarly, column A scrolls up and down, but not left or right.

❖ **To freeze titles:**

1. Click the cell that is in the first row and column to be scrolled. Everything above and to the left of the highlighted cell will be frozen. For example, to freeze row 1 and columns A and B, click **C2**.

2. Choose **Format Freeze Titles**. The freeze lines appear in the window.

Format Freeze Titles is a toggle command. Choose it again to release the frozen titles.

N O T E

If you want to freeze just rows but not columns, highlight a cell in column A. For example, to freeze rows 1 and 2, highlight cell **A3**. To freeze just columns but not rows, highlight the appropriate cell in row 1. To freeze column A, highlight cell **B1**.

Inserting and Deleting Rows and Columns

Sometimes you need to insert or delete a row or column after you have laid out your spreadsheet. The Insert menu lets you do both insertions and deletions.

❖ **To insert a column:**

1. Select the column to the right of the column you want to insert. For example, if you want to insert a column between columns C and D, select column D. You can select the entire column by clicking the column header.

2. Choose **Insert Row/Column**. Spreadsheet inserts a column before the selected column. All formulas and headers are adjusted to account for the new row.

Suppose you insert a new column C. Spreadsheet looks for any formula in the spreadsheet that refers to a cell in row C and adjusts it to refer to row D. Likewise, references to row D are changed to row E and so on.

❖ **To insert a row:**

1. Select the row that follows the row you want to insert. For example, if you want to insert a row between rows 4 and 5, select row 5. You can select the entire row by clicking the row header.

2. Choose **Insert Row/Column**. Spreadsheet inserts a row above the selected row. All formulas and headers are adjusted to account for the new row.

To delete a row or column, select the row or column and choose **Insert Delete Row/Column**. The selected row or column is deleted, and all formulas and headers are adjusted. Sometimes deleting a row or column causes certain formulas to produce the message *ERR* in their cells. This is because you deleted the end of a range reference. For example, if a formula refers to range E4:H8 and you delete column E, Spreadsheet can't adjust the range reference and displays *ERR*. (The same thing would happen if you delete column H, row 4, or row 8.) When you see the *ERR* message, you must adjust the formula yourself.

Edit Undo restores a deleted row or column, including any data it contained.

N O T E

You can insert or delete more than one row or column at a time. To insert multiple rows or columns, select as many rows or columns as you want to insert. For example, to insert four columns before column F, select columns F through I before you choose **Insert Row/Column**. To delete multiple rows or columns, select the ones you want to delete. Just press **Edit Undo**, and the rows or columns will be restored, with data, if you change your mind.

Moving and Copying Cells

You can move and copy cells using the toolbar. Or you can drag them using the mouse.

❖   **To move or copy using the toolbar:**

1. Select the cell or range of cells to be moved or copied.

2. Click the **Cut** or **Copy** icon. Works copies the selected cell(s) to the Clipboard. If you click the **Cut** icon, it will delete the cells from their current location.

3. Click the cell where you want to paste the moved or copied information. If you're moving a range, click the upper-left cell in the new range.

4.   Click the **Paste** icon. Works copies the cell(s) from the Clipboard to the new location.

If any formulas are included in copied cells, they are adjusted for the new location. For example, if the formula in E4 refers to cell E3 and you move E4 to F7, the formula is then adjusted to refer to F6. (Moved formulas are not adapted, though Works' documentation says that they are. This may be a programming error, and it might have been fixed by the time you read this. Try moving some formulas and see for yourself.)

❖   **To move or copy cells by dragging:**

1.   Highlight the cell(s) to be moved or copied.

2.   Position the pointer over the box surrounding the highlighted cells. Move it around slowly until it says *Drag*.

3.   Drag the cells to their new location. Press **Ctrl** to copy them; don't press any key to move them. As you drag, a black box the same size as the selected range moves with you so that you can see how much space you need. The mouse pointer changes from *Drag* to *Move* or *Copy*.

When you copy cell(s), formulas are adjusted accordingly. If you drop the cells on one or more cells that already contain information, the previous cells are replaced by the new ones. **Edit Undo** undoes a move or copy and restores former values of replaced cells.

Moving and Copying Values instead of Formulas

You can choose to move or copy the values in cells instead of their formulas. You have to use the Edit menu instead of the toolbar or the mouse to accomplish this.

❖   **To move or copy values instead of formulas:**

1.   Select the cell(s) to be moved or copied.

2.   Click the **Cut** or **Copy** icon in the toolbar. Works copies the cells to the Clipboard. If you click **Cut**, it also deletes them from their current location.

3. Click the cell where you want to paste the values.

4. Choose **Edit Paste Special**. The Paste Special dialog box opens (see Figure 10.6).

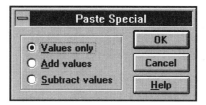

Figure 10.6 *Paste Special dialog box*

5. Click **Values Only** if it isn't already selected.

6. Click **OK**. Works pastes the values (not the formulas) into the spreadsheet.

Adding or Subtracting Pasted Values to Cells

The **Paste Special** command can also be used in another situation. When you are pasting moved or copied cells into a range that already contains data, the new cells by default replace the old ones. But if you use **Paste Special**, you can add or subtract the values in the new cells instead of replacing the old ones.

Let's take an example from the budget spreadsheet (Figure 9.2). Suppose you decide to consolidate the January through March columns. You can cut the January column, then paste it over the March column using **Paste Special** with **Add values** selected. Then cut the February column and paste it over March using the same technique. The March column is now a sum of the old January through March columns.

Filling Cells

In many spreadsheets, there are a set of cells that start off with the same value. For example, in the budget spreadsheet (Figure 9.2) row 3 shows monthly income. For many people, this value is the same every month. The Rent row might also have the same value every month, at least when you create the spreadsheet. When a range of cells have the same value, you only have to type the value once. Then you can *fill* the rest of the range with the value.

❖ **To fill a range:**

1. Select the range, making sure that the cursor is in the upper-left corner.

2. Type the value.

3. Press **Enter** (or otherwise record the value).

4. If the value represents currency, click the **Currency** icon. Works formats the value as Currency.

5. Choose **Edit Fill Right** (if it's a row) or **Edit Fill Down** (if it's a column). If it's a rectangle, choose one first, then the other. Works fills the selected cells with the value or formula in the upper left corner of the range.

If some of the cells already have values, they are replaced by the fill value. **Edit Undo** removes the filled values and restores any replaced values.

Filling with Formulas

You can fill a range with formulas in the same manner that you fill it with a specific value. Select the range, type the formula in the upper-left cell, and choose **Edit Fill Down** and/or **Edit Fill Right**. Works adapts the formula to each new location. For example, if the original formula in cell B12 says *=SUM(B3:B10)*, when it's copied to cell C12, Works changes it to read *=SUM(C3:C10)*.

Take a look at the spreadsheet in Figure 9.2 on page 231 and you can see how much time you can save by filling values and formulas. Several rows were filled from values in column B: Income, Rent, and Cable, along with others that don't show up in the figure. Several more rows were filled from formulas in column B: Savings, Household, Car, Other, and others that don't show up in the figure.

N O T E   If you want to copy or fill a formula without adapting cell references to their new locations, place a dollar sign in front of the row and column names. For example, E4 will not be adopted; in $E4, the column name will not be adapted but the row name will.

Filling with a Series

Sometimes you don't want to fill cells with identical values but with a series of values. For example, you might want to number a column of cells from 1 to 100. Or you might want to fill a row with the dates from January 1 through December 31. Spreadsheet can create the series for you.

❖   **To fill a series:**

1. Select the cells to be filled. Select them in one row or column. You can't fill a rectangular range with a series.

2. Enter the first number in the first cell.

3. Choose **Edit Fill Series**. The Fill Series dialog box in Figure 10.7 opens.

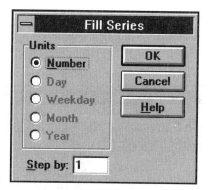

Figure 10.7 *Fill Series dialog box*

4. Type the amount of increase in the **Step by** box. For example, to fill the series 10, 20, 30,..., enter **10** in the first cell and set **Step by** to **10**.

5. Click **OK**. Spreadsheet fills the cells.

If the first cell contains a date, Spreadsheet fills the remaining cells with dates, but you must indicate whether you want to increase the day, the week-day, the month, or the year. For example, if the first cell contains *10/1/94* and you select **Day** and set **Step by** to 1, the series will read *10/2/94, 10/3/94,* and so on. If you increase the year, the series will read *10/1/95, 10/1/96,* and so on.

If you choose to increase weekdays, Spreadsheet increases the day but skips weekend days. For example, the series starting on *11/11/93* (a Thursday) would continue with *11/12/93, 11/15/93,* and so on.

Working with Named Ranges

You can assign a name to a range of cells and use the name in formulas instead of the range reference. This often makes formulas easier to understand. For example, the purpose of the formula =AVG(TestScores) is much clearer than =AVG(F14:F25). Creating and using a range name is much like creating a Bookmark in Word Processor. Range names also provide you with jump targets for the **F5** key, just as Bookmarks do in Word Processor.

❖   **To assign a name to a range:**

1.   Select the range.

2.   Choose **Insert Range Name**. The Range Name dialog box opens (see Figure 10.8). If a text cell is included in the range, Spreadsheet suggests the text as a range name. Otherwise the **Name** box is blank.

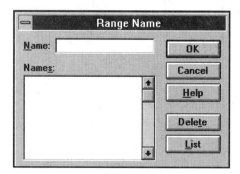

Figure 10.8 *Range Name dialog box*

3. Type a name of up to 15 characters for the range.

4. Click **OK**.

Managing Range Names

Once you have created a range name, it appears in the **Names** list whenever you choose **Insert Range Name**. You can delete a range name by clicking it in this list and clicking **Delete**. You can include a copy of the list in your spreadsheet by clicking the cell where you want it to start, choosing **Insert Range Name**, and clicking **List.**

Jumping to Range Names

Press **Shift+F5** to jump to the beginning of the next named range in the spreadsheet. You can jump to a specific range by using the following procedure.

❖ **To jump to a named range:**

1. Press **F5**. The Go To dialog box opens, showing the range name list.

2. Double-click the name of the range you want. Spreadsheet scrolls the spreadsheet as necessary to highlight the first cell in the range.

Sorting

Spreadsheet includes a facility to sort rows or columns of data. Suppose you have a project control sheet like the one in Figure 10.9. You have developed it in order by department, and within department, by project code. But now you want to take a look at projects by manager. You can sort the projects using the Manager column as your sort key.

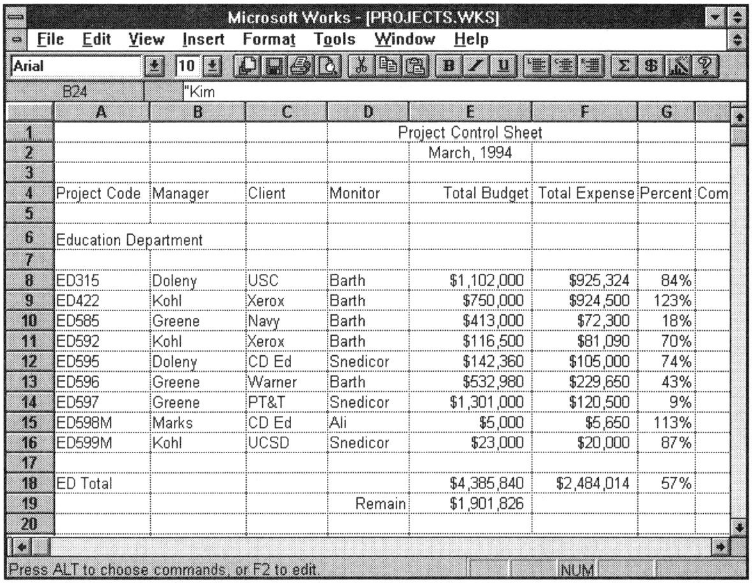

Figure 10.9 *Sample spreadsheet*

To sort a section of a spreadsheet, you start by selecting the cells that you want to use as the sort key. If you want to sort by client, for example, you select the cells in the Client column. Within the column, select only those rows that you want to sort; don't select the title rows, for example. (You can't help selecting spacing rows and subheading rows that are interspersed with data rows.) Then choose **Tools Sort Rows**. The Sort Rows dialog box shown in Figure 10.10 opens. If you want to sort the rows in descending rather than ascending order, click **Descend B**. Then click **OK** to sort the rows and adjust all formulas. If you don't like the result, **Edit Undo** undoes it for you.

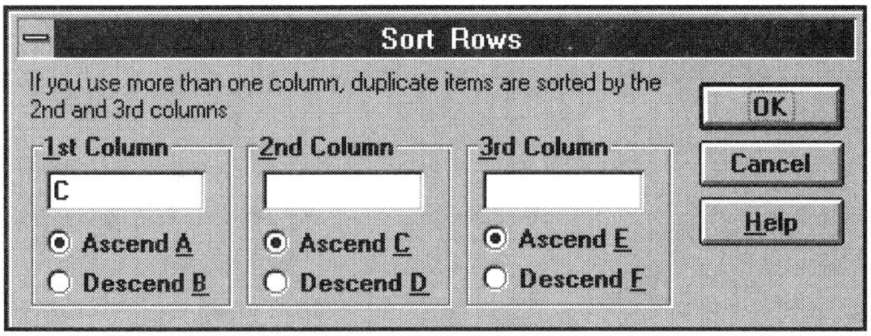

Figure 10.10 *Sort Rows dialog box*

NOTE

The column you selected determines the order of the rows, but it is not the only sorted column; Entire rows are sorted.

In all likelihood, you'll have to do some editing to make the new order presentable. You might have to insert spacing rows, delete old subheadings, add new subheadings, and so on. You might even have to add new rows to calculate sums and averages. Don't forget to use **Save As** if you want to make this into a new spreadsheet and keep the former (unsorted) one also.

Sometimes you want to sort by more than one key. For example, you might want to sort the spreadsheet in Figure 10.9 by project monitor. Rows belonging to the same project monitor should be sorted by the project manager. Figure 10.11 shows the result. To set up this sort, select the cells to be sorted in column D and choose the **Tools Sort Rows** command. In the Sort Rows dialog box, click the **2nd Column** box and type **B** to tell Spreadsheet to use the data in column B as a secondary key. You could also have a tertiary key.

	A	B	C	D	E	F	G	
4	Project Code	Manager	Client	Monitor	Total Budget	Total Expense	Percent	Com
5								
6	SI440M	Boane	Boeing	Ali	$5,050	$0	0%	
7	SI307	Kim	Xerox	Ali	$3,128,000	$2,357,100	75%	
8	SI435M	Kim	MIcrosoft	Ali	$7,500	$410	5%	
9	ED598M	Marks	CD Ed	Ali	$5,000	$5,650	113%	
10	SI428M	McKee	PT&T	Ali	$13,000	$7,560	58%	
11	SI434M	Rease	UC Med	Ali	$7,500	$500	7%	
12	SI436M	Rease	Navy	Ali	$3,000	$0	0%	
13								
14	ED315	Doleny	USC	Barth	$1,102,000	$925,324	84%	
15	ED585	Greene	Navy	Barth	$413,000	$72,300	18%	
16	ED596	Greene	Warner	Barth	$532,980	$229,650	43%	
17	ED422	Kohl	Xerox	Barth	$750,000	$924,500	123%	
18	ED592	Kohl	Xerox	Barth	$116,500	$81,090	70%	
19								
20	SI432	Boane	In-house	Jones, D.	$750,000	$110,000	15%	
21	SI427	Jiminez	Navy	Jones, D.	$73,000	$74,200	102%	
22	SI390	Rease	Boeing	Jones, D.	$3,000,000	$3,100,000	103%	
23								

Microsoft Works - [MONITORS.WKS]
File Edit View Insert Format Tools Window Help
Arial 10
A23

Press ALT to choose commands, or F2 to edit.   NUM

Secondary sort key   Primary sort key

Figure 10.11 *Sorting with two keys*

Splitting the Spreadsheet Window

You can split the Spreadsheet window into panes, just like the Word Processor window. But with Spreadsheet, you can also split the window vertically. In fact, you can split it both ways at the same time, creating four panes. This lets you look at up to four ranges at once. Figure 10.12 shows an example of a window with four panes.

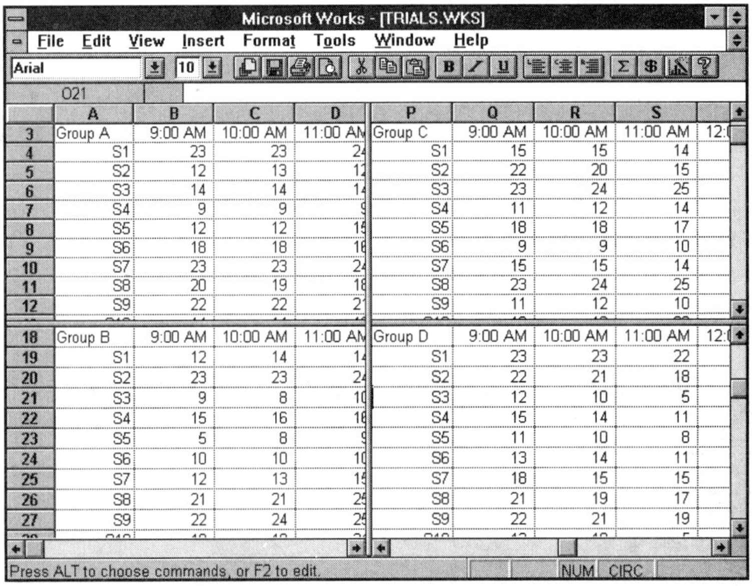

Figure 10.12 *Using four panes*

The Split box for splitting the window horizontally is located just above the up arrow on the vertical scroll bar. Remember that you double-click it to split the window in half. The Split box for splitting the window vertically is located to the left of the horizontal scroll bar. Double-click a split bar to end the split. (You can see the split boxes in Figure 10.11. They don't appear in Figure 10.12 because the window has already been split in both directions.)

Splitting the window makes it easier to move or copy data by dragging. You can drag a cell or a range of cells across a split bar into another part of the spreadsheet and drop it there.

N O T E

If you open multiple spreadsheets, you can drag data from one sheet to another to move or copy it.

Summary

This chapter has shown you how to:

- ❖ Edit a spreadsheet
- ❖ Locate cells using the **Go To** and **Find** functions
- ❖ Select an individual cell and a range of cells
- ❖ Change the value in a cell and recalculate automatically or manually
- ❖ Protect certain cells from being changed
- ❖ Control gridlines and titles
- ❖ View formulas instead of values in the cells.
- ❖ Insert and delete rows and columns.
- ❖ Move and copy cells within a single pane, across panes, and to other spreadsheets
- ❖ Create and use ranges
- ❖ Sort rows

In the next chapter, you'll learn how to dress up your spreadsheets using features such as fonts, color, borders, and shading.

CHAPTER 11

Formatting a Spreadsheet

A spreadsheet stuffed full of data can be pretty rough reading if you don't format it with guide-lines, white space, and so on. The values themselves often need to be edited with dollar signs, commas, minus signs (for negative values), and other symbols. This chapter shows you how to:

- ❖ Apply numeric formats to data
- ❖ Select fonts and font enhancements
- ❖ Align the data in cells
- ❖ Select borders and shading for cells
- ❖ Use **AutoFormats** to apply professional designs to your spreadsheets
- ❖ Format spreadsheet pages with margins, headers, footers, page breaks, and so on

Formatting Cell by Cell

Spreadsheet data is formatted on a cell-by-cell basis, with each cell having its own format, which may or not be the same as any neighboring cells. You don't have to designate the format of every cell separately, however; you can assign them in ranges. In addition, Spreadsheet makes certain formatting assumptions based on the data you enter, so you often don't have to do any extra formatting at all.

The format of a cell has two major components: (1) the external appearance of the cell and (2) the layout of the data in the cell. The external appearance is determined by choices you make on the Format menu, much as you format characters and paragraphs in Word Processor. It controls features such as the font, borders, alignment, and shading.

The data layout is determined largely by the type of data the cell contains. You can enter three general kinds of data into a cell: (1) text, (2) numbers, and (3) formulas. Text data is affected by the external formatting but receives no additional formatting; what you type is what you get. Numeric data is formatted for such layouts as currency, fixed decimal, percent, and fraction. Formulas are not formatted themselves, but their results are formatted as numeric data.

Dates and true/false values are considered to be types of numbers, as you'll see shortly.

N O T E

Every cell has a numeric format associated with it. If the cell contains a number or a formula, the numeric format determines the layout of the result. If the cell contains text, the numeric format is ignored. But if you replace the text with a number or formula, the numeric format is immediately applied.

The Numeric Formats

Sometimes you don't have to specify the desired format of a cell. When you enter certain types of data into a cell, Works recognizes the data and assigns the format accordingly. As you saw in the last chapter, if you enter **January**, Works assigns Date format to the cell, but if you enter **$45.00**, Works assigns Currency format to the cell. But in many other cases, you must specifically select the format you want.

Figure 11.1 shows the dialog box that opens when you choose **Format Number**. The radio buttons on the left side of the box show all the numeric formats. Many of these formats have additional options.

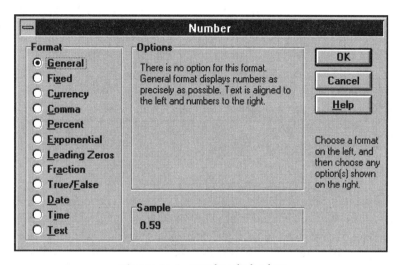

Figure 11.1 *Number dialog box*

To assign a format to one or more cells, select the cells and choose **Format Number**. Then click the desired format and select any options you want in the Options box, if appropriate. The Sample box at the bottom of the dialog box shows the current value of the cell that contains the cursor as laid out by the selected format. It changes as you try various format options. Each of the formats is explained in the following sections.

N O T E

The following discussion assumes that your computer is set up for U.S. numeric formats. If your system is configured for some other country, then the currency symbol, thousands separator, decimal point, and other numeric formats (including date and time formats) might be different. See Windows Control Panel in the Main group for information on changing country formats.

General Format

General format presents each number as precisely as possible. Trailing zeros after a decimal point are suppressed (12.00 becomes 12), but each number will have at least one digit before the decimal point, even if it's a zero (.59 becomes 0.59). Negatives are expressed with a minus sign (-12), and numbers that are too large to fit in the cell are displayed using scientific notation (360000000000 becomes 3.6E+11); the formula bar shows the actual value when you select the cell. Dollar signs, commas, and percent signs are not displayed.

N O T E   *General format* numbers appear in scientific notation if they have too many digits to fit in the cell or if they have more than 11 digits (counting the decimal point as a digit in this case), regardless of how big the cell is. See Exponential format, which follows, for more details on scientific notation.

General format is Spreadsheet's default format. When you open a new spreadsheet, all the cells have General format until you start entering data and selecting other formats. If you enter data that Spreadsheet doesn't recognize as another type, it is formatted in General format. (Once you format the cell as another type, however, you have to specifically select General format to return to it.)

Fixed Format

Fixed format includes a decimal point and a fixed number of decimal places in each number. Works rounds off longer decimal fractions to the fixed number of places. Commas, dollar signs, percent signs, and plus signs are not displayed. Negative numbers are displayed with a minus sign. Numbers too long to fit in the cell are displayed as a series of pound signs (#); the formula bar shows the actual value when you select the cell.

Figure 11.2 shows how the Number dialog box looks when you select Fixed format. Notice that you can specify the number of digits in the Options section. The default number of decimal places is 2, as shown, but you can enter any number between 0 and 7. As you change the number of decimals, the Sample changes to show the result.

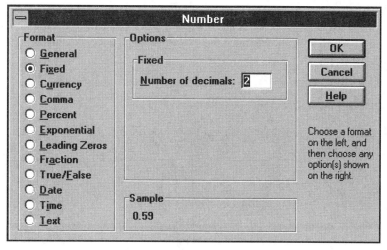

Figure 11.2 *Number dialog box with **Fixed** selected*

The following list shows how values are displayed in **Fixed format** with one decimal place:

Value as entered	Formatted value
12	12.0
.59	0.6
-3.62	-3.6
(459.27)	-459.3
7%	.1
45,389,223.99	45389224.0

NOTE

7% becomes .1 because Spreadsheet converts 7% into a decimal fraction, .07, then rounds that to .1.

If you set the fixed number of decimal places to 0, all numbers are rounded off to the nearest integer: 12.3 becomes 12 and 0.7 becomes 1.

Spreadsheet never assigns Fixed format automatically. If you type a number as 12.3, for example, Spreadsheet formats it according to the current numeric format of the cell. You must select the cell and select Fixed format specifically if you want to use it.

Currency Format

Currency format precedes each number with a dollar sign ($). Values larger than 999 are edited with commas ($10,231.67). Values smaller than 1 have a leading 0 before the decimal point ($0.50). Negative values are displayed in parentheses, not with a minus sign. Values too large to fit in the cell are displayed as a series of pound signs (#); the formula bar shows the actual value when you select the cell.

Figure 11.3 shows the Number dialog box with Currency format selected. As you can see, you can specify the number of decimal places, and you can choose to express negative values in red instead of parentheses. The default number of decimal places is 2, but you can specify any number between 0 and 7. Works rounds each value to the number of decimal places specified.

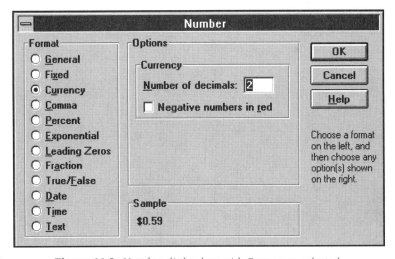

Figure 11.3 *Number dialog box with* **Currency** *selected*

The following list shows how values are interpreted in Currency format with two decimal places:

Value as entered	Formatted value
12	$12.00
.593	$0.59
-3.628	($3.63)
(459.2)	($459.20)
7%	$0.07
45389223.99	$453,892,24.99

Works assigns Currency format automatically if you type a currency symbol with a number. If you type a number with no decimal fraction ($59), Works uses 0 decimal places in the format. If you type any number of decimal places in the value ($59.12345), Works uses 2 decimal places in the format ($59.12).

NOTE

If you use the **Currency** icon to assign Currency format to one or more cells, 2 decimal places are used, regardless of the number of decimal places that were typed.

Comma Format

Comma format is the same as Currency format, except it doesn't insert a currency symbol. The following list shows how numbers are interpreted in default Comma format:

Value as entered	Formatted value
12	12.00
.5904	0.59
-3.627	(3.63)
(459.21)	(459.21)
75.2%	.75
45389223.99	45,389,224.99

Spreadsheet never assigns Comma format automatically. If you enter a value as **23,145,890.65,** Spreadsheet interprets and displays it according to the current numeric format of the cell.

Percent Format

Percent format interprets numbers as percentages, multiplying them by 100 and adding a percent symbol (%). Two decimal places are displayed by default, but you can specify a different number. Negative values are expressed by a minus sign. Dollar signs, commas, and plus signs are not displayed. Values too large to fit in the cell are displayed as a series of pound signs (#); the formula bar shows the actual value when you select the cell.

The following list shows how values are displayed in Percent format to one decimal place:

Value as entered	Formatted value
12	1200.0%
.59	59.0%
-3.62514	-362.5%
(25%)	-25.0%

Spreadsheet assigns Percent format to a cell automatically if you type a percent symbol after the value. You can type a space before the percent symbol, but Spreadsheet removes the space when it formats the value. If you enter a number with no decimal places (59%), the format uses 0 decimal places, but if you enter any number of decimal places (59.1%), the format uses 2 decimal places (59.10%).

Exponential Format

Exponential format expresses numbers in scientific notation to save space when a lot of digits are involved. Very large numbers, such as 165,000,000,000, and very small numbers, such as .0000000569, are often expressed in Exponential format.

Works converts a number to Exponential format by moving its decimal point so that there is one and only one significant digit before it. The remaining significant digits follow the decimal point, rounded off according to the number of decimal places you have selected. An exponent is added to the value to indicate the number of places the decimal point should be moved to identify the actual value. For example, E+5 means to move the decimal place five places to the right, while E-7 means to move the decimal place seven places to the left. Thus, 1.65E+11 would be interpreted as 165,000,000,000, and 5.69E-8 would be interpreted as .0000000569.

By default, Exponential format uses two decimal places, but you can specify any number between 0 and 7. Negative numbers are expressed with a minus sign. Exponential numbers too large to fit in a cell are displayed as a series of pound signs (#); the formula bar shows the actual value when you select the cell.

Works never assigns Exponential format to a cell automatically. Even if you enter a number in Exponential format, it is converted to the format of the cell. For example, **2.1E+14** entered in a cell with Comma formatting is converted to 210,000,000,000,000.00. If that doesn't fit in the cell, it's displayed as pound signs, but the formula bar shows the actual number.

Numbers in General format that have too many digits are displayed in Exponential format, but the cell still has General format.

NOTE

Leading Zeros Format

Leading Zeros format is just like General format except that leading zeros are not suppressed. You'll use Leading Zeros format primarily in situations where the number in question is not really a numeric value but some type of identifying number. For example, an international telephone number might start with 0, and it would be important to force Spreadsheet to show that 0. The same might be true for a part number, serial number, account number, and so on.

In many cases, Text format is more appropriate for this type of data than Leading Zeros format.

NOTE

Figure 11.4 shows the Leading Zeros dialog box. When you select the Leading Zeros format, you must indicate the total number of digits you want the number to have, including leading zeros as well as significant digits. The default is 1, which is rarely the right number. For example, if you enter **0145** and select Leading Zeros format with the default of 1 digit, the result will be 5. You need to set the number of digits to 4 to show the value as 0145. The maximum number of digits is 8.

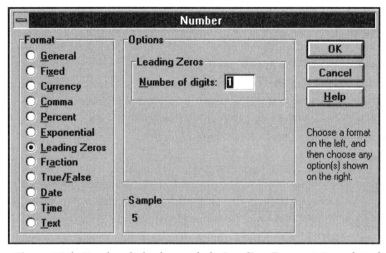

Figure 11.4 *Number dialog box with the* **Leading Zeros** *option selected*

The Leading Zeros format does not display decimal points, decimal places, commas, currency symbols, or percent symbols. Negative values are expressed by a minus sign. Values too large to fit the cell are displayed as **#####**; the formula bar shows the actual value when you select the cell. Works never assigns Leading Zeros format automatically.

Fraction Format

Fraction format displays a number as an integer and fraction, as in 3 3/7. If you enter a number in Decimal format, as in 5.26, and select Fraction format, Spreadsheet converts it as accurately as possible. For example, 5.26 is converted to 5 13/50.

As you can see in Figure 11.5, you can specify that the fraction be rounded to the nearest 1/2, 1/3, 1/4, and so on. For example, if you select to round 5.26 to the nearest 1/32, the result is 5 8/32, which Spreadsheet reduces and displays as 5 1/4. You can also choose not to reduce the fraction, in which case the fraction is displayed as 5 8/32. If you don't want to round the fraction, choose the default **All Fractions** option.

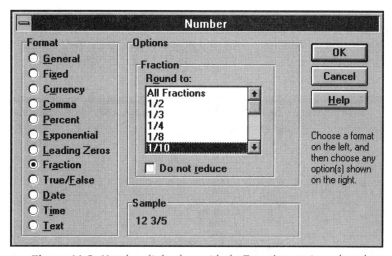

Figure 11.5 *Number dialog box with the **Fraction** option selected*

You can see the results of your choices on the current value in the **Sample** box.

N O T E

To avoid confusion with dates, a fraction must have an integer. Values between 0 and 1 have a 0 integer, as in 0 5/8. Negative values are expressed with a minus sign. Values too large to fit in the cell are expressed as a series of pound signs, but the actual value is displayed in the formula bar when you select the cell.

True/False Format

True/false values are used in certain of the Spreadsheet functions. A 0 value is displayed as *FALSE*; any other numeric value is displayed as *TRUE*.

Date Format

Date format interprets a value as a date. You can choose from a variety of date options (see Figure 11.6). The list box shows today's date in each of the formats. The **Sample** box shows the value of the current cell in the selected format. Watch the Sample change as you try out the various date options.

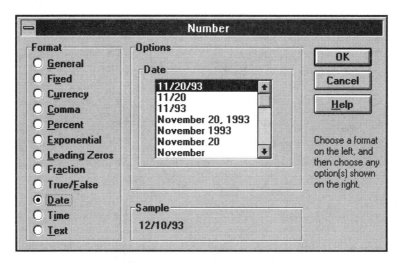

Figure 11.6 *Number dialog box with* **Date** *selected*

If a cell has some other format and you type a value using one of the date formats, Works automatically assigns Date format to the cell, using the option closest to the value you entered. Once a cell has been assigned Date format, you can enter a date using any of the optional formats, and Works converts it to the selected format. If you omit the year, Works assumes the current year, so "10/5" would be interpreted as 10/5/*yy*, where *yy* is the current year. If you omit the day, Works assumes the first day of the month, so "November" would be interpreted as 11/1/*yy*.

N O T E

Works accepts dates between January 1, 1900 and June 3, 2079. Any dates outside this range are interpreted as text.

A value in the format *nn/mm* might be interpreted as the month/day or the month/year, depending on the value of *mm*. If *mm* is equal to or less than the number of days in the month, it is interpreted as *month/day* of the current year. If it's greater than the number of days in the month, it's interpreted as the first day of *month/year*. So "10/31" is interpreted as October 31, of the current year, but "11/31" is interpreted as November 01, 1931.

WARNING

In all these cases, the value displayed in the cell depends on the date option chosen regardless of how you typed the value. For example, if you have chosen the month name only, then the cell would say merely *October* or *November* and you might not be aware that the year is 1931, not the current year. For this reason, unless you are displaying the month, day, and year, it's wise to enter all three items when you enter a date.

If you enter dates using the names of the months, as in January 1, 1995, you can abbreviate the month name to three letters or more. January can be abbreviated as Jan, Janu, Janua, and so on. Years between 1900 and 1999 can be abbreviated to the final two digits.

If you accidentally type a nondate value in a cell with Date format, the number is interpreted as the *n*th day after January 1, 1900. Thus, the value 366 is interpreted as December 31, 1900, the value 7259 is interpreted as November 15, 1919, and so on.

To insert the current date into a cell, press **Ctrl+;** (semicolon). Once entered, this date will not change unless you specifically replace it. If instead you want the date to be updated every time the spreadsheet is recalculated, use the formula **=NOW( )**. If you enter this formula before the Date format has been assigned to the cell, you'll see the serial number that Works uses to compute the date and time. As soon as you select the Date format, the current date appears.

Time Format

Time format is similar to Date format, but displays the value in the cell as a time. Figure 11.7 shows what the Number dialog box looks like with Time format selected. The list box shows the current time in each of the formatting options.

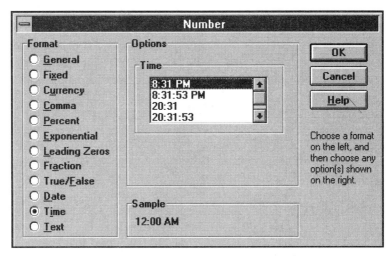

Figure 11.7 *Number dialog box with* **Time** *selected*

Works recognizes times and assigns Time format automatically. For example, if you enter a number followed by **AM** or **PM**, or enter a number using one of the time formatting options, as in **2:00**, Works automatically assigns Time format to the cell, selecting the option that is closest to the value you typed.

Once a cell has been associated with Time format, you can enter the time using any of the formatting options. For example, if you have chosen the *hh:mm* AM/PM option, you could enter 2:14 in the afternoon as **2:14 PM** or **14:14**. For morning times, you can enter **AM** or leave it out. Both AM and PM can be entered in lower-case or upper-case, with or without a separating space. You can omit leading zeros in each section, as in 5:6:7 for 5:06:07. If you specify AM/PM, you can enter just the hours, as in **2 AM**. If you omit the AM/PM desig-nator, you must include at least hours and minutes, but you can omit the sec-onds if they are **:00**. Illegal values (such as **25:00**) are displayed as midnight (**0:00:00**) or as text, depending on the value. Values too large for the cell are displayed as a string of pound signs.

To insert the current time into the cell, press **Ctrl+Shift+;** (semicolon). Once entered, this time will not change unless you specifically replace it. If instead you want the time to be updated every time the spreadsheet is recalculated, use the formula **=NOW( )**. If you enter the formula before Time format has been assigned to the cell, the serial number that Works uses to compute the date and time appears in the cell. As soon as you select Time format, the current time appears.

Text Format

The *Text format* option appears in the numeric format list so that you can tell Works that a value that looks like a number is really text. Use it when you want a number to be treated as text, such as part number or a social security number.

Once you have entered a value, and Works has decided that it is a number, selecting Text format in the Number dialog box has no effect. You must select Text format before entering the number. If you enter the number first, enter it again (after selecting Text format) to convert it. Alternatively, you can insert a quotation mark (") in front of the number in the formula bar.

NOTE

You can tell when a number is displayed in Text format because it is left justified and a quotation mark appears in front of its value in the formula bar.

Other Formatting

Figure 11.7 shows an example of how you can dress up a Spreadsheet with external formatting. You can use fonts, borders, colors, and shading not only to make a spreadsheet more attractive, but also to clarify sections of data. This is one of the main reasons for creating a textual table, such as the one in the figure, in Spreadsheet instead of Word Processor, as you can set borders and shadings on a cell-by-cell basis instead of on a paragraph-by-paragraph basis. So you can have three separate underlines in one row, for example, as you can see in row 4 in Figure 11.8. Notice also that shading (as in rows 6, 11, and 14 in the figure) is not available in Word Processor.

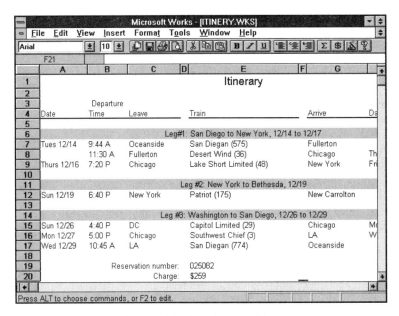

Figure 11.8 *Sample spreadsheet*

Fonts

Formatting the external appearance of spreadsheet data is done on a cell-by-cell basis. Select the cells you want to format, then select the font, font size, and font style (**bold**, *italic*, and <u>underline</u>) from the toolbar just as you do in Word Processor. You can select color and the strikethrough style by choosing **Format Font and Style**.

If you try to select a font or one of the formatting tools and get a message that this tool is unavailable at this time, the focus is currently in the formula bar. Press **Enter** to return the focus to the cell, then try again.

Alignment

By default, text data is aligned on the left and numeric data is aligned on the right. You can change the alignment of any cell to left, center, or right by using the toolbar. Other alignment options are available via the **Format Alignment** command, which opens the Alignment dialog box shown in Figure 11.9.

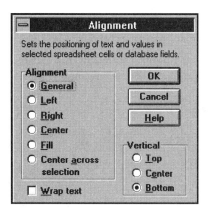

Figure 11.9 *Alignment dialog box*

General Alignment returns the selected cells to the default, with text on the left and numbers on the right. Left, center, and right alignment are the same as they are on the toolbar. The other alignment options are explained in the following sections.

Filling Cells

The **Fill** option fills the cell with whatever value is already in the cell. For example, if the cell contains a pound sign (#), it repeats the pound sign to completely fill the cell from left to right. If cells to the right are also selected and are blank, it fills those cells with the same character. Use this feature to create a row of asterisks (*), pound signs, equal signs (=), and so on.

Centering Text across a Row of Cells

The **Center across selection** option centers the text located in the first selected cell across the row of selected cells. In the example in Figure 11.8, the word "Departure" in row 3 is actually in cell A3, but it is centered across cells A3:A5. The messages in rows 6, 11, and 14 are centered across columns A through I.

❖ **To center text across a range of cells:**

1. Type the text in the leftmost cell. (If you put it in any other cell, it won't work.)

2. Select the range of cells, which should all be in one row. (All the others should be blank.)

3. Choose **Format Alignment**. The Alignment dialog box opens.

4. Click **Center across selection**.

5. Click **OK**. The Alignment dialog box closes, and the text in the first cell is centered across all the selected cells.

You can undo the centering across cells immediately by choosing **Edit Undo**. Later on, you can undo it by selecting the cells again and choosing **General** or **Left Alignment**.

Wrapping Text

Wrapping text is another major reason for creating textual tables in Spreadsheet instead of Word Processor. Figure 11.10 shows an example of a table with wrapped text. As you can see, the text entries in the cells require more than one line apiece. It's very difficult to create this type of table in Word Processor. You have to break the text into columns yourself, inserting tabs to line everything up correctly. If you revise the text, you might have to retype the entire table. But in Spreadsheet, creating such a table is easy.

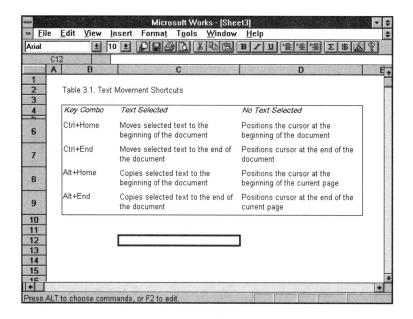

Figure 11.10 *Wrapped text*

By default, when text won't fit in a cell, it doesn't wrap to the next line. Instead, it spills over into the neighboring cells. If it's left aligned, it spills into the cells to the right. You can see an example of this in row 2 of Figure 11.10. The caption for the table is typed in cell B2; it spills over into C2. Right-aligned text spills over into the cells to the left. Figure 11.8 has an example in row 19. The heading "Reservation number:" is right-aligned in cell C19; it spills over into cell B19. Center-aligned text spills over on both the left and the right so that it remains centered on the cell that actually contains it.

There's nothing wrong with letting text spill over into neighboring cells as long as you don't plan to use those cells. In fact, that's the one way you can create captions, labels, annotations, and so on, that cut across the table's columns. (The other way is to center text across several columns, as you've already seen.)

The problem arises when you want to put text in the neighboring columns too. If a neighboring column is not blank, Spreadsheet chops off the text instead of spilling it over. Figure 11.11 shows what the table in Figure 11.10 looked like before the text was wrapped. You can see that all the values in column C were cut off.

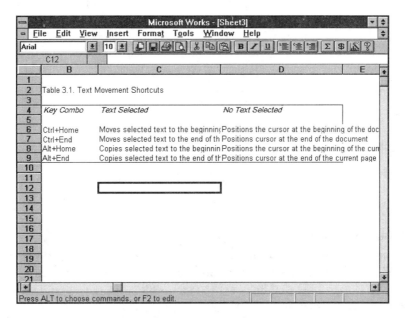

Figure 11.11 *Table text before wrapping*

Wrapping text turns each cell into a paragraph; the cell edges are the margins of the paragraph. By default, Spreadsheet adjusts the row height as needed to accommodate the cell with the most lines in each row. To wrap text, select all the cells involved, choose **Format Alignment**, and check **Wrap Text**. You can use any of the other alignment options along with text wrapping, so you can wrap left-, center-, or right-aligned text, filled text, and so on.

Figure 11.12 shows what the same table looks like after wrapping the text in the range C6:D9. Rows 6 through 9 have been expanded automatically, and all the narrative entries fit in their cells. The table is much clearer now.

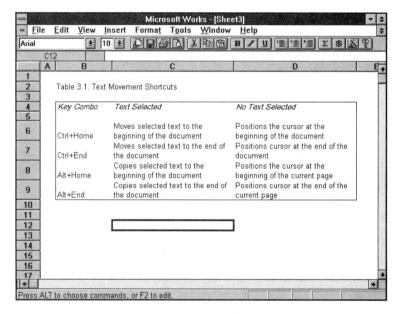

Figure 11.12 *Table text after wrapping*

Vertical Positioning

But it's still not right. Notice that the entries are positioned at the bottoms of their cells, which is the default positioning. You can see this most clearly in cells B6:B9, which have only one line each. In tables like this, text should be aligned at the top not the bottom of each cell. To position text at the top, select the desired cells, choose **Format Alignment**, and click **Top** in the Vertical group. Figure 11.13 shows the result.

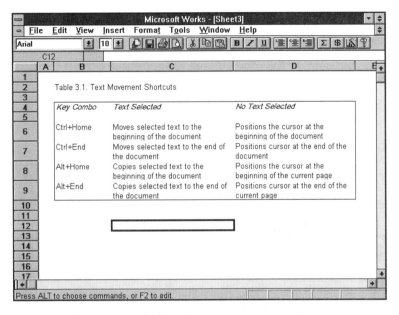

Figure 11.13 *Table after positioning text at the top*

Inserting Some White Space

The table in Figure 11.13 is almost ready, but there's one more problem—the rows are a little too close together. When Spreadsheet adjusts rows to fit the text they contain, it doesn't allow for any extra spacing between rows. Most tables look better with a little white space between the rows. You can drag the row separators to expand them a bit. Since the text is now aligned at the top of the cells in the range C6:D9, expanding the rows puts the extra space at the bottom of each cell. The result is the table in Figure 11.10.

When you're creating a narrative table, you don't have to do it step-by-step as shown here. The following procedure shows how to do it more efficiently.

❖ **To create a narrative table:**

1. Set up the columns and titles.

2. Select the range to contain the narrative text.

3. Choose **Format Alignment**. The Alignment dialog box opens.

4. Click **Wrap Text** to place an *X* in the checkbox.

5. Click **Top** in the Vertical group.

6. Click **OK**.

7. Type the narrative text. The rows wrap and expand as you type them.

8. When all the text is typed, adjust the row heights to provide some extra space between entries.

Other Ways to Insert White Space

Sometimes the simplest way to insert some space into a spreadsheet is to insert a blank row or column. For example, in Figure 11.13, row 5 is a spacing row. Figure 11.8 shows several spacing rows; in addition, columns D and F are spacing columns.

In most cases, you can put some white space between cells by expanding the height and width of the cells. But sometimes, a spacing row or column is a better choice. In Figure 11.8, for example, column D was inserted simply to break the line in row 4 to separate the "Departure" section from the "Train" section. Column F was inserted for a similar reason.

Also in Figure 11.8, row 5 was inserted to provide some white space between rows 4 and 6. Expanding row 4 and/or row 6 wouldn't work because the underline in row 4 and the shading in row 6 would move with their rows, and you wouldn't get any white space.

NOTE

Inserting a column after the fact can mess up your titles that are centered across columns. You may have to re-center them after inserting a new column.

You can also insert spacing rows and columns in a numeric table. Don't worry about blank cells in the middle of a range influencing the results of **SUM** or **AVG**; both functions ignore blank cells in a range reference.

N O T E

If you reference a blank cell individually with **AVG**, the cell is treated as a 0, and that does influence the result of the average. But as long as the blank is part of a range, the cell is ignored.

Figure 11.14 is an example of a numeric spreadsheet that uses spacing rows and columns. Notice, in particular, column G, which provides some white space between columns F and H. Expanding column F would not provide the same spacing because its data is right aligned. Expanding column H would provide some white space, but the line in row 3 would extend into the space, which isn't as neat as the way it's done here. At the right side of the window, you can just see column K, providing a break in the lines under Week 1 and Week 2 (not shown).

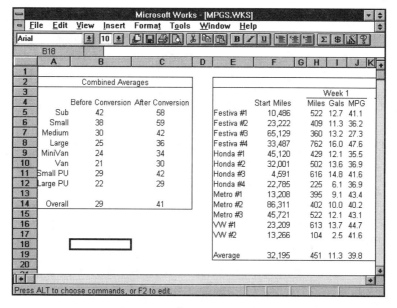

Figure 11.14 *MPGs spreadsheet*

N O T E This spreadsheet is an example of a common practice among spreadsheet users—it incorporates several related spreadsheets in one file. On the left, you see the Combined Averages spreadsheet, which summarizes data from several detailed spreadsheets. On the right, you can see the beginning of a detailed spreadsheet; this particular one contains weekly MPG figures for subcompact cars before conversion. Not shown in the window are similar detailed spreadsheets for the other automobile categories, before and after conversion. All in all, this file contains 17 related spreadsheets. The user has assigned a range name to each spreadsheet and moves around in the file by jumping to range names.

Borders

You place borders around cells the same way you do around paragraphs in Word Processor. If you select a single cell, the border runs along the edges of the cell. If you select a range, the border runs along the edges of the range. Figure 11.14 provides a good example of a range border. The range A2:C14 was selected, then an outline border was chosen. Instead of every cell being outlined individually, the entire range was outlined. Then the range A2:C2 was selected and a bottom border was chosen.

When you choose a border for a range, Spreadsheet actually defines the border cell by cell. In Figure 11.14, for example, cell C13 is defined with a right border only, cell C14 has a right and bottom border, cell B14 has a bottom border, and so on.

You draw borders using the **Format Border** command, which opens the Border dialog box shown in Figure 11.15. This dialog box works just like its Word Processor counterpart. By default, it draws an outline border around the selected cell(s), so if you don't want an outline, be sure to select some other border, turn off the default border, or click **Cancel**.

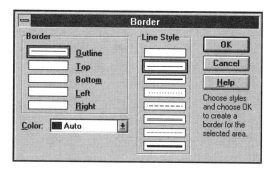

Figure 11.15 *Border dialog box*

Several editing actions can mess up your current borders, and you may find that you have to redraw them. Inserting a row or column in an area that has a border can interrupt or duplicate the border. Copying or filling from a cell with a border copies the border as well. Moving a cell with a border moves the border. Cutting cells or deleting a row or column with a border removes the border. Whenever you need to fix a border, choose the affected cells, choose **Format Border**, and correct the border options.

Shading

Shading also helps to enhance the readability of a spreadsheet. Choose the **Format Patterns** command to apply shading to the selected cell or range (see Figure 11.16). The **Pattern** drop-down list provides a number of shading patterns, including solid, various densities of dotted patterns, and stripes running in various directions. The pattern you select shows up in the **Pattern** box and the **Sample** box. The shading in Figure 11.8 uses a solid pattern.

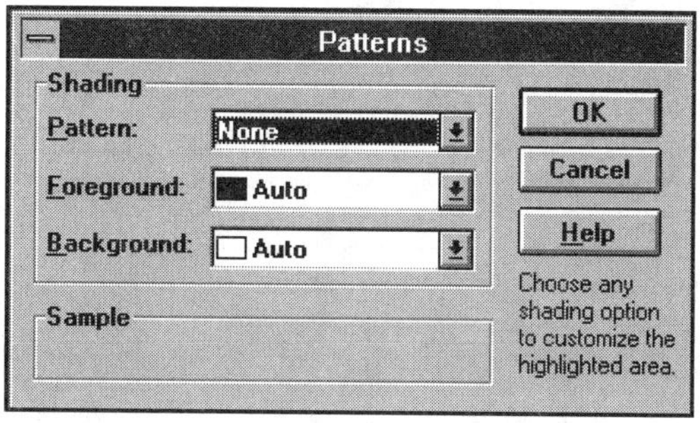

Figure 11.16 *Patterns dialog box*

The **Foreground** and **Background** drop-down lists let you select colors for the pattern. If the pattern includes dots or stripes, **Foreground** determines the color of the dots or stripes while **Background** determines the color of the field behind them. If you choose the solid pattern, **Foreground** determines its color. The colors you select show up in the **Pattern** box as well as the **Sample** box, so you can experiment until you find the combination you like. If you're working with a black-and-white system, you can choose black, white, light gray, and dark gray colors. The shading in Figure 11.8 is light gray.

Like borders, shading can be affected by editing actions. You might have to correct shading after moving, copying, inserting, or deleting cells.

AutoFormats

If you're not a graphic designer, you might feel somewhat daunted by the task of formatting a spreadsheet to look sophisticated and legible. Works includes a number of automatic formats to give you some expert help. Figure 11.17 shows the AutoFormat dialog box, which opens when you choose the **Format AutoFormat** command. As you select each format in the list, the **Sample** box shows you what it looks like on some sample data.

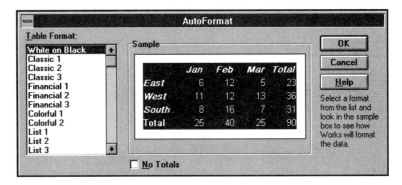

Figure 11.17 *AutoFormat dialog box*

AutoFormat removes any other formatting you have done to a range. For example, if you have added a border or centered a column, **AutoFormat** undoes it. You can add your own formatting to a range *after* using **AutoFormat**, if you wish.

The **AutoFormats** are designed for numeric tables with column titles in the top row, row titles in the left column, a total or averages column on the right, and a total or averages row at the bottom. If your table has no totals or averages, click **No Totals** so that **AutoFormat** won't format the right-hand column and the bottom row differently from the rest of the data.

The first format in the list, **White on Black**, simply reformats the selected cells to present white text on a black background. The top row and the left column—presumably the titles—are in ***bold italics***. The title in the bottom row is not italicized unless you click **No Totals**.

Figure 11.18 shows a before and after example of **Classic 1**. You can see that the data was set up originally to take advantage of the **AutoFormat** structure, with the titles at the top and left, and averages at the right and bottom. **AutoFormat** added borders and enhanced the titles to create an attractive, if simple, table. **Classic 2** and **Classic 3** add color and shading to the table.

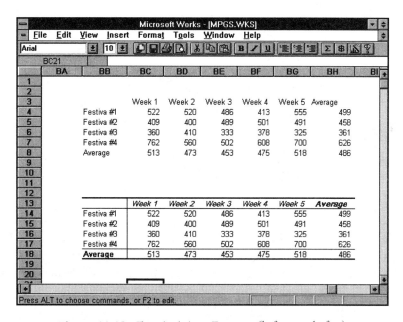

Figure 11.18 *Classic 1 AutoFormat* (before and after)

By the way, **AutoFormat** cannot analyze the data in a table to determine the location of the titles and borders. Regardless of the data in the table,

AutoFormat treats the top row and left column as titles, and if **No Totals** is unchecked, the right column and the bottom row are treated as totals.

The **Financial AutoFormats** are designed for financial data. Figure 11.19 shows the effect of **Financial 1.** The column titles are in gray this time, and dollar signs have been added to the first and last rows. Borders have also been added. **Financial 2** and **Financial 3** are similar to **Financial 1** but add a little color to the format.

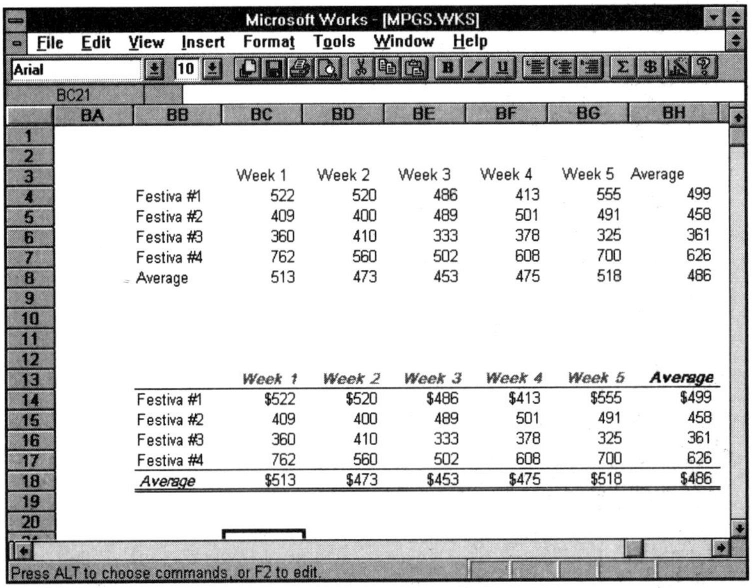

Figure 11.19 *Financial 1 AutoFormat* (*before and after*)

Colorful 1 and **Colorful 2** use color to set off the titles and totals. Lists 1 through 3 are designed for larger tables, where it might be hard to follow the data all the way across a row. They use various techniques (such as colored stripes) to mark the rows, much like the classic "computer paper," so that they are easier to scan.

At the bottom of the list box (not shown in Figure 11.17) are **3D Effects 1** and **3D Effects 2**, which use light gray shading combined with white and dark gray borders to create modern-looking tables that have a 3-dimensional appearance. Figure 11.20 shows **3D Effects 1** at the top and **3D Effects 2** at the bottom.

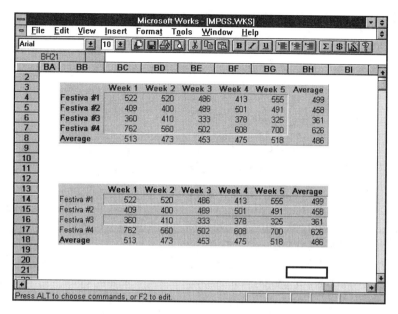

Figure 11.20 *3D Effects AutoFormats*

N O T E

Once you see how the experts do it, you can probably create your own 3D effects in tables that don't match the basic AutoFormat setup of titles at the top and left and totals at the right and bottom.

Page Formatting

Just like a Word Processor document, a spreadsheet can run to multiple pages. On your monitor, it all appears to be on one sheet of paper; you scroll around to see the various areas. But it might take several pages to print it.

You can format your pages in Spreadsheet just like you do in Word Processor. The **File Page Setup** command lets you set margins, including header and footer margins. The **View Headers and Footers** command lets you create headers and footers, which might include special characters like page numbers, the date, the time, and so on.

Landscape Orientation

Many spreadsheets fit better sideways on a page. You can set up your document to be printed in *landscape mode* (that is, sideways) as opposed to the normal *portrait mode*.

❖ **To print in landscape mode:**

1. Choose **File Page Setup**. The Page Setup dialog box opens.

2. Click the **Source, Size, and Orientation** tab. The Source, Size, and Orientation page appears.

3. In the **Orientation** group, click **Landscape**. The **Sample** box switches to landscape orientation. So does the icon in the **Orientation** group.

4. Click **OK**. The Page Setup dialog box closes. You won't see any difference until you print or preview the spreadsheet.

To return to portrait mode, repeat the above procedure, clicking **Portrait** in Step 3.

NOTE

Some printers can't handle landscape mode.

Breaking the Spreadsheet into Pages

If a spreadsheet won't fit on one page, Spreadsheet breaks it into pages, fitting as many rows and columns as possible on each page. It has no way of knowing where good page breaks might be. But you can tell it specifically where you want the pages to break.

❖ **To insert a page break:**

1. Select a row or column where you want the page to break. (You can select the entire row or column by clicking the header.)

2. Choose **Insert Page Break**. A dotted line indicates the page break.

A horizontal page break goes all the way across the spreadsheet, from column A to column IV. Similarly, a vertical page break goes all the way down the spreadsheet.

Figure 11.21 shows the MPG spreadsheet set up with page breaks to identify the print areas. You can see page breaks after row 19 and column D. Cells A1 through D19 will be printed on page 1. Works moves down the spreadsheet so that page 2 is the data that is below row 19 in columns A through D. It keeps going down the spreadsheet until it runs out of data and page breaks. Then it returns to the top and starts printing the data in columns E through whatever, rows 1 through 19. Again, it works down the spreadsheet, then returns to the top and moves to the next page to the right. It stops when there are no more page breaks and no more data.

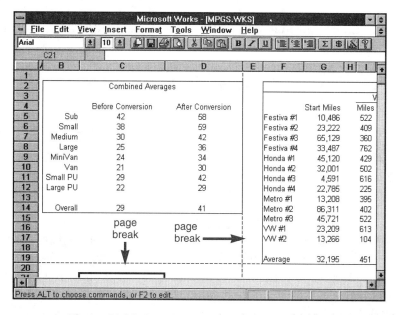

Figure 11.21 *Inserting page breaks in a spreadsheet*

To remove a page break, highlight the row or column and choose **Insert Remove Page Break**. This command is available only when a row or column containing a page break is selected.

NOTE

You can see how the pages are laid out without printing them by using **Print Preview**. Just click the **Print Preview** icon on the tool-bar.

Setting the Print Area

If you're having trouble breaking a complex spreadsheet into pages, there's another solution. You can set up a range as a *print area*. When you print the spreadsheet, only that area will print.

❖ **To set a print area:**

1. Select the range that you want to print in one print job.

2. Choose **Format Set Print Area**. A message asks you to confirm the operation.

3. Click **OK**. You won't see any difference in the spreadsheet, but when you print it, only the selected range will be printed.

NOTE

If you want to print only part of a spreadsheet, such as the Combined Averages table in Figure 11.21, set it up as a print area.

A print area doesn't have to be just one page. You can use page breaks within a print area to divide it into several pages.

Once you have set a print area, it remains in effect until you set another print area. If you want to return to printing your whole spreadsheet, you have to set the entire spreadsheet as the print area.

Summary

In this chapter, you have learned how to:

- ❖ Format a spreadsheet
- ❖ Select the numeric format for a cell
- ❖ Apply external formatting such as fonts, alignment, borders, and shading
- ❖ Use the **AutoFormats** to take advantage of professional designs
- ❖ Format and print pages

The **AutoFormats** aren't the only way to create professionally designed spreadsheets. In the next chapter, you'll see a number of Spreadsheet templates, along with some other special Spreadsheet features.

CHAPTER **12**

Special Features

This chapter shows you how to use several special Spreadsheet features, including the AutoStart Templates that involve spreadsheets. Specifically, you'll learn how to:

- ❖ Hide columns and rows in a spreadsheet
- ❖ Use Spelling Checker in a spreadsheet
- ❖ Use the AutoStart spreadsheet templates
- ❖ Create your own spreadsheet templates

305

Hiding Columns and Rows

You have seen how to bring together two parts of a spreadsheet by splitting the window, but sometimes it's easier to hide the intervening rows or columns. All you have to do is reduce their width or height to 0. Figure 12.1 shows an example, where rows 13 through 21 have been hidden.

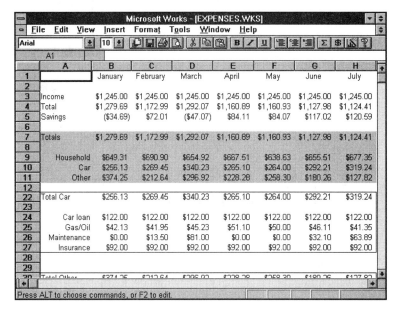

Figure 12.1 *Hidden rows*

❖ **To hide rows:**

1. Select the rows to be hidden.

2. Choose **Format Row Height**. The Row Height dialog box opens. The default height of 12 is displayed in the text box.

3. Replace the default height with **0**.

4. Click **OK**. The Row Height dialog box closes, and the selected rows disappear.

❖ **To hide columns:**

1. Select the columns to be hidden.

2. Choose **Format Column Width**. The Column Width dialog box opens. The default width of 10 is displayed in the text box.

3. Replace the default width with **0**.

4. Click **OK**. The Column Width dialog box closes and the selected columns disappear.

While the rows and/or columns are hidden, they won't be printed or copied to the Word Processor, either. Use this feature to bring together separated data for printing or embedding in a report, as well as to hide sensitive information from unauthorized readers who need to see the rest of the spreadsheet.

Don't worry about hidden rows and columns affecting totals, averages, and other formulas that refer to them. Their values are still accessible to Spreadsheet.

NOTE

❖ **To reshow hidden columns or rows:**

1. Select a range that includes the hidden columns or rows.

2. Choose **Format Column Width** or **Format Row Height**. The appropriate dialog box opens with the default column width or row height displayed in the text box.

3. Click **OK**. The hidden columns or rows reappear at the default width or height. (The rest of the selected range also has the default width or height.)

4. Adjust the width or height of the affected rows, if desired.

Spelling Checks

You have already seen how to use Spelling Checker with Word Processor. The same feature is available with Spreadsheet and is used in the same way. Start by selecting the range you want to check or, if you want to check the entire spreadsheet, select any individual cell. There's no **Spelling Check** icon on the toolbar, so choose **Tools Spelling** to start the check. The Spelling dialog box appears, and you respond to it in the same way.

Spreadsheet Templates

Works includes a variety of AutoStart Templates that are spreadsheets. Some help you with difficult calculations (such as monthly loan payments), but most involve relatively simple totals. Their main benefit is in providing professional-looking forms for your business, home, or classroom. Included are everything from fax cover sheets to personal financial statements. The following list briefly describes each spreadsheet template that Works provides.

Sales Invoice (AutoStart Business group, Billing category)	You fill in your company name and address, the customer's name and address, and the details of the items sold. (Works calculates the totals.)
Service Invoice (AutoStart Business group, Billing category)	Similar to the Sales Invoice, but includes sections for parts and labor.
Account Statement (AutoStart Business group, Billing category)	You fill in your company name and address, the customer's name and address, and the details of purchases and credits. (Works calculates the totals.)
Business Budget (AutoStart Business group, Business Planning category)	Fill in the details of your monthly income and expenses, budgeted and actual. (Works calculates the totals as well as the amounts over or under budget.) Several charts are available based on the data in this spreadsheet.
Breakeven Analysis (AutoStart Business group, Business Planning category)	Fill in the details of costs and sales. (Works calculates the breakeven point.) A Breakeven bar chart contrasts monthly sales with monthly expenses.
Cash Flow Statement (AutoStart Business group, Business Planning category)	Fill in January's beginning balance. Then supply the monthly details of receipts and disbursements. (Works calculates the totals, cash flow, and balances.)

Personal Financial Statement (AutoStart Business group, Business Planning category)	Fill in the details of your assets and liabilities. (Works calculates your net worth.)
Income Statement (AutoStart Business group, Business Planning category)	Fill in the details of your company's monthly income, expenses, and taxes. (Works calculates totals and prepares a Profit and Loss chart.)
Fax Cover Sheet (AutoStart Business group, Documents category)	Fill in your information and the recipient's information, add a message.
Mortgage and Loan Analysis (AutoStart Business group, Expenses category)	Fill in principle, interest, term, and so on. (Works calculates the monthly payments, total interest, and loan cost.)
Purchase Order (AutoStart Business group, Expenses category)	Fill in your information, the vendor's information, and the details of the items to be purchased. (Works calculates the totals.)
Weekly Time Sheet (AutoStart Business group, Management category)	Fill in the daily check-in and check-out times and wage information. (Works calculates the regular hours worked, overtime hours worked, and wages due.)
Job Estimate (AutoStart Business group, Sales category)	Fill in detailed materials and labor estimates. (Works calculates the totals.)
Order Form (AutoStart Business group, Sales category)	Fill in your company's information and print copies to send to your customers so they can order your products. Or fill in ordering information to order items from other companies.
Price List (AutoStart Business group, Sales category)	Fill in pricing details for your products.

Monthly Sales Goals (AutoStart Business group, Sales category)	Fill in sales information for each product you want to track. (Works calculates variances from goals and provides a Monthly Income chart.)
Grade Book (AutoStart Education group, Productivity category)	Fill in student names and scores. (Works calculates letter grades, averages, and class averages.)
Class Schedule (AutoStart Education group, Productivity category)	Fill in the details of subjects and instructors to create a daily class schedule.

Using Templates

To use a template, choose **Use a Template** in the Startup dialog box. Then choose a group and a category, and finally, double-click the name of the template in the list box. An unnamed document opens containing whatever data is contained in the template. You fill in the rest of the data. Whatever you fill in does not affect the template, just the new document you are now preparing. Be sure to save it often to preserve your new spreadsheet in a file on disk.

An AutoStart Example

Figure 12.2 shows an example of a typical AutoStart template, the Purchase Order form, which demonstrates how you use a spreadsheet template. The text in cells A2:A7 appears in red on your screen. You are supposed to replace it with your company's name, address, and so on. Similarly, you replace the text in cells D7:D11 with the vendor's name and address.

In each cell below, add the data indicated by the label. For example, click **A14**, click the formula bar to place the cursor in the data, then add the name of the person ordering the items on the purchase order.

Figure 12.3 shows the bottom half of the same form. (Some rows are hidden so you can see the entire section.) In the A26:F43 range, you list the items being ordered. For example, click cell A26 and type an item number. Press **Tab** and type a quantity. Press **Tab** and type a description. Press **Tab** and type the price for one item. Spreadsheet automatically calculates the total in cell G26 and the subtotal in cell G44. When you fill in the Tax rate in cell E45, it calculates the

Tax in cell G45. You fill in Shipping and Handling in cell G46 and Other costs in cell G47, and it calculates the Total amount in cell G48. As you add more items to the list, the totals are constantly updated.

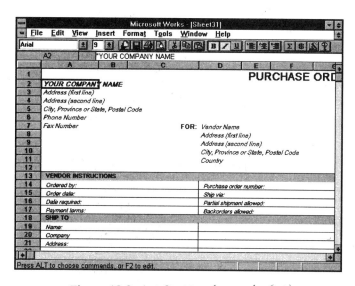

Figure 12.2 *AutoStart purchase order (top)*

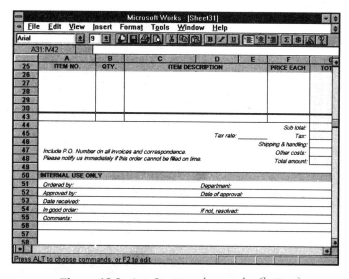

Figure 12.3 *AutoStart purchase order (bottom)*

N O T E The cells that Spreadsheet calculates are shaded. They are yellow on a color monitor. Most of the AutoStart spreadsheet templates use yellow shading to signal cells that are calculated for you. Some of the templates protect the formula cells so that you can't replace them, but many of them are not protected.

The cells in the bottom part of the form, labeled Internal Use Only, are meant to be filled in when the items are received. They can be filled in by hand on the printed purchase order, or you can reopen the spreadsheet and enter the appropriate data into the cells.

Creating Your Own Template

If you're using Works to support a business, you'll probably use Spreadsheet to create many of your own forms, such as the Purchase Order form. You can easily turn any spreadsheet into a template.

❖ **To convert the current spreadsheet into a template:**

1. Choose **File Save As**. The Save As dialog box opens.

2. Click the **Template** button. The Save As Template dialog box opens.

3. Type a name for your template. (This is not a filename; it can have up to 30 characters, including spaces.)

4. Click **OK**. Works creates an entry for the template in the Custom group, the Custom category.

SHORTCUT If you plan to use any of the AutoStart Templates on a regular basis, fill in your personal or company data that will be the same every time and resave the spreadsheet as a template.

Summary

In this chapter, you have learned how to:

- ❖ Hide rows and columns
- ❖ Check the spelling in your spreadsheet
- ❖ Use the AutoStart spreadsheet templates
- ❖ Create your own spreadsheet templates

Are you ready to generate some charts and graphs based on your spreadsheet data? The next chapter shows you how.

CHAPTER 13

Spreadsheet Charting

Spreadsheet includes a very flexible charting feature to develop bar charts, line charts, pie charts, and so on. You can create charts almost instantaneously by accepting all the default options, or you can do extensive tailoring to develop only the chart you need.

This chapter shows you how to:

❖   Create a new chart based on a range of data in your spreadsheet

❖   Work with the 12 basic chart types provided by Works

❖   Tailor a chart

❖   Manage charts: save, copy, print, delete, and so on

❖   Locate and view charts created by the AutoStart templates

Setting Up Data for a Chart

Before you can generate a chart, you need to select a range of data on which Works will base the chart. Sometimes the range is one row or one column, in which case there's little problem in selecting it. But sometimes you need to select several rows or columns that aren't adjacent to each other in the spreadsheet. For example, you might want to select the title row (to provide labels for the chart) and the totals or averages row (to provide the data for the chart), but not the rows in between.

There are two basic ways to bring together the necessary rows and columns. One is to hide intervening rows or columns, as you learned in the previous chapter. Works ignores hidden data when generating a chart. The other is to copy all the necessary data to an empty area in the spreadsheet, creating a mini-spreadsheet that is set up especially for the chart. If you do this, be sure to use **Paste Special** to copy **Values only** if the data contains formulas. If you copy the formulas themselves, they will be adapted to the new location and probably won't calculate the right results.

Generating a Chart

To generate a chart, select the desired range and click the **New Chart** icon on the toolbar (see Figure 13.1). The New Chart dialog box lets you select the type of chart you want, add a title, and change some of the default parameters.

The drop-down list shows the types of charts Works can create. The Bar chart is the default, as shown in Figure 13.1. You can see a small version of the selected chart at the lower right of the screen. It actually uses the data from the spreadsheet, although the labels are more abbreviated than they will be in the real chart. This sample chart changes instantly as you select chart types and the other options in the dialog box.

In the **Finishing touches** group, you can add a title to the chart. The title appears centered at the top of the chart. Works lets you type as many characters as you want in this text box, but it uses a maximum of 49 characters in the title, so you might as well learn to limit your titles to 49 characters. You can add a subtitle later, if you wish.

If you click **Add border**, Works draws an outline box around the chart. No other types of borders are available. If you click **Add gridlines**, Works draws dotted gridlines on the chart. Figure 13.2 shows the New Chart dialog box with a title, border, and gridlines. You can see them all in the sample chart.

New Chart icon

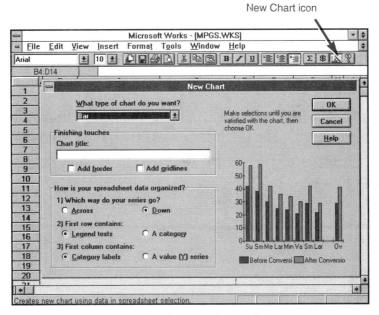

Figure 13.1 *The New Chart dialog box*

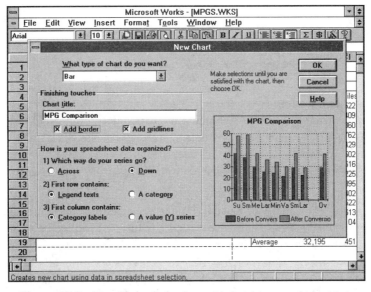

Figure 13.2 *New Chart dialog box with finishing touches added*

Categories and Series

Works makes some basic assumptions about the way the selected data is organized. Figure 13.3 shows the data that produced the sample chart in Figure 13.2 so that you can see some of the assumptions that Works made.

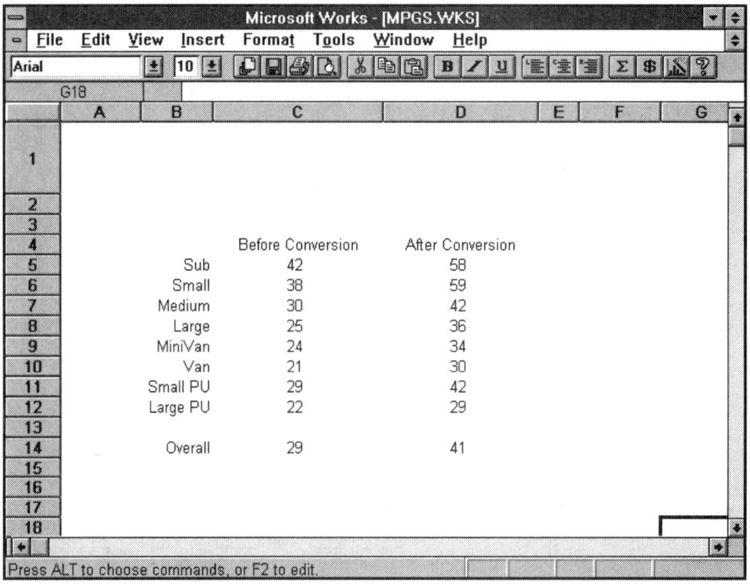

Figure 13.3 *Data for sample bar chart*

Most charts are based on two factors: *categories* and *series*. The categories determine what is placed on the horizontal axis (also called the X axis) of the chart. In the sample data, each row represents a category of cars: sub, small, medium, and so on. You can see that each category produced a group of two bars in the chart, and that each group is labeled with the title of the row from the spreadsheet.

The reason each category has two bars is because this particular spreadsheet has two series. The series data is so called because it produces a related series of points or bars along the horizontal axis. In Figure 13.2, all the dark bars belong to the first series, labeled Before Conversion, and all the light bars belong to the second series, labeled After Conversion. You can see in Figure 13.3 that the series data and labels came from the columns in the spreadsheet.

The data in the sample spreadsheet is taller than it is wide; that is, it has more rows than columns. In such cases, Works assumes that the rows represent the categories and the columns represent the series. If the selected data has more columns than rows, Works assumes that the columns represent the categories and the rows represent the series. You can override the assumption by clicking **Across** or **Down** under **Which way do your series go?** If you're not sure which way is correct, try each option. You'll see the results immediately in the sample chart in the New Chart dialog box. The correct option is usually obvious.

For most chart types, if Works finds text data in the first row and column, it assumes they are titles and should be used to label the chart. If it finds numbers in the first row and/or column, it assumes they are numeric data and should be used in the body of the chart. You can see under **First row contains** and **First column contains** what assumptions Works has made. If an assumption is wrong, you can change it by clicking the other option.

In most types of chart, the titles for the series data are used to create the legend at the bottom of the chart, which explains the colors or patterns used to identify each series in the chart. If no series titles are provided, Works labels the legend with "Series 1," "Series 2," and so on. These are not very meaningful labels, but you can change them later.

In most types of chart, the titles for the categories are used to label the horizontal axis of the chart. If no category titles are provided, the categories are not labeled. You can add labels later.

Blank Rows and Columns

Notice in Figures 13.2 and 13.3 that the spacing row (row 13) results in an empty category in the chart. This works out well in the bar chart, as it separates the overall averages from the detailed averages. But in other types of charts, a blank category or series could be very undesirable. In a line chart for example, a blank category would cause the line to suddenly dip to zero. Remove or hide blank rows or columns to eliminate this problem.

Creating the Chart

When you have selected all your options, click **OK**. The New Chart dialog box closes and a chart window appears on your screen (see Figure 13.4). Notice that the title bar shows the name of the spreadsheet as well as the generic name of the chart.

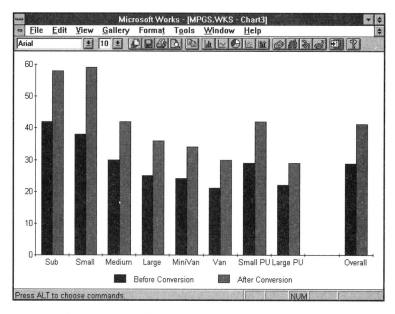

Figure 13.4 *A bar chart*

When a chart window is active, the Spreadsheet Charting program takes over the screen. You can see in Figure 13.4 that the toolbar and menu bar are different from Spreadsheet's. Charting's tools and menus let you modify and manage the charts that belong to a spreadsheet. You'll learn how to use many of its features in this chapter.

In Figure 13.4, the chart window is maximized. If you restore its normal size, you can see both the chart window and the Spreadsheet window. You can resize or tile the two windows so that you can work with both at once. When you resize the window, Works resizes the chart to fit in the window. The labels might become abbreviated, the proportions might change, and so on. Use **Print Preview** to see what the chart will actually look like when printed or embedded in a Word Processor document.

Works uses different shading patterns and chart symbols when displaying or printing a chart in black and white. If you have a color monitor and black-and-white printer, choose **View Display as Printed** to see the chart in the same black and white color scheme it will be printed in. It might look quite different from the color version.

N O T E

You can't edit the chart directly. That is, you can't select an object in the chart and change it, move it, resize it, and so on. However, you can modify almost everything in the chart via dialog boxes. You'll see how later in this chapter. But first, let's explore the various types of charts available.

The Chart Types

Works offers 12 basic chart types, including *area* charts, *line* charts, *bar* charts, and *pie* charts. Most of these basic types also have a number of variations. When you're working with the New Chart dialog box to create the original chart, you can choose only the 12 basic types, but once the chart window is open, you can choose variations on the basic types.

The following sections show you the 12 basic types and their variations. It would take too much space to explain each type and each variation in detail, or to explain when each one is the best chart to use. When you have a set of data that you want to chart, you can try out various charts until you find the one that does the best job for you.

Area Charts

An area chart shows the *relative* changes of values over a period of time. Figure 13.5 shows an example that tracks the population of an urban area for a period of 100 years. You can see not only how the total population has changed, but also the waxing and waning of the various ethnic groups that make up the total population.

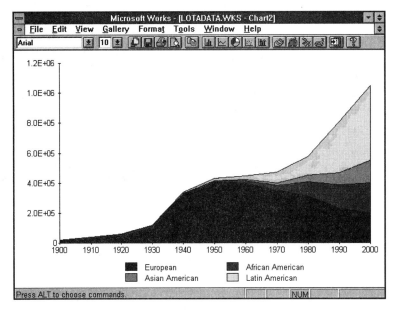

Figure 13.5 *Sample area chart*

N O T E The population numbers are so large that Charting couldn't fit them along the vertical axis and used scientific notation instead. You'll learn later how to change the labels on the vertical axis.

Figure 13.6 shows the variations that are available for area charts. You get to this dialog box by choosing **Gallery Area**. Click one of the variation buttons to convert your chart to that format.

Variation 1 is the basic chart, which you can return to if you decide you don't like another variation. Variation 2 depicts all data as it relates to the total, so that the top of the chart is a straight line representing 100%. Variation 3 is the basic chart with drop lines added to emphasize the years. Variation 4 adds gridlines to the basic chart. Variation 5 moves the series labels into the chart itself instead of the legend at the bottom. This variation would not be appropriate in the population example because some of the areas are too small to hold a label.

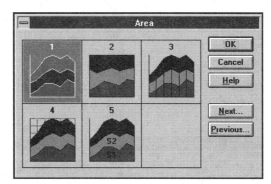

Figure 13.6 *Area chart variations*

Works also offers a 3D area chart, which is much like the basic chart, but it is drawn using 3D techniques. It looks much more sophisticated than the flat chart. Figure 13.7 shows the same data in a 3D chart.

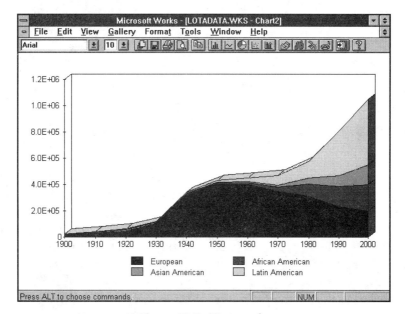

Figure 13.7 *3D area chart*

You can select a 3D area chart from the New Chart dialog box (Figure 13.2); all the 3D charts are at the bottom of the list of chart types. Or, if you have already created another type of chart and want to convert it to a 3D chart, click the **3D Area Chart** icon on the toolbar. (It looks like a 3D area chart.) A dialog box similar to the one in Figure 13.6 opens, and you can select which style of 3D area chart you want. Some of the variations are simply 3D versions of the flat charts, but some of the variations depict the areas as separate objects. Figure 13.8 shows an example of this type of 3D area chart.

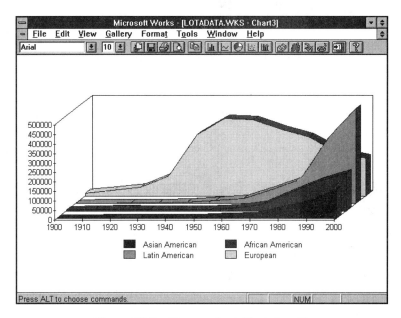

Figure 13.8 *3D area chart (Variation 4)*

When you use one of the 3D variations that places some areas behind other areas, as in Figure 13.8, it's important that the larger areas be at the back so they don't obstruct the smaller areas. You might find it necessary to go back to your spreadsheet and sort the rows or columns to bring the smaller areas to the front of the chart and put the larger areas at the back. (The first row or column in the range becomes the first series in the chart, which is in front. The second row or column becomes the second series, and so on.)

Bar Charts

Bar charts help you compare data such as the before and after results you have seen previously in the MPG chart. Figure 13.9 shows the variations that are available for bar charts. You can open the Bar dialog box from any chart window by clicking the **Bar Chart** icon in the toolbar, which looks like a bar chart.

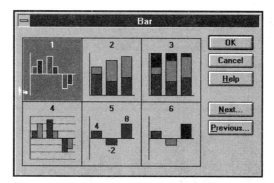

Figure 13.9 *Bar chart variations*

Variation 1 is the basic bar chart; notice that you can depict negative values in the chart. Variation 2 is a stacked bar chart, which shows the relationship of each series to the total of the category. Stacked bar charts are more appropriate for data where it makes sense to total the categories (such as the population data used for Figure 13.7). A stacked chart would not be appropriate for the MPG data, where adding up the average miles per gallon before and after conversion produces a meaningless total.

Variation 3 is similar to Variation 2, but presents the items in each category as percentages of the total for that category. The bars in this variation are always the same height, because each one represents 100% of the total for that category.

Variation 4 adds horizontal grid lines to the basic chart. Variation 5 labels each bar with the numeric value it represents. Variation 6 is used with a single series, showing each bar in a different color or pattern. For example, you might create a bar chart based on the after conversion column of the MPG data (Figure 13.3). The chart would show the MPG averages for the various categories of converted cars.

Works also offers 3D bar charts. You can select a 3D bar chart to start with in the New Chart dialog box (the 3D charts are at the bottom of the list), or you can convert any chart to a 3D bar chart by clicking the **3D Bar Chart** icon in the toolbar, which opens a dialog box very similar to the one in Figure 13.9. Some of the 3D variations present the series in separate rows instead of side by side. Figure 13.10 shows an example of one of these variations.

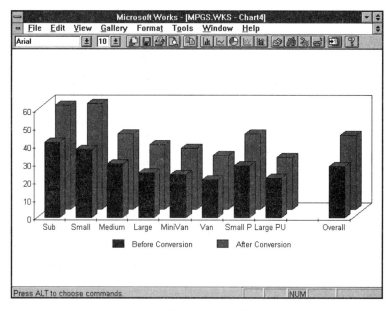

Figure 13.10 *3D bar chart (Variation 6)*

Line Charts

A *line chart* is used when you want to depict trends over time. Figure 13.11 shows a typical line chart, in which the population growth in three cities is contrasted. Each cell from the spreadsheet is represented by a marker in the line.

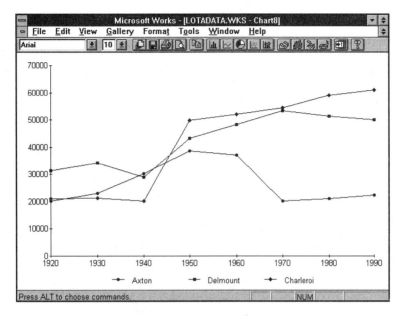

Figure 13.11 *Line chart*

Figure 13.12 shows the variations that are available for line charts. You can open this dialog box by clicking the **Line Chart** icon on the toolbar. Variation 2 shows the lines without the markers, whereas Variation 3 shows the markers without the lines. Variation 4 adds horizontal gridlines to the basic chart, and Variation 5 adds both vertical and horizontal gridlines to the basic chart. Variation 6 is used with stock market data, indicating high, low, and closing values over a period of time.

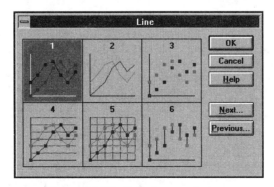

Figure 13.12 *Line chart variations*

Works also offers 3D line charts like the one in Figure 13.13. Variations add various types of gridlines to the basic 3D chart.

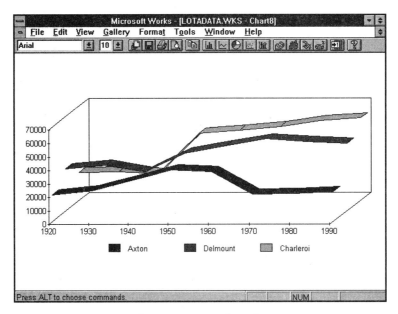

Figure 13.13 *3D line chart*

Stacked Line Charts

A *stacked line* chart is somewhat like a combination of an area chart and a line chart. It stacks the lines on top of each other to add them up, like an area chart does, but it depicts them as lines instead of areas. Figure 13.14 shows an example based on the same data Figure 13.7 was based on. Variations on the stacked line chart add various types of gridlines to the basic chart.

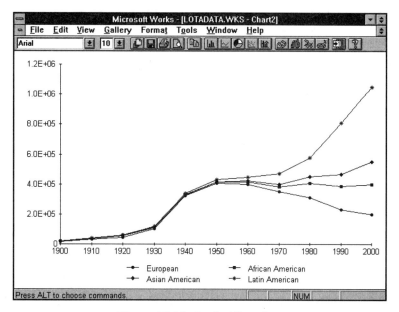

Figure 13.14 *Stacked line chart*

There is no toolbar icon for stacked line charts. Either choose **Stacked Line** from the New Chart dialog box when you first create the chart, or choose it from the Gallery menu to change the chart.

Scatter Charts

Scatter charts show how two factors interact. For example, you could plot the relationship between age and the incidence of heart attacks in a group of people. Figure 13.15 shows an example based on hypothetical data. Age is plotted on the horizontal axis and number of heart attacks is plotted on the vertical axis.

You can plot more than one series in a scatter chart. Works uses different colors for each series, or, in a monochrome system, a different shaped marker. Figure 13.16 shows what a scatter plot might look like if you plotted age with heart attacks for smokers, people who don't smoke but live with smokers, and people not exposed to smoke. (All the data is hypothetical.)

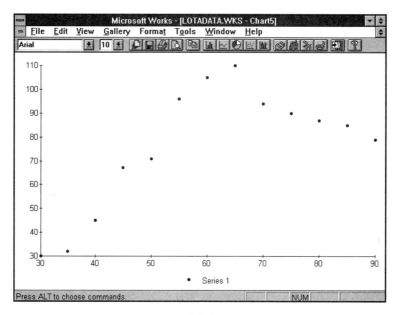

Figure 13.15 *Scatter chart*

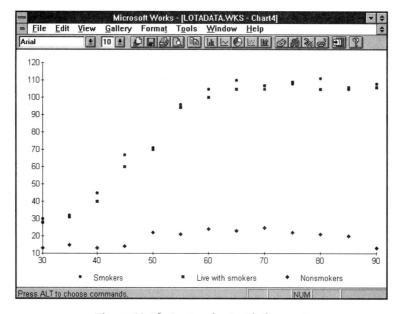

Figure 13.16 *Scatter chart with three series*

Variations on the scatter chart add various types of gridlines to the basic chart. One variation connects the markers with lines, making the chart look something like a line chart.

Combination Charts

Combination charts mix line and bar charts. They generally serve the same purpose as line charts, but showing some series as bars and some as lines makes certain data stand out. The AutoFormat Income Statement template includes a profit and loss combination chart like the one in Figure 13.17. You can see that plotting the Profit after Tax series as a line over the income and expenses bars has a very dramatic effect.

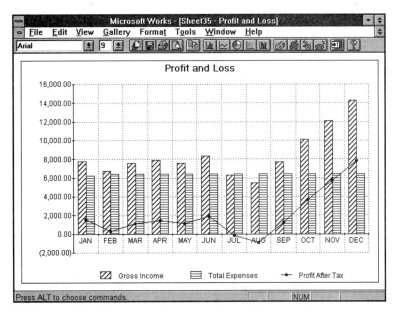

Figure 13.17 *Profit and loss combination chart*

Variations for the combination charts include right vertical axes and stock market line charts over bar charts.

Radar Charts

A *radar* chart is something like a circular line chart. It shows the values in a series relative to a central point rather than stretched out along an axis. The final point in the radar chart is connected to the first point to complete the circuit. Suppose you plot monthly average rainfall data in three cities. Figure 13.18 shows what the radar chart might look like. You can see the variations in rainfall patterns clearly on the radar chart.

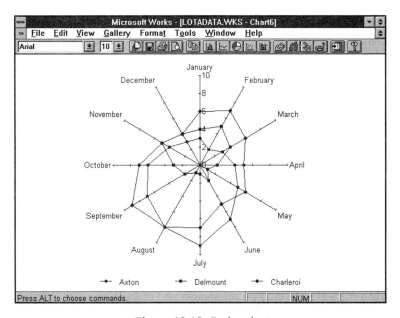

Figure 13.18 *Radar chart*

Radar chart variations show only the markers or only the lines, suppress the radiating axes, and add gridlines.

Pie charts

A pie chart shows the proportion of items that make up a whole. Figure 13.19 shows an example taken from an expense spreadsheet. In this case, the total expenses fall into five categories, with child care taking up almost one-third of the expenses. Pie charts are based on a single series only. If you select more than one series, Works uses only the first one.

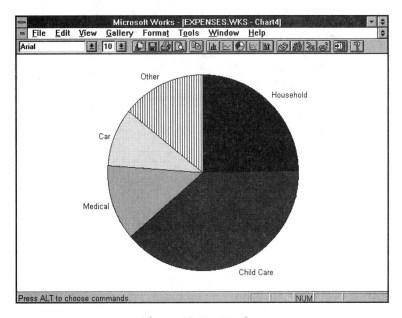

Figure 13.19 *Pie Chart*

Figure 13.19 shows one of the pie chart variations. The basic pie chart looks just like the one in the figure but has no labels. Other variations include exploded slices and percentages for each slice. Pie charts come in a 3D version also. Figure 13.20 shows the 3D version of the variation that explodes the first slice, with no labels.

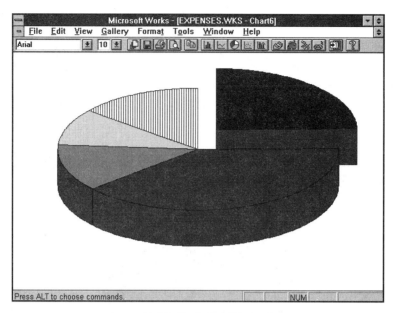

Figure 13.20 *Exploded 3D pie chart*

The toolbar includes both a flat **Pie Chart** icon and a **3D Pie Chart** icon. Click the icon to open the dialog box where you can select one of the variations.

Tailoring Charts

Once you have a chart, you can tailor almost everything it contains, from the range it is based on to the colors and patterns used to plot the data.

Tailoring Titles and Labels

You can add or change a chart's title and add a subtitle. You can also change all the labels and legends.

Titles

Figure 13.21 shows the Titles dialog box, which you use to add, change, or delete titles. You can also see examples of all four types of titles in the chart in the background. Choose **Edit Titles** to open this dialog box.

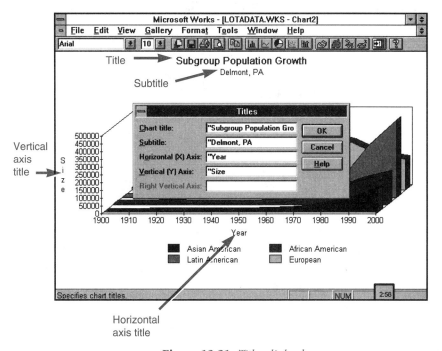

Figure 13.21 *Titles dialog box*

Legends

Figure 13.22 shows the Legend/Series Labels dialog box, which opens when you choose **Edit Legend/Series Labels**. You use this box to add or modify the text that is used in the legend at the bottom of the chart. If you click **Auto series labels**, Charting uses its generic legend text: "Series 1," "Series 2," and so on. When this option is unchecked, the values in the **Series Labels** boxes are used.

Each Series Label text box can contain a cell reference or text. If it contains a cell reference, as the first three series in the figure do, whatever value is in that cell is used as the legend for the indicated series. If a box contains text, as the fourth series in the figure does, that text becomes the legend.

In flat area charts, you can click **Use as area labels** to place the series labels in the areas themselves instead of in a legend. Don't get too excited by the prospect, however. They usually don't fit very well and end up looking pretty bad.

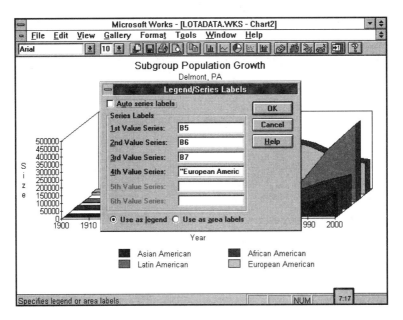

Figure 13.22 *Legend/Series Labels dialog box*

If you don't want to include a legend, don't just blank out these text boxes. You'll end up with a bunch of unlabeled pattern swatches at the bottom of the chart. Instead, choose **Format Add Legend**, which is a toggle command that displays or suppresses the legend.

Category Labels

Unfortunately, you can't supply the category labels in a text box as you can supply the legend labels. Category labels must come from the spreadsheet. You can designate which cells to use, however. If you don't want to build titles into your spreadsheet, or you don't want to use the built-in ones, create a range somewhere else that contains the desired category titles. Then open the chart and choose **Edit Series**. Figure 13.23 shows the Series dialog box.

At the bottom of the box is a text box labeled **Category (X) Series**. The range in that box identifies the location of the category labels. If it's blank, there are no category labels. Type the correct range reference in the box to label your categories along the horizontal axis.

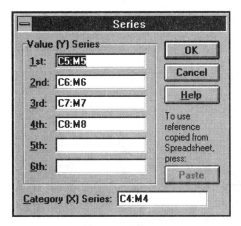

Figure 13.23 *Series dialog box*

 N O T E If you create a range of category labels somewhere away from the main portion of your spreadsheet, be sure to use **Format Set Print Area** to print your main spreadsheet only. Otherwise, your category labels will be printed, too.

Data Labels

Certain types of charts can have labels in the data area, showing the actual values that were used to plot the markers or bars. Figure 13.24 shows an example of a bar chart with data labels. To add data labels to a chart, choose **Edit Data Labels**. (If this option is dimmed, the chart type doesn't permit data labels.) In the resulting Data Labels dialog box, check **Use Series Data** to add the data labels to the chart.

Data labels look pretty good on a bar chart, but they can make a mess on other types of charts, such as a line chart with four or five lines that are fairly close together. In the combination chart generated by the Income Statement template, for example, the template includes data labels in the chart. I removed them in Figure 13.17 because many were unreadable and, at points, interfered with the category labels. To remove data labels, choose **Edit Data Labels** and uncheck **Use Series Data**.

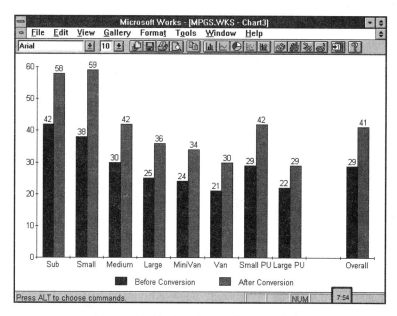

Figure 13.24 *Bar chart with data labels*

Changing Fonts

You can change the fonts of any chart text. You might want to do this just to enhance the attractiveness of the chart, but more importantly, a smaller font can make labels more readable. An abbreviated label in a large font might be spelled out fully in a smaller font. Labels that crash together on the X or Y axis or provide conflict in the data area might cause fewer problems in a smaller font.

The Charting program recognizes two font groups in a chart: the title, and everything else. If you select the title and change the font, only the title is changed. Click the title to select it. If you change the font when the title is not selected, everything else is changed.

The subtitle is not part of the title. Its font is changed when you change everything else.

N O T E

Change the font just as you change it in Word Processor or Spreadsheet. You can select a different font name and size on the toolbar. All other font changes are done using the **Format Font and Style** command.

Changing Colors, Patterns, and Markers

You don't have to use Charting's default colors, shading patterns, and markers for your chart data. You have complete control over the design of your chart. Look back at Figure 13.17, for example. The bars in that chart use striped patterns instead of shades of gray.

Patterns and Colors

Choose the **Format Patterns and Colors** command to open the Patterns and Colors dialog box shown in Figure 13.25. In the example, the only colors available are black and white because **View Display as Printed** is in effect to prepare the chart for a black-and-white printer. If you're viewing the chart in color, a full range of colors is listed in the **Colors** box.

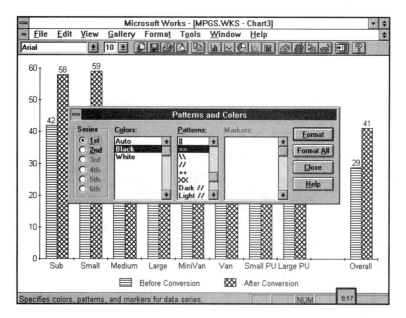

Figure 13.25 *Patterns and Colors dialog box*

❖ **To change colors and patterns:**

1. Choose **Format Patterns and Colors**. The Patterns and Colors dialog box opens.

2. In the **Series** box, click a series that you want to change.

3. Click a color in the **Colors** box.

4. Click a pattern in the **Patterns** box.

5. Click **Format**. You will see the selected series change in the chart behind the dialog box. The dialog box remains open so you can continue to change patterns and colors.

6. Repeat Steps 2 through 5 until you have selected colors and patterns that you like for all your series.

7. Click **Close**.

Changing Markers

When a chart contains markers, the Patterns and Colors dialog box also lets you change markers. Figure 13.26 shows an example. Since the chart in question is a stacked line chart, the items in the **Patterns** list box now pertain to lines, not bars. You can select the color for a line, the pattern for the line, and the marker symbol that is used in the line.

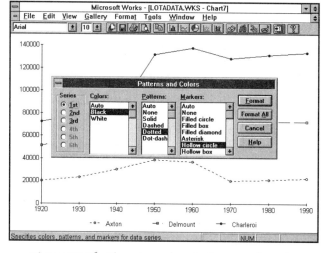

Figure 13.26 *Changing colors, patterns, and markers*

Adding Lines to a Chart

You can add several types of lines to a chart, to enhance both attractiveness and readability. Figure 13.27 shows an example of a chart with gridlines, droplines, and a border.

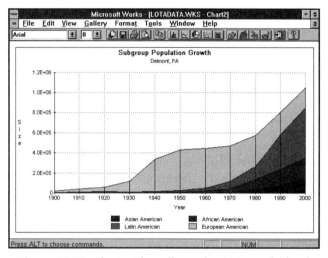

Figure 13.27 *Chart with gridlines, droplines, and a border*

Gridlines are displayed as dotted lines in the open area of the chart. You can display vertical gridlines, horizontal gridlines, or both. *Droplines*, which are available only with flat area charts, are solid vertical lines in the data area. The *border* is the outline around the entire chart.

❖ **To add vertical gridlines and/or droplines to a chart:**

1. Choose **Format Horizontal (X) Axis**. The Horizontal (X) Axis dialog box opens.

2. To add vertical gridlines, check **Show Gridlines**.

3. To add droplines to a flat area chart, check **Show Droplines**.

4. Click **OK**.

❖ **To add horizontal gridlines to a chart:**

1. Choose **Format Vertical (Y) Axis**. The Vertical (Y) Axis dialog box opens.

2. Check **Show Gridlines**.

3. Click **OK**.

Special Pie Chart Features

Pie charts have a couple of features not found in other charts. You can explode one or more slices, for example, and you can label the slices with data, text, and/or percentages.

Data Labels

When you choose **Edit Data Labels** for a pie chart, the dialog box looks like Figure 13.28. As you can see in the figure, you can request two labels per slice. The second label is enclosed in parentheses next to the first label. In the sample pie chart behind the dialog box, the first label is the text from the first column in the selected range, and the second label is the value from the second column in the selected range.

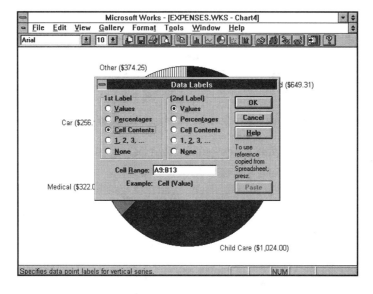

Figure 13.28 *Data Labels dialog box for pie chart*

Exploding Slices

You can explode either the first slice or all slices in a pie chart by choosing one of the chart variations. But if you want to explode some other combination of slices, you have to use the Patterns and Colors dialog box. Figure 13.29 shows what this dialog box looks like for a pie chart. Notice the **Explode Slice** check-box in the lower left corner.

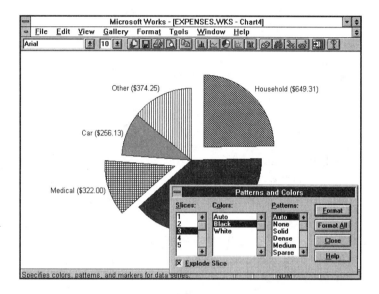

Figure 13.29 *Patterns and Colors dialog box for a pie chart*

❖ **To explode a slice:**

1. Choose **Format Patterns and Colors**. The Patterns and Colors dia-log box opens.

2. In the **Slices** list box, click the number of the slice you want to explode.

3. Click **Explode Slice**.

4. Click **Format**. You will see the slice move in the chart in the back-ground.

5. Repeat Steps 2 through 4 for each slice you want to explode.

6. Click **Close**.

Changing the Data for the Chart

After you see your chart, you might find that you want to change the data it is based on. After you have put a lot of work into tailoring a chart, you don't want to throw it out just to change the data. You can change the data for the current chart. You can edit the selected series, add more series, or remove one or more series.

Return to the spreadsheet window to change the data. If you make changes to a series that is already plotted in the chart, the chart is updated automatically. But if you want to add a new series to the chart or replace an existing series with a different range of cells, you have to use the **Paste Series** command to make the change.

❖ **To replace or add a range to an existing chart:**

1. In the spreadsheet, highlight the range you want to copy to the chart. If you are replacing a row or column of data, do not select the title for the row or column. Select the data cells only.

2. Click the **Copy** icon in the toolbar. Works copies the selected range to the Clipboard.

3. Switch to the chart you want to change.

4. Choose **Edit Paste Series**. The Paste Series dialog box opens (see Figure 13.30).

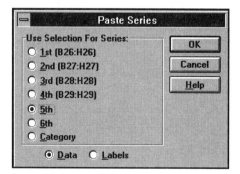

Figure 13.30 *Paste Series dialog box*

5. If you want to replace a series with the selected range, click the series to be replaced. If you want to add a new series to the chart,

click the first unused series. (In the example, the fifth and sixth series are currently unused.) If the selected range represents a new category, click **Category**. If the selected range represents labels instead of data, click **Labels** at the bottom of the box, then indicate which labels should be replaced.

6. Click **OK**. The chart changes to reflect the new data.

If you replace the wrong range, there is no **Undo** function, but you can return to your former chart by closing the spreadsheet without saving changes and reopening it.

❖ **To delete a series from a chart:**

1. Open the chart.

2. Choose **Edit Series**. The Series dialog box opens (see Figure 13.23).

3. Delete the range reference of the series you want to remove from the chart.

4. Click **OK**.

Managing Charts

Charts belong to the spreadsheets they are based on. There are no separate chart files. If you want to access a chart, you must open its spreadsheet. This section shows you how to manage the charts that belong to a spreadsheet.

In the next chapter, you'll learn how to copy charts to other documents.

N O T E

Saving a Chart

You save a chart by saving the spreadsheet it belongs to. Until you save the spreadsheet, you are in danger of losing the chart, so save often. You can save the entire spreadsheet and all its charts by clicking the **Save** icon from the spreadsheet window or any of its chart windows.

Closing a Chart

You close a chart by closing its window, just like any other document window. When you close a spreadsheet, you also close all the open charts belonging to it.

Reopening a Chart

To reopen an existing chart, you must open its spreadsheet. Then choose the **View Chart** command, which displays a list of all the charts belonging to the spreadsheet. Double-click the chart you want.

Working with Multiple Charts and the Spreadsheet

If you have multiple spreadsheets and multiple charts open, each is in a separate document window. You can tile them, cascade them, minimize them, or otherwise organize them in Works' work area. If you want to switch to a spreadsheet or chart you can't see, pull down the Window menu for a list of all the open document windows.

Renaming a Chart

When you create a new chart, the Charting program assigns it a generic name: Chart1, Chart2, and so on. After you create two or three charts for the same spreadsheet, you might have trouble remembering which chart is which. You can assign more meaningful names to your charts to avoid confusion. In fact, it's a pretty good idea to assign a meaningful name to every chart, regardless of how many there are in the spreadsheet. When you open the spreadsheet a month from now, you might not remember what Chart1 is, but "Before Conversion" is pretty clear. A chart name can have up to 15 characters, including spaces.

❖ **To rename a chart:**

1. Choose **Tools Name Chart**. (You can do this from any chart belonging to the spreadsheet.) A dialog box lists all the charts belonging to the current spreadsheet.

2. Click the chart you want to rename.

3. Type a new name in the text box.

4. Click **Rename**. The new name replaces the former name in the list. The dialog box stays open so you can rename other charts if you wish.

5. Click **OK** to close the dialog box.

Deleting a Chart

You can delete a chart when you don't want it any more. In fact, if you already have eight charts in a spreadsheet, you won't be able to create any new charts until you delete at least one of the existing ones.

❖ **To delete a chart:**

1. Choose **Tools Delete Chart.**

2. A dialog box lists all the charts belonging to the spreadsheet.

3. Click the chart you want to delete.

4. Click **Delete**. The chart is removed from the list and is deleted from the spreadsheet. The dialog box stays open so you can delete more charts if you wish.

5. Click **OK** to close the dialog box.

Copying a Chart

Sometimes the easiest way to create a new chart is to duplicate an existing one and adapt it.

❖ **To duplicate a chart:**

1. Choose **Tools Duplicate Chart**.

2. A dialog box lists all the charts belonging to the spreadsheet.

3. Click the chart you want to duplicate.

4. Type a name for the new chart in the text box at the bottom of the dialog box, unless you want Works to assign a generic name.

5. Click **Duplicate**. The new chart is created and added to the list. The dialog box stays open so you can duplicate more charts if you wish.

6. Click **OK** to close the dialog box.

Printing a Chart

To print a chart, activate its window and click the **Print** icon in the toolbar. You can preview it first by clicking the **Print Preview** icon instead.

AutoStart Template Charts

In the previous chapter, you were introduced to the AutoStart spreadsheet templates. Some of these templates include charts, such as the one in Figure 13.17, which comes from the Income Statement template.

When you're working with a template, you can find out if it has any charts associated with it by choosing **View Chart**. If the command is dimmed, there are no charts associated with the current spreadsheet. If some charts are listed, double-click their names in the list box to see them. If you don't quite like the design of the chart, you can adapt it just as you do with the charts you create yourself.

Summary

This chapter has shown you how to:

❖ Use the Spreadsheet Charting tool to create charts based on your spreadsheet data

❖ Create a new chart, tailor it, save it, print it, and otherwise manage it

❖ Work with the 12 basic chart types: bar, area, line, scatter, and so on

In the next chapter, you'll see how to integrate your spreadsheet and its charts into a Word Processor document.

CHAPTER **14**

Exchanging Data

A major advantage of using an up-to-date Windows application such as Works for Windows version 3.0 is its capability of exchanging data with other applications. Works lets you move or copy text from one document to another, as well as between Works and other applications. You can also embed objects, such as a graphic, a spreadsheet range, or a chart, in a Word Processor document. (You have already learned how to embed WordArt, Note-It, ClipArt, and Microsoft Drawing graphics.) In addition, you can *link* an object back to its source so that, if the source changes, the copy is updated automatically. You'll find this particularly handy for including spreadsheet data and charts in a Word Processor report.

In this chapter, you will learn how to:

❖ Copy and move text between Word Processor and Spreadsheet and between Works and other applications

349

❖ Create and embed new objects (including spreadsheets and charts) in a Word Processor document.

❖ Embed existing objects (including spreadsheets and charts) in a Word Processor document.

❖ Manage embedded objects.

❖ Link objects (including spreadsheets and charts) to a Word Processor document.

❖ Manage links.

❖ Convert a graphic object into a Microsoft Drawing.

Copying and Moving Text

You can move or copy a block of text from one place to another in the same document, to another Word Processor or Spreadsheet document, or to a document belonging to another application that handles text. For example, you can move or copy text from Word Processor to the Windows accessories called *Write, Notepad, Paintbrush,* and *Cardfile.* You can also copy blocks from those applications to Word Processor.

When you copy a block of text within Word Processor, it retains any character formatting information such as font and style. If you include paragraph markers in the block, the paragraphs retain their formatting also. But when you copy to another application, such as Windows Write, formatting information is generally lost, as other applications format their text and paragraphs differently. But some applications, such as Microsoft Word for Windows, which is a kissing cousin of Microsoft Works for Windows, retain the original formatting.

When you move or copy a block of text, the copy in the destination document behaves just like all the other text in that document. It is no longer considered a separate block. You can position the cursor in it, select any part of it, edit it, check its spelling, and so on. As you'll see later in this chapter, this is quite different from embedded or linked objects.

Once a copy has been made, there is no lingering association between the source and the copy. Any changes you make to the copy have no effect on the source and vice versa.

Moving and Copying within Word Processor or Spreadsheet

You have already learned how to move or copy a block of text within a Word Processor document or among Word Processor documents. After selecting the text, you can copy or cut it to the Clipboard, then position the cursor and paste from the Clipboard. Or you can drag and drop the selected text. You use the same techniques to move or copy a range of cells within a Spreadsheet document or among Spreadsheet documents.

Moving and Copying Data between Word Processor and Spreadsheet

You can copy text or numeric data from Word Processor to Spreadsheet using the same techniques. The number of cells that are filled depends on whether the block of data includes tabs and carriage returns. The first column of the first paragraph goes into the upper-left cell of the destination range. Each tab in a paragraph starts a new cell to the right. Each carriage return starts a new row underneath the upper-left cell.

Suppose, for example, that you drag three paragraphs with no tabs and drop them on cell A5. The first paragraph goes into A5, the second paragraph goes into A6, and the third paragraph goes into A7.

Now suppose that you drag the following two paragraphs, in which the columns are separated by tabs:

25	**27**	**29**
31	**35**	**39**

If you drop the block on cell A5, the data fills the range A5:C6, with the 25 going into cell A5 and the 39 going into cell C6.

Word Processor's text and paragraph formatting are not carried over to Spreadsheet; the pasted data is formatted according to Spreadsheet's default formatting techniques. That is, text data is left aligned, numeric data is right aligned, numbers preceded by dollar signs are assigned the Currency format, and so on.

Moving or copying text in the other direction—from Spreadsheet to Word Processor—is not quite as simple. If you use the usual techniques, the data will be embedded in the report. As you'll soon see, embedded data is quite a different animal. There is a way to move or copy spreadsheet cells into Word Processor so that they become normal text. The following procedure shows you how.

❖ **To move or copy spreadsheet cells into Word Processor as unformatted text:**

1. Open both documents.

2. Select the cells to be moved or copied.

3. To move the cells, click the **Cut** icon on the toolbar. To copy the cells, click the **Copy** icon on the toolbar. (The spreadsheet window must be active.) Works cuts or copies the selected cells to the Clipboard.

4. Click the Word Processor document. Works activates the Word Processor document window.

5. Position the cursor where you want to paste the cells.

6. Choose **Edit Paste Special**. The Paste Special dialog box opens (see Figure 14.1).

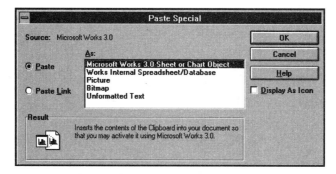

Figure 14.1 *Paste Special dialog box*

7. Double-click **Unformatted Text**. Works converts the contents of the Clipboard into normal text, using tabs and carriage returns in place of cells, and pastes the result into the active document at the cursor position.

Now you can edit the pasted text just as if you had typed it from scratch. There is no longer any relationship between it and the spreadsheet it came from.

Moving and Copying among Other Applications

You can probably move or copy text to and from any Windows application you have that handles text and includes the **Dynamic Data Exchange** (DDE) feature. Dragging and dropping might not work with every application, but you should always be able to use the Clipboard. The following procedure shows you how to move and copy text between Word Processor and another Windows application via the Clipboard.

❖ **To move or copy text from a Works document to another application:**

1. Open the source document in Word Processor.

2. Select the block of text to be moved or copied.

3. Click the **Copy** icon to copy the block or the **Cut** icon to move the block.

4. Open the target document.

5. Position the cursor where you want to insert the block.

6. In the target window, choose **Edit Paste**. (If the target application has a **Paste** icon on a toolbar, you can use that.) The block should be inserted in the document at the cursor position.

If you try to move or copy something that isn't text into a Word Processor document, such as a graphic, it will probably be linked or embedded instead of simply inserted. If you move or copy a spreadsheet range, some applications might interpret it as text, whereas others might interpret it as a graphic. You can usually use the **Paste Special** feature to force the target application to recognize the spreadsheet as unformatted text.

Embedding Objects

When you do a straight move or copy, the pasted text becomes a normal part of the destination document's text. But an embedded object is not normal text, even if it contains text. It retains the same features that it had in the source document—formatting, graphics, and so on—even when the destination document doesn't offer those features. It's as if you are pasting a miniature version of the source application itself into the host document, and in many senses, that's exactly what happens. You could think of it as a small window from the source application inserted into the target document.

As you'll recall from the embedded objects you have already worked with, such as Note-Its and WordArt, an embedded object is a single unit. When you select it, handles appear around it, and you have to manipulate the entire object. You can't, for example, move or delete part of it.

When you embed an object, Works copies not just the object's data, but some programming information as well. Enough information is included to enable the host document to display and print the object as it appeared originally in the source application. You will also be able to edit the object without leaving the destination document. If you open the embedded object for editing, you might see a window from the source application (as with Microsoft Draw), a dialog box might appear (as with Note-Its), or the current application's menu bar and toolbar might be replaced (as with WordArt). When you close the embedded object, the normal document window returns. As you can imagine, the programming information occupies a lot of space; embedded objects add significantly to the size of the destination document file. You'll also find that an application runs more slowly when it's displaying a document with a lot of embedded objects.

The tremendous advantage of embedded objects, of course, is that you can copy *any* information into a document—graphics, a sound clip, a video clip, a spreadsheet range or chart—even though the destination has no such facilities on its own. And once they're embedded, you can move, copy, and edit them without leaving the destination document.

Managing Embedded Objects

Although you have already learned how to manage embedded objects, the following notes should serve as a reminder:

❖ Click an object to select it; handles appear around the object when it is selected.

❖ Drag a selected object to move it. When it is embedded in the text, you can move it only to some other position in the existing text. When it is embedded on the page, you can move it anywhere on the page.

❖ Press **Ctrl** while you drag an object to copy it.

❖ You can also move and copy objects using the Clipboard commands.

❖ Drag an object's handles to resize it.

❖ Choose **Format Picture/Object** and open the **Text Wrap** page to change an object from being embedded in the text (**In-Line**) to being embedded on the page (**Absolute**), and vice versa.

❖ Position an object in the header or footer to print it on every page. You can embed it in the header or footer text, or position it absolutely in the header or footer margin.

❖ Press **Delete** to delete an embedded object. Deleting an object affects the destination document only; it has no effect on the original source of the object.

Some objects can be played, or executed, by double-clicking them. For example, you can listen to a sound clip or watch a video clip by double-clicking the icon that appears on the page. You've already seen how to "play" a Note-It—that is, display the note that it contains—by double-clicking it. When you're done playing the object, click anywhere to return to the normal view.

You can edit any embedded object by selecting it and choosing **Edit *object-name***. For example, if a spreadsheet object is selected, you would choose **Edit Works Sheet or Chart Object**. (The selected object always appears as the last command on the Edit menu.) If it's not a playable object, you can also edit it by double-clicking it. For example, to edit an embedded spreadsheet, you would just double-click it. But since double-clicking plays a playable object, you have to use the Edit menu to edit such objects.

When you open an object for editing, what happens depends on the type of object; you might see an editing window or dialog box, or the current window might change to let you edit the object. When you're done editing, close the window or dialog box or, if there is none, click outside the object to return to the normal window. Your changes to the object are not saved on disk until you save the document, just like any other changes that you make to the document.

N O T E

Editing changes do not affect the original object nor any other copies of the same object; only the copy that you open for editing is changed.

Embedded objects are not displayed in Draft view, although a dotted box indicates where they are. Draft view scrolls faster because Works doesn't have to take the time to display the contents of embedded objects. You can still select and manipulate an object in Draft view, including opening it for editing or playing it. Both Normal and Page Layout views display the contents of embedded objects.

The **Edit Undo** command pertains to object manipulation just as it does to other editing. For example, immediately after inserting an object, **Edit Undo** removes it; immediately after deleting an object, **Edit Undo** restores it; if you edit an object, **Edit Undo** restores the unedited version.

Embedding an Existing File

There are several ways to embed an object in a document. Perhaps the most straightforward is to embed an entire file that already exists somewhere else. For example, you might embed a complete spreadsheet from Works Spreadsheet, a complete drawing from Windows Paintbrush (or some other graphics program), a sound clip or a video clip. The following procedure shows you how to do this.

❖ **To embed a complete file from any Windows application:**

1. Position the cursor where you want to insert the object.

2. Choose **Insert Object**. The Insert Object dialog box opens.

3. Click **Create from File**. The dialog box changes so that you can select or identify a file (see Figure 14.2.)

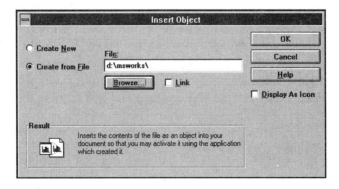

Figure 14.2 *Insert Object dialog box (for an existing file)*

4. If you know the complete reference for the file, including the path, replace or edit the text in the **File** text box and skip to step 5. Otherwise, click the **Browse** button. The Browse dialog box opens (see Figure 14.3).

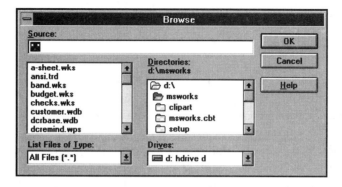

Figure 14.3 *Browse Dialog Box*

5. Click the correct drive in the **Drives** box, double-click the correct directory in the **Directories** box, and double-click the correct file name in the file list. The Browse dialog box closes, and the name of the file appears in the Insert Object dialog box.

6. Click **OK**. The Insert Object dialog box closes, and the object is embedded at the cursor position.

What you see for the embedded object depends on the source. You might see the actual data, such as a graphic, a spreadsheet, or some text, or you might see an icon representing the object. If it's an icon, then you can double-click it to view or play the object. When you print the document, the icon will be printed, not the contents of the object.

Linking and embedding require both the source and the target applications to include Windows' **Object Linking and Embedding (OLE)** feature. Works for Windows includes **OLE**, but some of the applications included in your Windows accessories, such as Write and Cardfile, don't. If you try to embed an object from a source that doesn't offer **OLE**, Windows uses an intermediary OLE program called Object Packager to create the object. Object Packager always embeds an icon for the object in your document, so you won't be able to print the contents of the object with your document. It also opens an editing window for the object so you can see its contents. Close the window by normal means to return to your document.

If you want to include printable text from an application that doesn't offer **OLE**, such as Write or Cardfile, copy it to your document using the plain vanilla copying techniques described at the beginning of this chapter.

When you insert a complete Works spreadsheet using this technique, Works opens a Spreadsheet window (see Figure 14.4.) in the default object size—which is pretty small for a window. Crammed into that space are a horizontal scroll bar, a vertical scroll bar, part of the message bar, and some row and column headers. There are two ways that you can expand the object to show the data you want. You can resize the window and scroll around until you find the data area you want to display. Or you can click outside the window to close it, which leaves a small part of the spreadsheet itself in the object. Then expand the object until the desired area is showing.

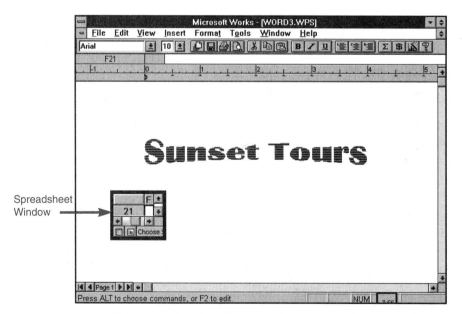

Figure 14.4 *Spreadsheet Window as an object in a word processor document*

Creating and Embedding a New Object

You don't have to create a file separately before you embed it. Windows' **OLE** function lets you create a new object at the time that you embed it. You have already done this with Microsoft Draw, WordArt, and Note-Its. The following procedure shows you how to do it with any **OLE** application.

❖ **To create and embed a new object:**

1. Position the cursor where you want to embed the object.

2. Choose **Insert Object**. The Insert Object dialog box opens (see Figure 14.5). The list box shows all the applications on your system that support **OLE**.

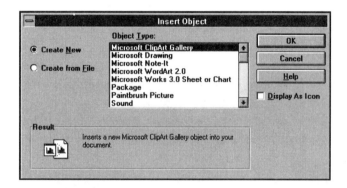

Figure 14.5 *Insert Object dialog box (for a new object)*

3. Double-click the application you want to use. The result depends on the application. You might see a window or a dialog box, or the application's menu bar and toolbar might take over the target application's window, with the object displayed in a small object window (as with WordArt).

4. Create the object.

5. Close the window or dialog box, if there is one, or click outside the object window. The new object is embedded in the document.

N O T E

You don't save the object as a separate file. It doesn't get a file of its own, but it exists solely within the target document. Save the target document soon to save the new object on disk.

You can use the previous procedure to embed a new spreadsheet, but Word Processor also gives you a special command to embed a new spreadsheet. This is a particularly handy way to create a narrative table while you are working on a document. The following procedure shows you how.

❖   **To create and embed a new spreadsheet or table:**

1.   Position the cursor where you want to embed the new spreadsheet or table.

2.   Choose **Insert Spreadsheet/Table**. The Spreadsheet/Table dialog box opens (see Figure 14.6).

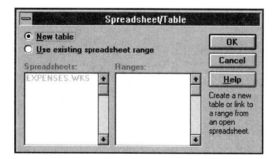

Figure 14.6 *Spreadsheet/Table dialog box*

3.   Click **New table**.

4.   Click **OK**. A spreadsheet object window appears in the document and the Spreadsheet menu bar and toolbar replace Word Processor's in the document window (see Figure 14.7).

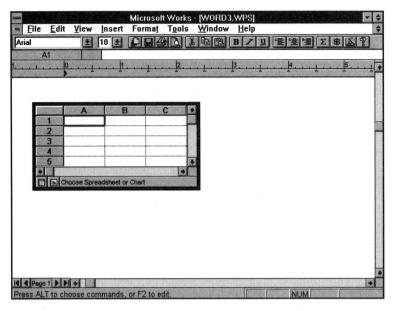

Figure 14.7 *A Spreadsheet Editing window in a word processor document*

5. Create the spreadsheet. You can resize the window to reveal more or fewer cells.

6. Click outside the object window to close it and embed the spreadsheet data in the document.

If you really want to embed a chart, not the spreadsheet itself, use the following procedure.

❖ **To create and embed a new chart:**

1. Follow steps 1 through 5 from the previous list.

2. Select the range to create the chart.

3. Click the **Chart** icon in the lower-left corner of the window. The New Chart dialog box opens (see Figure 13.1).

4. Select the desired options and click **OK**. The dialog box closes, and the chart appears in the editing window. The Charting menus and toolbar replace the Spreadsheet menu and toolbar in the document window.

5. Resize the chart, if desired, and tailor it as necessary.

6. Click anywhere outside the object window to close the window and embed the chart.

You can also start this procedure by choosing **Insert Chart**, which is nearly the same as choosing **Insert Spreadsheet/Table**.

In all of the above cases, you can edit the embedded object by double-clicking it to reopen the object window and provide the appropriate menus and toolbar. If you need to edit the data on which a chart is based, double-click the chart to open the object window, then click the **Spreadsheet** icon in the lower-left corner of the window. After editing the data, click the **Chart** icon again to return to the (updated) chart.

If you delete an object that was created just to be embedded, you delete the only copy of it. **Edit Undo** will recover it, but once you proceed to something else, **Undo** forgets it, and it is then gone permanently.

Selecting Part of a File to Embed

So far, you have been embedding complete files, but you can select just a section of a file to embed. For example, from a graphics file containing 200 clip art drawings, you can select and embed just one drawing. Or you can select and embed a specific range from a spreadsheet. You use these procedures also to embed spreadsheet charts.

You use the Clipboard or drag-and-drop to embed selections from other applications. In many cases, a simple copy procedure results in an object being embedded because there's no other way for the target document to display the copied material. For example, if you select a spreadsheet range and drag it to a Word Processor document, or if you copy and paste it, it will be embedded. The same is true for a graphic from Windows Paintbrush or another graphics program.

You can't select part of a chart for embedding, but you can copy a whole chart to the clipboard. The following procedure shows you how to embed a chart in a Word Processor document.

❖ **To embed a chart in a Word Processor document:**

1. Open the target document and the spreadsheet containing the chart.

2. Open the chart.

3. Drag the mouse from the chart to the target document. Works embeds the chart at the cursor position.

4. Resize the chart as desired.

Linking

Linking is similar to embedding, but instead of inserting all the editing information in the target document, Works stores a reference to the source document, called a *link*. Each time you open the target document, Works asks if you want to reread the data from the source document, so that any changes that you have made to the source document are carried over to the target. If you open a linked object for editing, you switch to the source application; you can't edit just the copy in the target document.

Suppose you have a project expenses spreadsheet that is updated daily, and you include it and its charts in a weekly project status report. If you link the spreadsheet and its charts to the status report, you'll always print the latest version when you print the report.

The advantage of linking over embedding lies in the automatic updates. If you simply embed an object, then revise the source that it came from, the embedded object is not updated automatically. You would have to replace the embedded object manually with the newer version. But if you link it, the object is updated every time you update the source. This is especially important when a source document provides data for many different target documents, as you might not remember to update them all manually when you modify the source.

A linked object takes up less room than an embedded object because the linked object doesn't need all the editing information stored with it. You don't edit the object in the target document, you edit it at its source.

Earlier, you saw how you can create new objects during the embedding process. There's no such thing as creating a new object for linking. You can link existing data only.

NOTE

Both the source and the target application must support **OLE**, but not all **OLE** applications can link.

A linked object looks like an embedded object and is managed in the same way. There are, however, some additional management tasks, such as updating a link. You'll learn about them after you learn how to link.

Linking Complete Files

In general, you link a complete file in the same way that you embed one, but you check the **Link** checkbox. The following procedure shows the details of linking a complete file.

❖ **To link a complete file:**

1. Position the cursor where you want to insert the object.

2. Choose **Insert Object**. The Insert Object dialog box opens.

3. Click **Create from File**. The dialog box changes so that you can select or identify a file (see Figure 14.2).

4. If you know the complete reference for the file, including the path, replace or edit the text in the **File** text box and skip to Step 5. Otherwise, press the **Browse** button. The Browse dialog box opens (see Figure 14.3).

5. Click the correct drive in the **Drives** box, double-click the correct directory in the **Directories** box, and double-click the correct file name in the list box under **Source**. The Browse dialog box closes, and the name of the file appears in the Insert Object dialog box.

6. Click **Link**.

7. Click **OK**. The Insert Object dialog box closes and the linked object is inserted at the cursor position.

Now you can resize the object, embed it on the page instead of in the text, and so on.

Linking to Selections from Files

When you want to link to a selection from another file or application, you start by copying the selection, then you use the **Paste Special** command to paste it because the Paste Special dialog box includes a **Paste Link** option.

❖ **To link to a selection into Word Processor:**

1. Open the source document and select the data to be linked.

2. Choose **Edit Copy** (or click the **Copy** icon if there is one).

3. Return to the target document and position the cursor.

4. Choose **Edit Paste Special**. The Paste Special dialog box opens (see Figure 14.1).

5. Click **Paste Link**.

N O T E

If the **Paste Link** option is dimmed, the source application doesn't support **OLE** linking.

6. Click **OK**. The linked object is inserted at the cursor position.

Word Processor gives you some special commands to link a Word Processor document to a chart or a named spreadsheet range. The following procedures show you how to do this.

❖ **To link to a chart:**

1. Open the spreadsheet containing the chart.

2. Return to the Word Processor document and position the cursor.

3. Choose **Insert Chart**. The Insert Chart dialog box opens (see Figure 14.8), listing all the open spreadsheets.

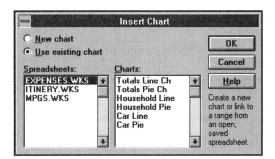

Figure 14.8 *Insert Chart dialog box*

4.   If more than one spreadsheet is listed, click the one you want. The charts belonging to the selected spreadsheet are listed in the **Charts** box.

5.   Double-click the chart you want. The Insert Chart dialog box closes and the linked chart is inserted at the cursor position.

6.   Resize the chart as desired.

❖   **To link a named spreadsheet range to a Word Processor document:**

1.   Open the source spreadsheet.

2.   Open the Word Processor document and position the cursor where you want to insert the link.

3.   Choose **Insert Spreadsheet/Table**. The Spreadsheet/Table dialog box opens (see Figure 14.6).

4.   Click **Use existing spreadsheet range**. All the open spreadsheets are listed in the **Spreadsheets** box.

5.   Click the name of the spreadsheet you want to use. The selected spreadsheet's named ranges are listed in the **Ranges** box.

6.   Double-click the name of the range you want to insert. The linked range is inserted at the cursor position.

7.   Resize the range as desired.

Managing Links

When a Word Processor document includes a link, the **Links** command becomes available on the Edit menu. You use this command to do things such as change from automatic to manual updating, update a link manually, and change the source of a link.

Editing Linked Data

Unlike embedded data, which you edit right in the target document, you edit linked data in the source document. You can open the source document by the usual means (such as the Startup dialog box), or you can double-click the linked object. The source application starts up, and the document containing the linked object is opened in its usual editing window.

After you change the source document and save it as usual, you'll see the effect in any documents that are linked to it. If a linked document is already open, you'll see the change right away. If not, the document is updated the next time you open it, unless you choose not to do so, as explained in the next section.

Automatic or Manual Updating

Updating links is not completely automatic. You can bypass it when you open a document, and you can turn it off. By default, when you open a document that contains at least one link, a message asks if you want to update the links. If you respond "Yes," Works rereads the source file for every link in the document, thus incorporating any changes that you have made to the source documents. If you respond "No," none of the links are updated. (You can still update individual links manually, as you'll see soon.)

You can turn off automatic updating for a specific link. This affects only what happens if you change the source data while the linked document is already open. By default, the linked document is updated as soon as you change the source. But if you select manual updating, the linked document is updated only when you enter an **Update Now** command. However, if you open a linked document and choose "Yes" in response to the update links question, all links are both updated regardless of their automatic or manual settings.

❖ **To request manual updating for a link:**

1. Open the document containing the link.

2. Choose **Edit Links**. (If this command is dimmed, the current docu-
    ment does not include any links.) The Links dialog box opens (see
    Figure 14.9). All the links in the current document are listed.

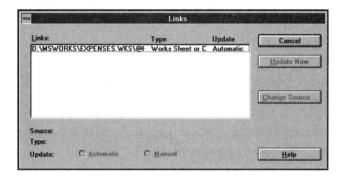

Figure 14.9 *Links dialog box*

3. Click the link you want to change. The dialog box changes to show
    the information for the selected link (see Figure 14.10).

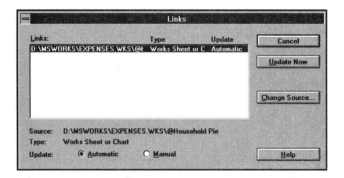

Figure 14.10 *The Links dialog box with a link selected*

4. In the update section, click **Manual**. The Manual option is selected,
    and the **Cancel** button changes into a **Close** button.

5. Click **Close**. The Links dialog box closes.

❖ **To update a link manually:**

1. Open the document containing the link.

2. Choose **Edit Links**. The Links dialog box opens (see Figure 14.9). All the links in the current document are listed.

3. Click the link that you want to update. The dialog box changes to show the information for the selected link (see Figure 14.10).

4. Click **Update Now**. Works updates the link. (You may be able to see the results behind the dialog box if the linked object is showing.) The dialog box stays open so you can manage more links, if desired.

5. Repeat Steps 3 and 4 for any other links you want to update.

6. Click **Close**. The dialog box closes.

If you decide to return to automatic updates for an object, select the link in the Links dialog box and click **Automatic**.

Changing the Source of the Link

If you move or rename a file that is linked to other documents, the links become invalid. You'll need to delete the linked objects or tell Works where the file is now located. You use the Links dialog box to tell Works where to find a moved or renamed file.

❖ **To change the source of a link:**

1. Open the document containing the link.

2. Choose **Edit Links**. The Links dialog box opens (see Figure 14.9). All the links in the current document are listed.

3. Click the link you want to change. The dialog box changes to show the information for the selected link (see Figure 14.10).

4. Click **Change Source**. The Change Source dialog box opens (see Figure 14.11). In the **Source** text box, the path and name of the source file are highlighted, but the chart name or range name is not.

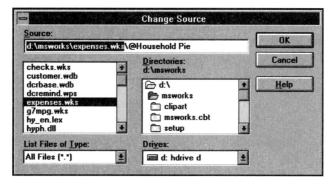

Figure 14.11 *Change Source dialog box*

5. You can overtype the highlighted text with the correct path and file name, or you can choose the desired file from the **Drives**, **Directories**, and file list boxes.

If the link includes a chart or range reference, the new file should include a chart or range of the same name. If not, the results can be unexpected. Works warns you if the specified file doesn't include the referenced data.

N O T E

6. Click **OK**. If other links in the same document refer to the file that you have just replaced, Works asks if you want to change all relevant links to the new file.

If you delete a source file, the link is broken. As long as you don't try to update the link, the last updated version of the data is available in the target document. If you try to update the link, a message warns you that the source is missing and the link can't be updated. You can fix the problem by deleting the linked object or by identifying a new source for it with the previous procedure.

Converting Note-Its and Other Special Objects into Drawings

As you have seen in earlier chapters, Works provides a range of previously designed graphics that you can embed in your documents: Note-Its, ClipArt, and even spreadsheet graphs. Once you have inserted such an object, you might want to tailor it for your own needs. For example, some of the Note-Its could be good attention-getters for a newsletter or a flyer if you could put text in them. Figure 14.12 shows an example.

Figure 14.12 *Using a Note-It as a graphic*

As other examples, some of the ClipArt drawings might fit in better with your letterhead in a different color, with a label, or with a slight adaptation. You might even want to combine two or more of the ClipArt drawings. What's more, if you could modify a chart outside of the Charting program, you could insert area labels that fit in the available areas, add callouts and labels to point out special features, and so on.

You can edit any embedded graphic by copying it to Microsoft Draw, making the changes, and reinserting it in the document. The following procedure shows you how this is done.

❖ **To edit an embedded graphic using Microsoft Draw:**

1. Select the graphic object.

2. Click the **Copy** icon.

3. Choose **Insert Drawing**. The Microsoft Draw window opens.

4. In the Draw window, choose **Edit Paste**. The graphic is pasted from the Clipboard to the Draw work area. It is broken down into as many drawing objects as possible. All the objects are selected. (In Figure 14.13, two drawing objects are selected: the yellow sticky note itself and the caption.)

5. Click a blank part of the Draw work area to deselect all the selected parts.

6. Modify the graphic as desired.

7. Choose **File Exit and Return to *document-name***. A message asks if you want to update the object.

8. Click **Yes**. The modified graphic replaces the original graphic. The object now belongs to Microsoft Draw instead of the application that originally created the graphic.

If the object was linked, as in a chart, it is no longer linked; it's just an embedded object.

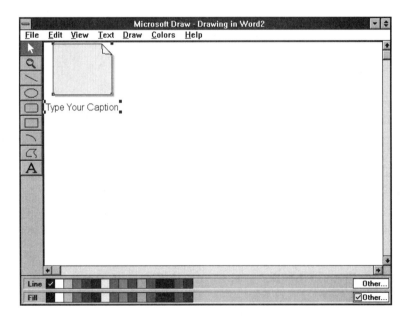

Figure 14.13 *Pasting a graphic object in Microsoft Draw*

Why You Can't Link or Embed Objects into Spreadsheets

OLE recognizes three kinds of applications: those that can be linked to (called *clients*), those that can be linked from (called *servers*), and those that can be both clients and servers. Word Processor can be both a client and server. Spreadsheet can be a server but not a client. In fact, you can neither embed nor link something into a Spreadsheet cell. So if you want to add your WordArt logo or some Note-Its to a spreadsheet, link it to a Word Processor document and add the graphics there.

Summary

This chapter has shown you how to:

- ❖ Embed and link objects, especially spreadsheet data and charts, into a Word Processor document
- ❖ Understand the differences among copying, embedding, and linking, and how you would perform each process
- ❖ Manipulate and revise embedded and linked objects
- ❖ Manage the links in a document
- ❖ Turn a ClipArt or Note-It graphic or a Spreadsheet chart into a Microsoft Draw graphic and tailor it for your own use

The next part of this book discusses the Works for Windows Database tool, and you'll find that it has many familiar features, such as embedded graphics and formulas.

PART IV

Database

CHAPTER 15

Introduction to Database

This chapter shows you how to create a new database and enter data in it. Specifically, you will learn how to:

❖ Design and create a new database form

❖ Enter formulas and data into a database

❖ Override a formula in a field

❖ Establish default values for fields

❖ Use both Form view and List view

❖ Manage database files

What Does Database Do?

Database helps you collect and organize a file full of data records. You have already seen an example of a database with the WorksWizards Address Book (see Chapter 3). Other examples might be employee pay records, customer credit records, and inventories.

Once you have created a database, you can update it by inserting, deleting, and modifying records. You can sort the records, use them to print form letters, enter a query to select a subset of records (such as all employees who worked overtime this week), and prepare reports based on the data. Figure 15.1 shows an example of a report drawn from a database.

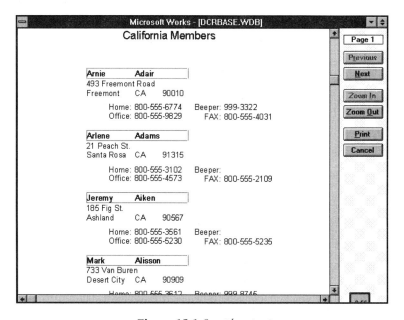

Figure 15.1 *Sample report*

Database interfaces with each of the other three Works tools. You have already seen how Word Processor works with Database to produce form letters, envelopes, and mailing labels. You can also copy, embed, or link lists and reports from Database into a Word Processor document. You can copy, embed, or link Spreadsheet ranges and charts into Database records. As you know, you can't embed or link things into Spreadsheet, but you can copy lists from

Database into a spreadsheet: Each field becomes a cell, and each record becomes a row. Information from a database can be used by Communications to dial telephone numbers.

You already know how to do many of the Database tasks. A field in a record is just like a Spreadsheet cell. You can enter text, a number, or a formula into it. Text and numbers are formatted just as they are in Spreadsheet, and you change the formatting in the same way (including external formatting such as fonts and alignment). In fact, you can work with the database records in List view, which looks and behaves much like a spreadsheet.

Another Database view, called *Form* view, presents records one at a time (see Figure 15.2). You can design this form any way you like. You can add graphics using the same features you have already learned with Word Processor: WordArt, ClipArt, Note-It, and Microsoft Draw. Borders and patterns help to organize the information attractively.

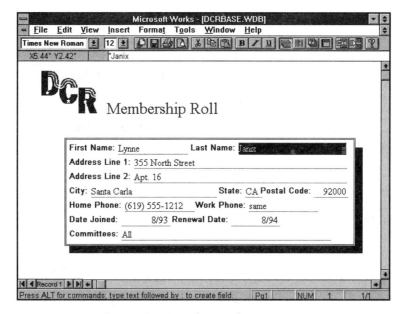

Figure 15.2 *Sample record in Form view*

Database includes many of the special features that you know and love: Spelling Checker, find and replace, sorting, hiding data, protecting data, and integrating with other tools and other applications. Several WorksWizards and AutoStart templates help you create databases. You'll learn how to use these special features in Chapter 17.

Only three tasks in Word Processor are completely new to you:

❖ Designing a new form for Form view (covered in Chapters 15 and 16).

❖ Querying the database (covered in Chapter 16).

❖ Designing and developing a report (covered in Chapter 18).

The Database Window

To start a new database, click the **Database** button in the Startup dialog box. Figure 15.3 shows what the Database window looks like right after you open a new database. Form view is selected by default; the form is blank because you haven't created it yet.

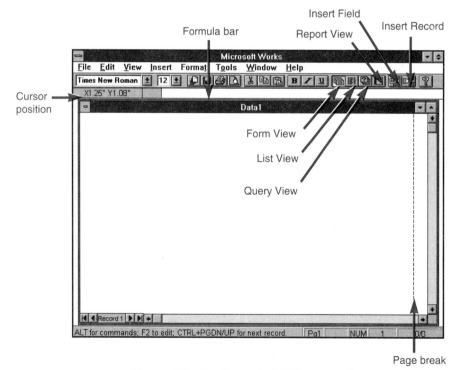

Figure 15.3 *Database window (Form view)*

The window includes a formula bar that works just like Spreadsheet's. At the left, instead of showing a cell reference, it shows the cursor position in terms of inches from the upper-left corner of the form. The toolbar includes icons to switch views, insert a new field, and insert a new record.

Instead of showing paging information, the horizontal scroll bar shows which record you're looking at and gives you icons to move forward and backward through the records. Since one form could run to several pages (you can see Database's default page break in the figure), the page number in the status bar identifies the location of the cursor within the current record.

Creating a Form in Form View

You create a new form by inserting and positioning fields, adding labels, and perhaps adding graphics. Figure 15.4 shows the beginning of a pay record form. The dotted lines are *fields*; this is where you enter the data. The text preceding each field, which always ends in a colon, is the *field name*. Text not associated with fields are *labels*.

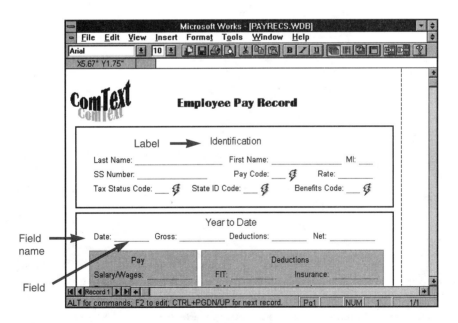

Figure 15.4 *Sample pay record form*

Creating a Field

All you have to do to create a new field is to position the cursor and type the field name (up to 15 characters). Be sure to type a colon at the end, as this is how Database knows it is a field name, not a label. When you press **Enter**, Database displays the Field Size dialog box (see Figure 15.5). It's hard to say exactly what the default width of 20 means; it's an approximation of how many characters can be displayed in the field, given the font and the font size. But if you want to type up to 20 characters in a field, including capital letters, you probably need to set it closer to 25. Default height 1 means that only one line can be typed in the field. If you set a larger height, you can type more than one line in the field.

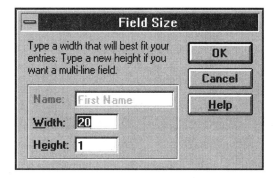

Figure 15.5 *Field Size dialog box*

 A field name can be up to 15 characters and cannot start with a double quotation mark or an apostrophe (single quotation mark). It must be terminated by a colon. Each field name must be unique within the record.

N O T E

After you click **OK**, the field appears on your database form. Click the field name to highlight it. You can then drag it to perfect its position. When you drag the field name, the field goes with it. If you decide you don't like the size, click the field (not the field name) and choose **Format Field Size** to adjust it.

Snap to Grid is on by default, so it's fairly easy to line up your fields in rows and columns. Choose **Format Snap to Grid** to turn off the grid, if desired, when fine-tuning.

N O T E

Creating Labels

Use labels to add descriptive text to your database form. You can place labels anywhere, and there is no limit on length. To create a label, position the cursor and type the text. As long as it doesn't end with a colon, Database knows it's a label and doesn't give it any special treatment. (No dialog box opens.) Press **Enter** or click somewhere when it's finished. You can then select it and drag it to fine-tune its position.

You can display a label instead of a field name by choosing the field name, choosing **Format Show Field Name** (to turn it off), and then inserting a label in its place. This way you can label a field with something longer than 15 characters.

N O T E

Adding Artwork

There are several graphics in the example in Figure 15.4. You probably recognize the company logo in the upper-left corner as a WordArt graphic. You might not have recognized the little lightning bolts as Note-Its (with blank captions); they're bright yellow on a color monitor. And, of course, you can recognize the borders around the sections and the shading patterns for the Pay and Deductions groups.

Embedding Various Types of Graphics

Figure 15.6 shows the Insert menu for Database. The bottom section should look pretty familiar to you. You can insert the same types of graphics in Database's Form view that you can insert into Word Processor. ClipArt, WordArt, Note-Its, and Drawings are all embedded so that you create, store, and edit them in Form View.

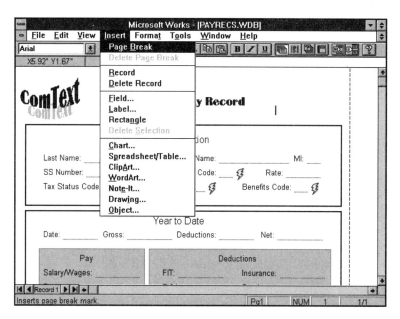

Figure 15.6 *Insert menu for Database*

The Note-Its in this example are used to provide details of the various codes necessary in the employee record. For example, an inexperienced data entry clerk could pop up a list of benefits codes by double-clicking the lightning bolt following the Benefits Code field. Another way of providing such information on screen, of course, is to simply include it as labels, so that it always shows, but it takes up a lot more space that way, and most people don't need it after entering data for an hour or so.

Adding Boxes and Patterns

You can box a section (or add rectangles as graphics) by choosing **Insert Rectangle**. A dotted square rectangle with handles appears somewhere on the screen, and you can drag it and resize it to enclose the area you want. Choose **Format Border** to select a different color and line style for the border. In the figure, the boxes around the main sections have a medium-thick border instead of the default hairline border. (What you can't see is that they are navy blue to match the navy blue ComText logo.)

After you have set up a box, you can select it and choose **Format Patterns** to add shading to it. In the figure, the boxes around the Pay and Deductions groups have dark gray borders and light gray shading.

When you first position a rectangle, it overlays any data underneath it. This makes it impossible to select the fields it covers. In fact, if you add shading, you won't even be able to see the fields. Select the rectangle and choose **Format Send to Back** to send the box to the back layer and let the fields and labels be on top.

Once you have inserted a rectangle, you can't insert any more fields in that area because you can't click the form to position the cursor without selecting the rectangle instead. But you can create the field somewhere else and drag it into the desired position.

You can see an example of a shadow box in Figure 15.2. This is created out of two overlapping rectangles. The following procedure shows you how to create a shadow box.

❖ **To create a shadow box:**

1. Choose **Insert Rectangle**. A default size rectangle appears somewhere on the page.

2. Position and size the rectangle to be the main box.

3. Choose **Format Patterns** and color the rectangle solid white.

4. If the rectangle is covering text, choose **Format Send to Back**. The overlaid text should reappear.

5. Press **Ctrl** and drag the border of the rectangle to create another rectangle slightly down and to the right of the existing rectangle. The new rectangle will be on top.

6. Choose **Format Patterns** and select a shadow color for the new rectangle.

7. Choose **Format Send to Back** to place the shadow behind the main rectangle.

Design Considerations

In deciding what fields to use and where to place them, consider how you are going to use the database. If you will be addressing letters, envelopes, and mailing labels, for example, you might want to include a title field (Mr/Mrs/Ms/Dr).

If you will be addressing people casually, you might want a nickname field so that you can start the letter with "Dear Jack" instead of "Dear Mr. Tabler" or "Dear John."

Any data that will be used as a sort key needs a field of its own. For example, if you want to sort your records by last name, be sure to have a separate last name field, instead of just a name field. If you will be sorting by postal code, as required for bulk mailings, you will need to have a separate postal code field and not just bury it in the address. The same is true regardless of the sorting method you choose.

You also need separate fields for any data that will be used to select records. For example, if you want to select the records of all employees who live in a particular state, the state needs to be a separate field. If you want to select all employees with more than 20 overtime hours, you have to separate out overtime hours in its own field.

Also keep in mind how you will enter data into the database. If you'll be using Form view, each time you complete a field, you press **Tab** to jump to the next field to the right. When you reach the end of a row, **Tab** takes you to the first field in the next row. Therefore, it makes sense to organize your fields so that it's natural to work across the rows rather than down columns. If people will be entering data from printed forms, you might want to lay out the on-screen fields in the same order as the printed fields.

If you'll be printing your database in Form view, the graphics, borders, and shadings print along with it. You might have to limit the bells and whistles to things your printer can handle.

Entering Data

After you finish creating the form, you're ready to start entering data into the records.

Entering Data in Form View

Click the first field and start typing. As soon as you type the first character, the focus goes to the formula bar and the **Cancel** and **Enter** icons appear. When you finish the first field, press **Tab** to record the data in that field and move the cursor to the next one. Works formats the first field according to the data you typed. (Remember that you can use **Format Number** to change it.)

You don't have to do the fields in order if you don't want to. You can click any field and type data in it. Clicking another field records the data in the current field. You also can move around the form with the arrow keys, but they don't move from field to field. You'll find yourself highlighting labels, field names, and so forth. It's better to use the mouse or the **Tab** key to move from field to field.

SHORTCUT

Shift+Tab tabs backward, to the preceding field.

Don't forget to start a formula with an equal sign. Refer to fields by their field names. For example, in Figure 15.6, the formula for Net might be **=Gross-Deductions**. The formula for Gross might be **=Salary/Wages+Bonuses+Commission+Other**. You can use the same functions you use in Spreadsheet, including **SUM**, **AVG**, and **NOW( )** for the date and time. **SUM** doesn't make much difference since there are no range references in Database; you might as well use plus signs, as in the previous formula for Gross.

Works assumes that a formula pertains not just to the current record but to every record in the database. It fills in all formulas automatically as soon as you create a new record by adding data to any field in the record. You can also use **Fill Right**, **Fill Down**, and **Fill Series** to copy text and numeric values to other records, but you have to be in List view to use these commands. List view is explained in the next section.

List View

Click the **List View** icon (see Figure 15.3) to switch to List view. Figure 15.7 shows an example, using the same database as Figures 15.4 and 15.6. As you can see, List view is much like a spreadsheet with the record numbers as row headers and the field names as column headers. No matter what sizes you have given the fields in Form view, they all have the default size when you first switch to List view. You can adjust the sizes just as you do in Spreadsheet.

	Last Name	First Nam	MI	SS Numbe	Pay Code	Benefits C	Date	Gross	S
1	Abernathy	Martin	G.	199-67-0221	4	A	11/27/93	22500	
2									
3									
4									
5									
6									
7									
8									
9									
10									
11									
12									
13									
14									
15									
16									
17									
18									
19									
20									

Figure 15.7 *List view*

SHORTCUT

Highlight all the columns, choose **Format Field Width**, and select **Best Fit** to let Works adjust the columns widths to fit the data they contain.

None of the graphics are carried over from Form view to List view. In fact, you can't embed anything in List view. Shadings and borders are not carried over, nor is any other external formatting such as fonts. The order of the columns are determined not by the order of fields in Form view, but by the order that you created the fields. If you don't like the order, you can change it:

❖ **To move a field in List view:**

1. Click the field header to select the entire column.
2. Click the **Cut** icon.

3. Click the field header of the field that should follow the moved field.

4. Click the **Paste** icon.

You can enter data in List view just as easily as Form view. In fact, if you're comfortable with Spreadsheet, you might find that you prefer it this way. You can also use the **Edit Fill** commands in List view, which aren't available in Form view.

Filling Down

In the example in Figure 15.7, suppose you are about to enter data for 200 employees, all with the same pay code as Martin G. Abernathy. You could select the Pay Code column in record 1, extend the selection down through record 200, and choose **Edit Fill Down**. The additional 199 records are added to the database with a 4 in the Pay Code field. Any formulas in record 1 are also copied to the new records, so you might see a lot of data appear when you choose the **Edit Fill Down** command.

WARNING

Don't fill an entire column (by selecting the column header) unless you actually intend to add more than 32,000 records to the database. It will take a long, long time for Works to create all the new records with the filled value as well as all the formulas, and the database will be huge, both in memory and on disk.

Filling a Series

Suppose your database includes a serial number, starting with 1 in the first record and continuing as you add records. If you intend to add 100 records today, type the 1 in the first record, select that field in the first 100 records, and choose **Edit Fill Series**.

Filling to the Right

You can also fill right if you have several adjacent fields in one record that have the same value. And you can use **Edit Fill Series** across a row if you have several adjacent fields that should contain a series of numbers.

Overriding Formulas

Sometimes one or more formulas don't pertain to a particular record. For example, an employee might request that a particular dollar amount be withheld from each paycheck for federal income tax. You can override any formula by typing an actual value (but not another formula) for the field. The same field in other records is not affected; the formula still pertains to those records. If you later delete the specific amount, the formula returns to the field.

Default Values

Since formulas can be overridden, you can use them to set up default values for fields. For example, suppose most of your employees have pay code 4. Instead of typing a 4 in the first record and filling it down, type the formula **=4** in the Pay Code field. This fills a 4 into the Pay Code field of each new record. For employees with a different pay code, just overtype the 4 with the actual value.

Managing Your Database

Each database is saved in a file, just like a Word Processor document and a Spreadsheet spreadsheet. Be sure to save your new database early and often to avoid losing data in case of a power outage or system hangup. When you name a new database, Works assigns the extension *WDB* (for Works DataBase) to it.

N O T E

You can print your database in any view. When you print in Form view, each record becomes one page (or more, if the form takes multiple pages).

In List view, Works prints as many records as possible on one page. The columns are not labeled unless you select **Page Setup** and turn on the **Print Record and Field Labels** option. When you use this option, the column and row headers are printed on every page.

SHORTCUT

You'll save time, paper, and ink by previewing the printout and fixing any problems before printing it on paper.

If the records have too many fields to fit on one page, Works prints as many pages as necessary to show all the columns. Sometimes you can get them all on one page by choosing **Page Setup** and selecting **Landscape** orientation. You'll get fewer rows per page, but at least each record will be intact.

Printing a large database from List view, even with column and row headers and landscape orientation, often does not produce a very attractive document. You'll get better results by generating a report, where you can specify your own headers and organize the rows and columns as you wish. You'll learn how to generate reports in Chapter 18.

Summary

This chapter has shown you how to:

- ❖ Create a new database and enter data in the records
- ❖ Design and create a form with fields, labels, and artwork
- ❖ Enter text, numbers, and formulas into the form
- ❖ Use both Form and List views
- ❖ Use the **Edit Fill** commands in List view
- ❖ Override a formula and set up default values for fields
- ❖ Save and print your database in both views

Now that you have a basic database, the next chapter shows you how to revise and improve it, as well has how to query it.

CHAPTER 16

Working with Databases

Now that you have a design and some initial records in your database, you'll want to start modifying it and updating the records. In this chapter, you'll learn how to:

❖ Select items (fields, field names, labels, and objects) in form view

❖ Format selected items

❖ Change the design of a form

❖ Locate records

❖ Insert new records

❖ Modify existing records

❖ Delete records

❖ Move and copy data between fields and between records

❖ Format pages for printing

❖ Display or suppress gridlines and field lines

❖ Query the database for records that match certain criteria

Selecting Items

In Form view, you can select embedded objects, rectangles, labels, field names, and fields. To select an individual item, click it. There are several ways to select multiple items, depending on whether they are adjacent to each other and whether they're enclosed in a rectangle. If they are adjacent and not enclosed, you can select them by dragging.

> ❖ **To select a group of items by dragging:**
>
> 1. Position the mouse pointer over a blank area outside, but near, one corner of the group.
> 2. Start dragging the mouse pointer. A rectangular marquee appears and moves with your mouse pointer.
> 3. Enclose the desired group in the marquee.
> 4. Release the mouse pointer. All items completely inside the marquee are selected.

This technique won't work if the items are inside a rectangle and you try to start the marquee inside the rectangle. When you click a blank area inside a rectangle, you select the rectangle. If you then start dragging the mouse pointer, you move the rectangle. (Choose **Edit Undo** to return it to its former position.) However, if you're careful to start the marquee outside the rectangle, you can drag it across the border and into the rectangle without selecting the rectangle. If you can manipulate the marquee so that only the desired items are completely enclosed, you will select the desired items.

N O T E

Be careful not to enclose the rectangle completely unless you want to select it too.)

If you can't enclose the items you want to select, hold down **Ctrl** and click them one at a time. You can select as many items as needed this way, and they don't have to be adjacent.

If you select a field name, only the name is selected; you have not automatically selected the field itself. Likewise, selecting a field does not automatically select the field name. Because they must stay together, moving or copying one also affects the other, but other operations, such as changing fonts, affect only the one that is selected. If you want to change them both, select them both.

In List view, select a single field by clicking it. Select adjacent multiple fields by dragging the mouse pointer across them. You can't select nonadjacent multiple fields.

Formatting

Database uses the same default formatting rules as Spreadsheet, and you override them in the same way.

Fonts

The font affects the appearance of the labels, the field names, and the fields. The default font depends on what fonts you have installed on your system, but it is probably a 12-point sans serif font. Use the **Fontname** and **Font Size** drop-down lists in the toolbar to change the font. Use the **Bold**, *Italic,* and **Underline** icons to select the font style. For other styles and for color, choose **Format Font and Style**.

If you change the font when nothing is selected, you establish a new default font. Any future labels, field names, and fields will be displayed in this font. If you change the font when something is selected, only the selected items are changed.

You can have different fonts for the field names and the fields themselves.

N O T E

Text Data

Text data is aligned on the left but otherwise not formatted. You can change the alignment with the **Format Alignment** command. You can choose **General**, **Left**, **Center**, or **Right** alignment. Other alignments available in Spreadsheet, such as **Justified**, are not available.

General alignment lets Works use its default alignment.

N O T E

Another alignment option is available in Form view: **Slide to Left**. This option affects the printed form only, moving the affected field left to fill in any blank space between it and the preceding field.

Numeric Data

Numbers are aligned on the right and formatted using the same defaults that Spreadsheet uses. You can change the alignment with the **Format Alignment** command, and you can select a different numeric format with the **Format Number** command.

Changing Views

You can select font, alignment, and numeric formats in either view. Font options affect all records, but only the current view. If you set the **Last Name** field to Times New Roman in Form view, for example, in List view the Last Name field still uses the same font it had before. Alignment options and numeric formats affect all records and both views.

If you want to change the format of a field in List view, you need to select the field in one record only. The format options automatically apply to all records.

N O T E

Page Formatting

As you have seen, Works breaks your databases into pages for printing. You can add formatting to the page—specifying page breaks and adding heading and footers.

❖   **To insert a page break in Form view:**

1.   Select an item (such as a field or a rectangle) that should immediately follow the page break.

2.   Choose **Insert Page Break**. Works inserts a horizontal page break before the selected item. (You can't insert a vertical page break in Form view.)

In List view, select a row or column by clicking the header. Then choose **Insert Page Break**. Works inserts the page break before the selected row or column.

Choose **File Page Setup** to open the Page Setup dialog box, where you can set margins, choose portrait or landscape orientation, choose the paper size, and so on. Your choices affect both Form view and List view. The options on the **Other Options** page are different for the two views, however, as you can see in Figures 16.1 and 16.2.

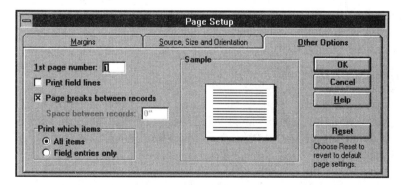

Figure 16.1 *Page Setup dialog box, Other Options for Form view*

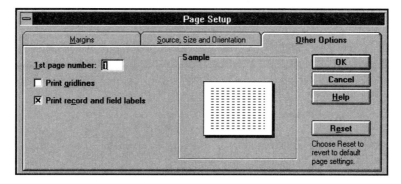

Figure 16.2 *Page Setup dialog box, Other Options for List view*

In Form view, you can print the lines underneath the fields, which are not printed by default. If you choose not to print each record on a separate page, you can specify the vertical spacing between records. You can also choose to print all the items on the form or the data in the fields only. You might want to print just the data if you're printing on preprinted forms, such as W2 forms.

In List view, you can choose to print gridlines and the record and field labels.

You can also add headers and footers to your pages with the **View Headers and Footers** command, which works just as it does in Word Processor except you can't have header and footer paragraphs. The headers and footers you define affect both views.

Gridlines and Field Lines

When you're working on your database, you may or may not find the gridlines (in List view) and the field lines (in Form view) helpful. You can turn them off and on by selecting **View Gridlines** or **View Field Lines**. This doesn't affect the way the database is printed, just the view on your monitor.

Redesigning the Form

It seems inevitable that, as soon as you finish designing a database, you have to change it. You already know how to add items (labels, fields, and so on) and how to reposition them. You also might need to change and delete items.

Deleting Items

In Form view, you can delete any item by selecting it and pressing the **Delete** key. If you select a field, only the data in that particular record is deleted; you must select the field name to delete the entire field from all records. Database asks you to confirm when you delete a field. Other types of items are deleted without question. Except for the data in a field, any item that you delete is deleted from all records. You can't undo a field deletion, but you can undo any other type of deletion.

You can't delete a formula from a field by pressing the **Delete** key. If you want to delete a formula, select the field and choose **Edit Clear Formula**. In List view, you have to choose the entire column by clicking the header for the field in order to make available the Clear Formula command.

N O T E

When a field contains a value that is overriding a formula, if you delete the value, the formula returns to the field.

Changing Items

You can change the text of a label or a field name, and you can change a formula in a field.

❖   **To change an item in Form view:**

1.   Select the item. Its contents appear in the formula bar.

2a. To replace the item completely, type the new text. The next text replaces the old text in the formula bar.

2b. If instead you want to adapt the current text, click the formula bar to place the cursor in it, then edit the item.

3.   Remove the focus from the formula bar to record the new value. (You could press **Enter** or **Tab,** for example.) The new text replaces the old on the form.

If you change a field name, Database automatically adapts any formulas that refer to that field.

❖ **To change a field name in List view:**

1. Select the field.

2. Choose **Edit Field Name**. The Field Name dialog box opens.

3. Type the new field name and click **OK**. The new field name replaces the old one. All views are affected by the change.

❖ **To change a formula in List view:**

1. Select any field containing the formula. The current formula appears in the formula bar.

2. Replace or edit the formula.

3. Remove the focus from the formula bar. (You could press **Enter**, for example). The new formula replaces the old one and all records are recalculated. The changed formula affects all views.

Updating Database Records

Most databases are constantly being updated—records are inserted, deleted, and changed on a daily basis. You can update your Database files in List view or Form view.

Locating a Specific Record

There are several ways to locate a specific record, depending on the view and whether you're looking for a specific record number or some data that the record contains.

❖ **To find a specific record number in Form view:**

1. Press **F5**. The Go To dialog box opens.

2. Type the record number and click **OK**. The specified record appears.

If you don't know the record number, then you'll probably be looking for a value, such as "Abernathy" or "199-67-0221." In List view, you often can just scan the list for the desired value, especially if the records are sorted according to the contents of that field. But you can search for the desired value in either view.

❖ **To find a specific value in a field in either view:**

1. Choose **Edit Find**. The Find dialog box opens (see Figure 16.3).

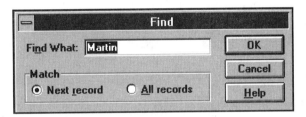

Figure 16.3 *Find dialog box*

2. Type the data you want to find. For example, if you want to find the record for Henry Martin, type **Henry** or **Martin**.

N O T E

In List view, you can limit the search to specific fields and/or records by selecting those columns and/or rows.

3. Click **OK**. Database locates the next field containing the specified value, highlights the field, and displays the record (in Form view) or scrolls the list as necessary to show the record (in List view).

4. If the desired record isn't found, press **F7** to repeat the search.

N O T E Database starts at the current cursor position and searches to the end of the current record, then searches the next record from beginning to end, and so on. In List view, this is equivalent to searching across rows, as opposed to searching down columns.

5. After locating and updating the desired record, you can press **F7** again to locate the next record containing the same value.

Locating a Specific Field in a Record

If you're working with a large record where you can't see all the fields on one screen, you might find it helpful to search for the field you want. You can search for a field name using the following procedure.

❖ **To find a field:**

1. Press **F5**. The Go To dialog box appears (see Figure 16.4). All the field names are shown in the list box.

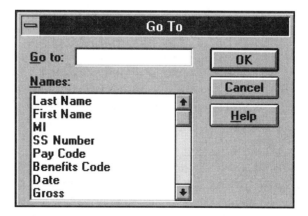

Figure 16.4 *Go To dialog box*

2. Double-click the desired field name. Database scrolls the record as necessary and highlights the requested field.

Inserting and Deleting Records

To insert a record in List view, select the record it should precede by clicking the row header, then choose **Insert Record/Field**. You can insert multiple records in one position by selecting as many rows as you want to insert records. To delete one or more records in List view, select them and choose **Insert Delete Record/Field**. You can undo both of these actions.

To insert a record in Form view, display the record it should precede and click the **Insert Record** icon in the toolbar (see Figure 15.3).

In both cases, the new record is blank. It doesn't even have any formulas yet. As soon as you enter the first value, formulas are also added.

Updating Records

Updating a record is a simple matter. Locate it, click a field to be changed, and edit or replace the value in the formula bar.

Moving and Copying Data

You can copy and move values between fields and between records. In List view, you can copy and move by using drag-and-drop techniques or by using the Clipboard. As a reminder:

- ❖ To move a value by drag-and-drop, select the value and drag it to another field. (The mouse pointer says *Move.*)
- ❖ To copy a value by drag-and-drop, press **Ctrl** while you drag it. (The mouse pointer says *Copy.*)
- ❖ To move a value via the Clipboard, click the value and click the **Cut** icon; then click the destination field and click the **Paste** icon.
- ❖ To copy a value via the Clipboard, click the value and click the **Copy** icon; then click the destination field and click the **Paste** icon.

You can't move or copy a value by using drag-and-drop techniques in Form view; when you drag a field, you drag the field name, too. Use the Clipboard to move and copy values in Form view.

Queries

Queries help you select a group of records that meet certain criteria. For example, you might want to list all employees with pay code 4 or with benefits code A. In fact, you can combine criteria to select all employees with both pay code 4 and benefits code A or to select all employees with either pay code 4 or benefits code A.

When you enter a query, Database hides any records that don't meet the criteria. You then treat the remaining records as if they constituted the entire database. You can view them in List or Form view, update them, print them, merge them with a Word Processor document, sort them, build a report based on them, and so on. When you're done with the query, you unhide the other records to return them to your database.

Each query you enter is assigned a name. You can recall a query at any time and apply it to the database again. For example, suppose you assign the name Temps to the query for all employees with pay code 7. Whenever you want to list just your temporary employees, reapply the Temps query.

Simple and Advanced Queries

Database offers two levels of queries: *simple* and *advanced*. A simple query has up to three criteria and is entered via the New Query dialog box (see Figure 16.5). Advanced queries have more than three criteria, and may have more complicated relationships between the criteria. You probably won't need to use advanced queries, at least at the beginning, and this book doesn't deal with them.

Creating a Simple Query

Choose **Tools Create New Query** to open the New Query dialog box. The text box at the top shows Database's default name for the query. If you think you'll use the query more than once, you'll probably want to replace this name with something more meaningful, such as Temps, Sophomores, or Overdue Accts.

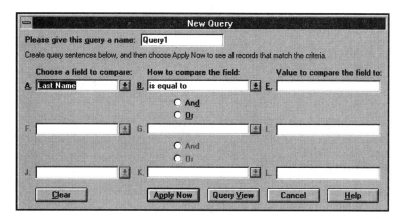

Figure 16.5 *New Query dialog box*

Writing a Query Sentence

Each row in the main part of the New Query dialog box creates a query sentence consisting of a field name, a comparison, and a value. For example, the following query selects all records with pay code 4:

Pay Code is equal to 4.

The following query sentence selects all employees who worked overtime this week:

Hours Worked is greater than 40.

The field name box is a combo box; you can type the name of the desired field in the text box or drop down the list box to select it. The comparison box is also a combo box. The possible comparisons are:

- ❖ is equal to
- ❖ is less than
- ❖ is greater than
- ❖ is not equal to
- ❖ is less than or equal to
- ❖ is greater than or equal to
- ❖ contains

The contains comparison locates fields that include a value but might contain other data as well. For example, suppose you have a database of marching band members, where the Instruments field lists all the instruments a musician can play. To find all your band members who play trumpet you could write this query:

Instruments contains trumpet

Multiple Query Sentences

Now suppose you want to list all band members whose last name begins with M. You can't say "Last Name is equal to M" because that would limit the selection to records where the last name field contains only an M. You can't say "Last Name is greater than M" because that would select not only people starting with M but also people starting with N, O, P, and so on. The query "Last Name contains M" would also select musicians who have an M somewhere else in their name, as in Smith and Ramirez. The answer lies in using two query sentences.

If you want to use another query sentence, click one of the connectors between the rows. If you click **And**, both sentences must be true for a record to be selected. If you click **Or**, a record is selected if either sentence is true. When you click a connector, the boxes that make up the next query sentence become available.

Suppose you want to list all musicians whose last names begin with M. The following query will do it:

Last Name is greater than M

   and

Last Name is less than N

Suppose you want to list all employees with a pay code of 5, 7, or 10:

Pay Code is equal to 5

   or

Pay Code is equal to 7

   or

Pay Code is equal to 10

Query Results

After you have created the query sentences, click **Apply Now**. The New Query dialog box closes and Works hides any records that don't match the query criteria. If you're in List view, you'll see the results right away. Figure 16.6 shows an example. Notice the record numbers in the row headers; you can see that many records are not shown.

	Last Name	First Name	MI	SS Number	Pay Code	Benefits Code	Date
8	Baker	George	C.	493-02-4563	3	C	11/28/93
20	Charles	Harry	Q.	198-32-7665	2	C	11/28/93
23	Frantz	Richard	E.	590-65-2918	3	C	11/28/93
25	Levitz	Dan	C.	762-83-7112	1	C	11/28/93
36	Muntner	Arthur	P.	871-34-7821	3	C	11/28/93
42	North	Lee	G.	194-29-3789	1	C	11/28/93
47	Ogden	Mark	S.	910-56-8923	1	C	11/29/93
48	Omar	Omar	C.	781-29-3823	2	C	11/29/93
52	Powers	Robert	A.	821-89-2893	1	C	11/29/93
55	Prince	Glenda	C.	309-29-1002	2	C	11/29/93
62	Ramirez	Pilar	D.	903-29-4783	1	C	11/29/93
69	Runnel	Roberta	M.	291-65-3892	2	C	11/29/93
80	Thomas	Yolanda		781-90-2367	2	C	11/29/93

Figure 16.6 *Result of a query (List view)*

In Form view, where you can see only one record at a time, you have to page through the records to examine the results. Of course, in either view, if you print or copy the database, only the unhidden records are used.

When you're ready to return to the full database, choose **View Show All Records**. To repeat a query, choose **View Apply Query** or press **F3** and select the name of the query from the list box.

Query Management

A query is automatically stored with the database. Database gives you several commands to manage queries. You have already seen **Tools Create New Query** and **View Apply Query**. The Tools menu (see Figure 16.7) includes additional query commands, which are explained as follows:

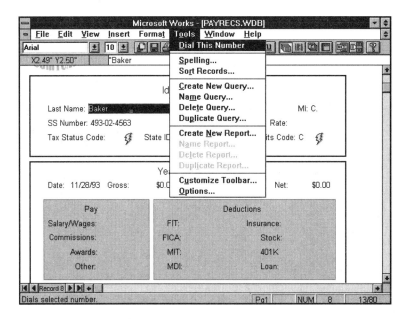

Figure 16.7 *Query commands on the Tools menu*

❖ **Name Query** Displays a dialog box where you can select a query and provide a new name for it.

❖ **Delete Query** Displays a dialog box where you can select and delete a query.

❖ **Duplicate Query** Displays a dialog box where you can select and copy a query. (You would then adapt the copy using advanced querying techniques.)

Summary

This chapter has shown you how to:

- ❖ Modify and query a database
- ❖ Change the design of a form, insert, delete, and update records, and move and copy data
- ❖ Create and apply simple queries
- ❖ Manage the queries belonging to a database

The next chapter covers a variety of Database features, such as sorting records and integrating Database records with Word Processor documents, as well as the WorksWizards and AutoStart Templates that create databases.

CHAPTER 17

Special Features

T he Database tool includes many of the same special features that you have learned to use with Word Processor and Spreadsheet, such as find and replace, Spelling Checker, and **OLE**. This chapter shows you how to apply them to Database and also discusses the professionally designed databases provided by WorksWizards and AutoStart Templates. You will learn how to:

❖ Exchange data with other Works tools: move, copy, embed, and link

❖ Exchange data with other applications

❖ Merge a database with a Word Processor document

❖ Sort a database

❖ Hide and show fields

❖ Protect forms and fields from being changed

❖ Find and replace data

411

❖ Spell check a database

❖ Use the WorksWizards and AutoStart databases

Exchanging Data with Other Tools and Applications

In Form view, Database works almost exactly like Word Processor in its ability to copy, embed, and link data. In List view, it is more like Spreadsheet; you can copy or link from it to other documents, and you can copy to it, but you can't embed or link objects into it from other sources.

This chapter briefly reviews the procedures involved in exchanging data and points out any features unique to Database. For complete explanations of how to exchange data, see Chapter 14.

Copying Data

You can copy data from other applications into Database fields, where it supplies the values for the fields. You can't do a straight copy to any other place in either List view or Form view. For example, you can't copy text from Word Processor or Spreadsheet to create a label or a field name. If you try to copy spreadsheet cells to a blank area on a form, they will be either embedded or linked, but they won't create or replace a label or a field name. You'll learn more about embedding and linking spreadsheet ranges later in this chapter.

Replacing a field value by copying a single cell from Spreadsheet or a single paragraph with no tabs from Word Processor causes no problems in either view. But you might get some unexpected results if you copy a range of cells or a text block that includes carriage returns and/or tabs. In List view, a range of spreadsheet cells (or the equivalent from a Word Processor document) replaces a comparable "range" of fields and records. In Figure 17.1, the spreadsheet range is three cells wide and seven cells down, so it replaces three adjacent fields in seven records. You may have applications where this facility comes in handy.

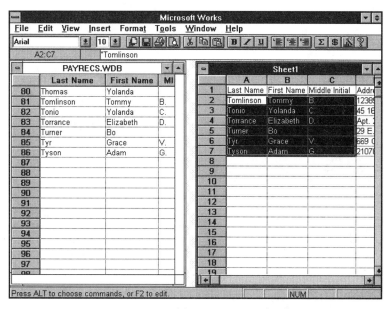

Figure 17.1 *Copying a spreadsheet range to a database in List view*

If you copy a range of spreadsheet cells (or the equivalent from a Word Processor document) to a record in Form view, fields are replaced as if you were in List view. You'll see the first cell's value replace the field where you paste the range. If the range is several cells wide, other fields in the same record are replaced. The effect on the fields depends on how the fields are arranged in List view, even though you're in Form view. If the range is several cells down, fields are replaced in the next several records.

Altogether, you have to be pretty brave and self-confident to copy a range of cells or a text block containing carriage returns and tabs to a database in Form view. You're much wiser to do it in List view, where you can see which fields and records are going to be affected.

You also can copy Database data to other tools and applications. If you copy a set of fields from List view to a Word Processor document, for example, the list is inserted in the document at the cursor position. In Figure 17.2, you can see that the fields from Abernathy Martin G. to Arkin Ella V. were copied to a document. Works inserted tabs between the fields and carriage returns between the records to create the rows and columns that appear in the document.

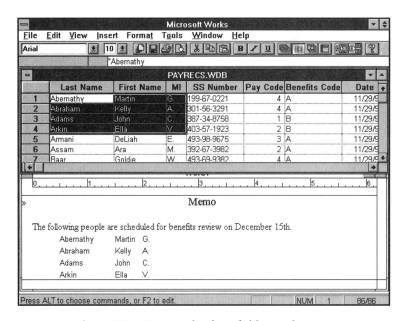

Figure 17.2 *Copying database fields to a document*

N O T E Later in this chapter, you'll learn how to hide fields and records so you can bring together the data you want to copy to another document.

In Form view, you can select a single item—a field name or a field value, for example—and copy it to another document. But you can't copy a multiple selection.

Suppose you're writing a letter and you want to copy the name and address from your address book. Open the address book in List view, locate the desired record, and select the fields that make up the name and address. Drag them to the letter and drop them in position. They will be strung out in one paragraph with tabs in between. Replace the tabs with carriage returns and you'll have an accurate name and address in your letter.

Use any of the standard methods to copy objects from one application to the other. Use drag-and-drop if it works, otherwise use the Clipboard.

Embedding Objects

You have already seen some examples of objects embedded in a Database form. You can embed the same types of objects, using the same procedures, that you embed in a Word Processor document. You can't embed objects in List view. When you embed an object in one record, of course, it shows up in every record.

Embedding New Objects

Use the Insert menu (see Figure 17.3) to embed most objects. With WordArt and Drawing, you'll create a new object before you embed it. You can also choose to create a new object from any **OLE** application via the **Insert Object** command. (Choose **Create New** in the dialog box.) Remember that the objects you create this way do not have separate files; they are stored within the database. If you want to create a new spreadsheet or chart just to embed in the form, choose **Insert Spreadsheet/Table** or **Insert Chart**. (Choose **New table** or **New Chart** in the dialog box.)

Embedding Existing Objects

You can embed existing objects, of course. Use **Insert Object** to embed a whole file. (Choose **Create from File** in the dialog box.) To embed part of a file, just drag the part you want and drop it on the form, or, copy and paste it. If it isn't normal text and it's from an **OLE** application, Works will embed or link it instead of simply copying it. (The dialog box lets you choose between embedding and linking.)

SHORTCUT

If you drag the mouse pointer from a chart window to a Database window in Form view, the chart will be copied and embedded or linked in the database form. A message asks if you want to link the chart; if you choose **No**, it's embedded.

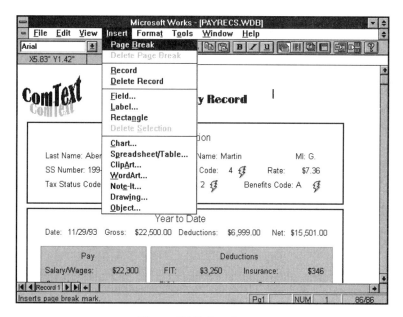

Figure 17.3 *Insert menu*

Managing Embedded Objects

Once an object is embedded in a form, you can move it, copy it, resize it, and delete it. If it's playable, you play it by double-clicking it. If it's not playable, double-clicking it opens it for editing. You can edit playable objects (as well as unplayable ones) by choosing **Edit *object-name***.

In a database form, an embedded object can overlay other items. You can bring it to the front or send it to the back using the Format menu.

Linking Objects

You link objects on a database form the same way you do in a Word Processor document. Use **Insert Object** to link an entire file; choose **Create from file** and click the **Link** checkbox. Use drag-and-drop to link part of a file; when Works asks if you want to create a link, choose **Yes**. If the source spreadsheet is open, you can also link a named spreadsheet range by choosing **Insert Spreadsheet/Table**; click **Use existing spreadsheet range** and the link is created automatically. Similarly, to link a chart, choose **Insert Chart** and click **Use existing chart**.

The **Edit Links** command (see Figure 17.4) lets you manage the links in a database. You can choose to update a particular link automatically or manually. If you're updating it manually, choose **Update Now** to update it. If you have moved or renamed the file containing the source of the linked material, choose **Change Source** to specify the new path or name for the source.

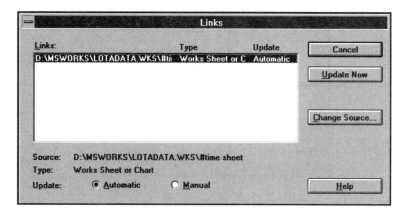

Figure 17.4 *Links dialog box*

To edit the source file, double-click the linked object. To delete a link, click it and press **Delete**.

Merging Database Data into a Word Processor Document

When you want to print a form letter, envelopes, or mailing labels using names and addresses from a database, you merge the letter with the database. Chapter 3 showed you how to use a WorksWizard to merge Database fields into a Word Processor document for printing. But you don't need to use the WorksWizard. You can use the **Insert Database Fields** command from Word Processor's window.

❖ **To merge database fields:**

1. With the cursor in the Word Processor document, choose **Insert Database Fields**. The Insert Field dialog box opens (see Figure 17.5).

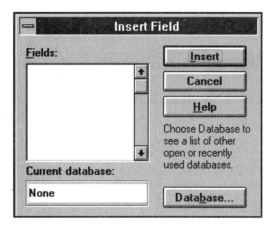

Figure 17.5 *Blank Insert Field dialog box*

2. If no databases are listed, or if the database you want is not listed, click **Database**. The Choose Database dialog box opens (see Figure 17.6).

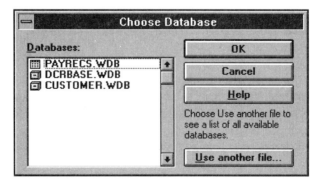

Figure 17.6 *Choose Database dialog box*

3.   Double-click the desired database. (If it's in a different directory and not listed in the dialog box, click **Use another file** and locate it in the directory tree.) The Insert Field dialog box returns with the selected database's fields listed (see Figure 17.7).

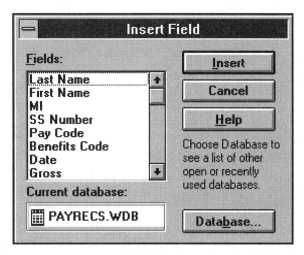

Figure 17.7 *Insert Field dialog box with open database*

4.   Double-click each field you want to use in the form letter. For each field you select, Works inserts a placeholder in the document. If you insert more than one, they are placed side-by-side to form one paragraph, separated by a single space.

5.   When you have inserted all the placeholders you need, click **Cancel** to close the dialog box.

6.   Insert carriage returns and text as needed to incorporate the placeholders into the document (see Figure 17.8).

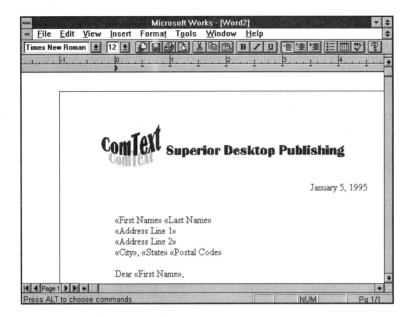

Figure 17.8 *Database placeholders in a document*

7. If you discover that you need more placeholders, repeat Steps 1, 4, 5, and 6.

Use Print Preview (see Figure 17.9) to see how your document looks with data substituted for the placeholders. Works might ask you to select the name of the database again while preparing the printed documents; be sure to select the same database that you used to select the placeholders.

When you merge a document and a database, Works prints one copy of the document for every unhidden record in the database. You can hide records that you don't want to merge. If you want to hide records, open the database before starting the previous procedure and do a query. Or you can manually hide records using the View Hide Record command.

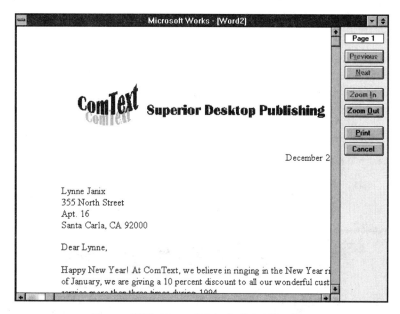

Figure 17.9 *Merged data in Print Preview*

❖ **To hide records manually:**

1. Select a record. (In List view, you can select several adjacent records if desired.)
2. Choose **View Hide Record**.

Don't forget to choose **View Show All Records** to unhide records again after the merge job is done.

Chapter 3 shows you how to print envelopes and mailing labels from a database.

N O T E

If you want to print data from more than one database record in a single copy of the Word Processor document, you can't use the merge facility. You must generate a report and insert that in the document. Chapter 18 shows you how to do that.

Sorting a Database

You'll probably keep your database in some kind of alphabetical or numeric order, but you might occasionally need to sort it into another order. For example, you might need to print letters, envelopes, or mailing labels in order by postal code for bulk mailing. Sorting a database is much like sorting a spreadsheet.

❖ **To sort a database:**

1. Choose **Tools Sort Records**. The Sort Records dialog box opens (see Figure 17.10).

Figure 17.10 *Sort Records dialog box*

2. In the **1st Field** box, choose the name of the field that should be used as the primary sort key.

3. Choose field names in the **2nd Field** and **3rd Field** boxes if desired. For example, if the first field is the Benefits Code field and you want to sort those records with the same benefits code according to pay code, choose **Pay Code** for the second field. If you want to choose those records with the same benefits code and pay code in alphabetical order by last name, choose **Last Name** as the third field.

4. Click **OK**. The records are sorted in the specified order.

You can undo a sort immediately with **Edit Undo**. If you do some editing after the sort, you have to resort the records to restore their former order.

Hiding Fields

You learned earlier how to hide fields in a spreadsheet. You can hide fields in a database the same way in List view. Select one or more fields and choose **Format Field Width**. Set the width to 0 and the fields no longer show up on the screen or in print.

❖ **To show a hidden field:**

1. Select the fields that surround the hidden field.

2. Choose **Format Field Width**. The Field Width dialog box opens with a default size of 10 for all selected fields.

3. Click **OK**. The dialog box closes and all selected fields, including any hidden fields in the selected range, are given the default size of 10.

4. Adjust the field widths of the individual fields.

You can't completely hide a field in Form view, but you can hide its field name by choosing **View Field Name** and you can reduce its field width to 1 by choosing **Format Field Width**.

Protecting Fields and Forms

When you develop a form that other people will use to develop and maintain a database, you might want to protect the form so that no one can change it. You can enter and change data in the fields in a protected form, but you can't alter the fields, the labels, the artwork, or the linked and embedded objects. You might also want to prevent people from entering or changing the data in particular fields. For example, if a field contains a formula, you might want to prevent someone from overriding it. If a field contains a serial number generated by a Fill Series command, you might want to protect it.

❖ **To protect a database form:**

1. In Form view, choose **Format Protect Form**..

You protect fields in Database the same way you do in Spreadsheet. All fields are protected by default; if you turn protection on, they are all protected. You must unlock the fields that you want to access.

❖ **To unlock a field:**

1. Select the field (in either view).

2. Choose **Format Protection**. The Protection dialog box opens (see Figure 17.11).

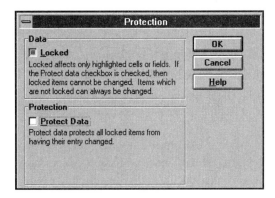

Figure 17.11 *Protection dialog box*

3. Click **Locked** to clear the checkbox.

4. Click **OK**.

❖ **To protect all locked fields:**

1. Choose **Format Protection**. The Protection dialog box opens.

2. Choose **Protect Data**.

3. Click **OK**.

Repeat this procedure to remove protection again.

Find and Replace

Database in List view includes the same find and replace facility that the other Works tools have. The Replace dialog box shown in Figure 17.12 opens when you choose **Edit Replace**. Enter the text to be replaced in the **Find What** field and the replacement text in the **Replace With** field. Click **Records** if you want to search down columns and **Fields** if you want to search across rows. Click **Find Next** to locate and highlight the next occurrence of the search text or **Replace All** to replace all occurrences without asking. If you use **Find Next** and Works finds an occurrence, click **Replace** to replace it, **Find Next** to skip it, **Replace All** to replace all the remaining occurrences, or **Cancel** to exit the Replace function.

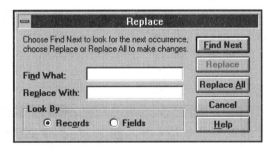

Figure 17.12 *The Replace dialog box*

Spelling Checker

You can use Spelling Checker in either view. It works just like it does in the other tools. It's a little disconcerting in Database because you can see the highlight flash around the fields as it examines each one.

Professional Database Designs

WorksWizards and AutoStart templates provide a number of professionally designed databases to make your life a little easier. This section explores some of the designs provided with Works.

WorksWizards

WorksWizards includes a number of database designs for business, home, and classroom use. You can choose the style of the form and, for some of the styles, the artwork. Almost all the databases have extra fields to choose from, including a comments field and four generic fields. With all but one (the Quick database), the form is protected so if you want to tailor it, you have to remove the protection first. You have already seen the Address Book database in Chapter 3. The other databases are described as follows.

❖ **Business Contacts** Similar to Address Book, but designed to keep track of business acquaintances: name, address, phone numbers, job title, contact history, and so on. Extra fields include special dates (birthday, anniversary, etc.).

❖ **Business Inventory** Designed to keep track of inventory items. In Figure 17.13, you can see the basic form (using the Cubed style) plus two of the extra field groups. The supplier information group is not shown.

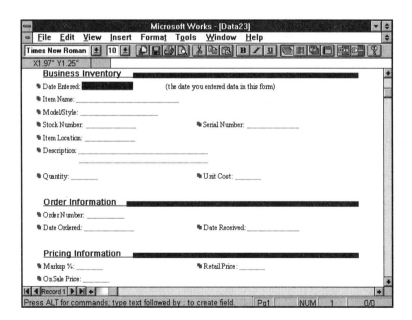

Figure 17.13 *WorksWizards Business Inventory database*

❖ **Customer Profile** Similar to Address Book, but includes information pertinent to customers. Extra fields include credit information and personal information (hobbies, employer, etc.).

❖ **Home Inventory** Designed to track personal possessions. Figure 17.14 shows the basic form plus the extra field groups (using Symbols style). Compare this to the AutoStart Templates Home Inventory described later.

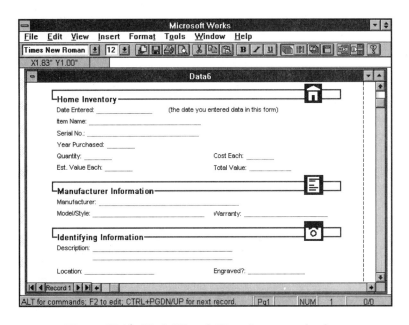

Figure 17.14 *WorksWizards Home Inventory database*

❖ **Membership Tracker** Designed to track members in a club or other type of organization. The basic fields include name and address information and date joined. Extra fields include membership status, member profile (age, ability level, etc.), guardian information, and medical information.

❖ **Quick Database** A generic database containing Fields 1 through 10 with no options except style. The form is not protected in this database so that you can readily replace the field names with more meaningful ones, add more fields, or remove unneeded fields. Use this WorksWizards to take advantage of the professionally styled forms, but insert your own fields.

❖ **Student Information** Designed to track students. The basic form includes name, homeroom, student ID number, and so on. Additional information includes class schedule and guardian information.

AutoStart Templates

Several of the AutoStart templates are databases. Some of them duplicate the WorksWizards functions, but use different designs. The forms are protected so that you can't change the basic form design without removing the protection. In some cases, fields containing formulas are protected so that you can't override them without removing the protection. (Protected fields are usually shaded yellow.) When you use the template, check **View Apply Query** to see what queries have been built into the template.

❖ **Accounts Receivable** Tracks your customer accounts. Figure 17.15 shows the top of the Accounts Receivable form. Additional fields in the lower part of the form track this month's activities. Includes Overdue and Last Notice queries (AutoStart Business group, Billing category).

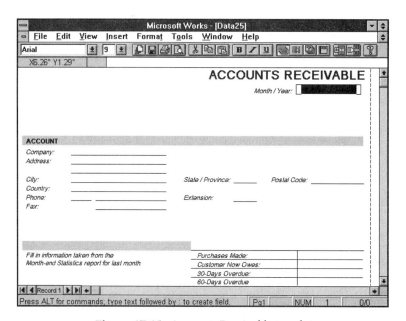

Figure 17.15 *Accounts Receivable template*

N O T E The Accounts Receivable database integrates with the Past Due Statement (see Figure 17.16), which is in the same group and category. The Cue Card that accompanies the Past Due Statement explains how to use it.

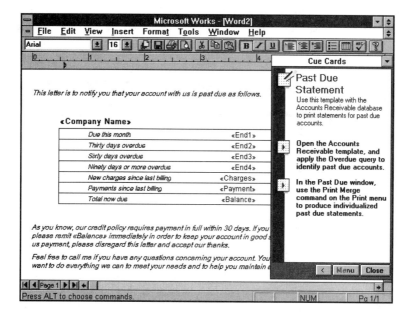

Figure 17.16 *Past Due Statement*

❖ **Membership Roster** Tracks members in a club or other organization, including name and address information, date joined, membership status, and so on (AutoStart Personal group, Addresses category).

❖ **Personal Directory** Acts as your personal address book, including fields for birthdays, anniversaries, and so on (AutoStart Personal group, Addresses category; also, AutoStart Education group, Productivity category).

❖ **Book Collection** Tracks your books—title, author, location, and so on (AutoStart Personal group, Household Management category; also, AutoStart Education group, Classroom Management category).

❖ **CD/Tape Collection** Tracks your CDs and audio tapes—title, artist, tracks, and so on (AutoStart Personal group, Household Management category; also, AutoStart Education group, Classroom Management category).

❖ **Household Inventory** Tracks your personal possessions, including a place to paste a picture of the item (which many insurance companies require). Figure 17.17 shows the form. If you have a scanner, you can insert the picture as an object in the database. Otherwise, print the database and paste pictures into the printed copy (AutoStart Personal group, Household Management category).

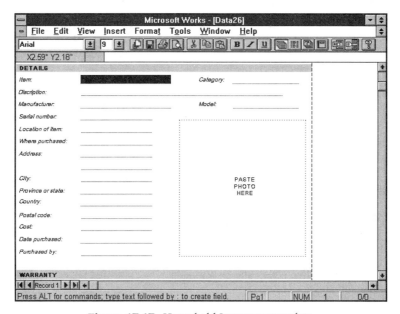

Figure 17.17 *Household Inventory template*

❖ **Recipes** Lets you record your favorite recipes, including ingredient list and instructions.

❖ **Video Collection** Similar to the CD/Tapes collection, but keyed toward videos—cast listing, tape speed, counter number, and so on (AutoStart Personal group, Household Management category; also, AutoStart Education group, Classroom Management category).

❖ **Credit Card Collection** Tracks your credit cards, including information on where to report a lost or stolen card (AutoStart Personal group, Personal Finances category).

❖ **Check Register** Helps keep your checkbook balanced. Figure 17.18 shows the complete form. When you create the database, enter your current account balance in the first record. From then on, as long as you enter all transactions (including service charges and other fees), Works tracks your checking account balance for you. If you have more than one account, keep a separate database for each one (AutoStart Personal group, Personal Finances category).

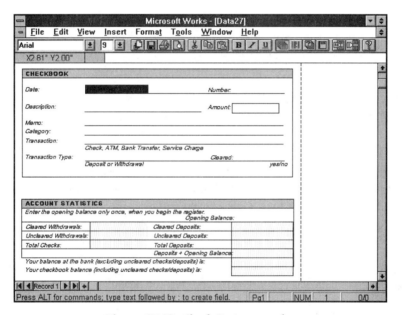

Figure 17.18 *Check Register template*

❖ **Student Records** Tracks students, including name, grade, scholastic standing, guardian and medical information (AutoStart Education group, Classroom Management category).

Don't forget that you can tailor any of these templates for your own use and resave it as a template. You can also turn any of your own databases into templates if you want to create more than one database file using the same design.

NOTE If you want to turn your database design into a template, do it after you enter formulas but before you enter specific data into the first record. That way, the formulas will be included in the template, but specific individuals won't.

Summary

This chapter showed you how to:

- ❖ Use a number of special database features
- ❖ Exchange data with other applications, including copying, linking, and embedding information as well as merging database information into Word Processor documents
- ❖ Hide and protect fields as well as protect (and unprotect) a form
- ❖ Use Works' replace feature and Spelling Checker

You also have been introduced to the WorksWizards and AutoStart databases, and have had a chance to examine the contents of several of them.

One of the major reasons for building a database is to generate reports on the data. Chapter 18 shows you how to generate these reports.

Reports

With Database's report facility, you can select information from a database, perform summaries and other statistics on it, and print the results or copy them to a Word Processor document. In this chapter, you will learn how to:

- ❖ Create a standard report
- ❖ Tailor the standard report
- ❖ Sort records in a report
- ❖ Group records in a report
- ❖ Integrate a report into a Word Processing document
- ❖ Manage reports

Introduction to Database Reporting

Figure 18.1 shows an example of a report generated by Database. Print Preview was used so that you can see the report with data filled in. The report in the example is based on a database with many more fields, but only certain fields have been selected for the report. You might develop several reports based on one database, each showing different types of information.

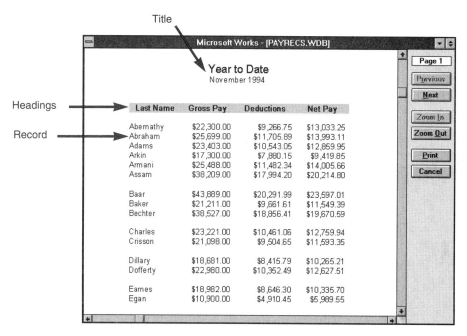

Figure 18.1 *Sample report (beginning)*

In Figure 18.1, you can see examples of a report title, column headings, and records, three basic elements of a report. You can tailor the formats of these items just as you do in a spreadsheet.

Figure 18.2 shows the last page of the same report, where the report summaries are printed. This particular report summarizes the number of records and the total Gross Pay, Deductions, and Net Pay.

Summaries

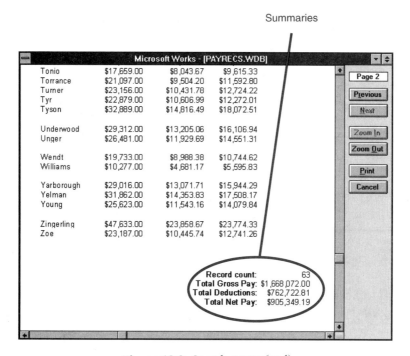

Figure 18.2 *Sample report (end)*

Creating a Standard Report

You start the process of creating a report by generating a standard report, and then tailoring it as desired. It takes several stages to develop a standard report.

The Tools Create New Report Command

You begin by choosing the **Tools Create New Report** command, which opens the **New Report** dialog box shown in Figure 18.3. Type a title for the report in the **Report Title** box. For example, for the report shown in Figure 18.1, you would type the title **Year to Date**. (The subtitle of November 1994 was added later.)

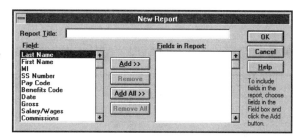

Figure 18.3 *New Report dialog box*

Next, select each field that you want to include in the report, in the desired order. (You don't have to select them in the same order that they appear in the list box.)

❖ **To select a field:**

1. Click the field name in the list box.

2. Click the **Add>>** button. The field name is listed in the **Fields in Report** box, and the highlight moves down one field in the **Field** box so that the next field is ready for selection.

SHORTCUT

If you want to use all the fields in the database, in the order shown, just click the **Add All>>** button.

If you change your mind about a field, select it in the **Fields in Report** box and click the **Remove** button. To remove them all, click **Remove All**. When you have selected all the fields you want, click **OK** to continue.

Selecting Statistics

When you click the **OK** button in the New Report dialog box, the Report Statistics dialog box opens (see Figure 18.4). You use this dialog box to select the statistics that you want to print for each field in the report. The sample report in Figure 18.2 uses the Count statistic for the **Last Name** field and the

Sum statistic for **Gross**, **Deductions**, and **Net**. You can select more than one statistic for a field.

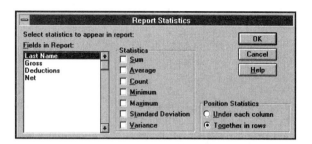

Figure 18.4 *Report Statistics dialog box*

❖ **To select statistics for a field:**

1. Click the field name in the **Fields in Report** list box.

2. Click each statistic you want for that field. An *X* appears in each checkbox that you select.

If you change your mind about a statistic, click it again to remove the *X* from the checkbox.

N O T E

The **Position Statistics** group gives you two choices for where the statistics will be printed in the report. They always come at the end, of course. If you choose **Together in rows**, the statistics are displayed in a block of rows at the end of the report, like the example in Figure 18.2. If you choose **Under each column**, they are printed with the columns they are based on. Figure 18.5 shows the same report as in Figure 18.2, but using **Under each column** instead of **Together in rows**.

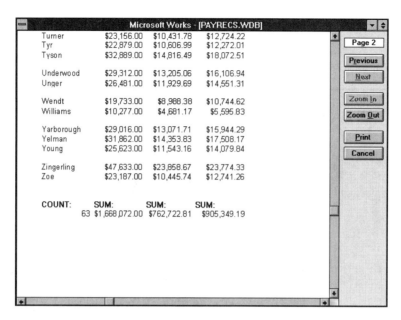

Turner	$23,156.00	$10,431.78	$12,724.22	
Tyr	$22,879.00	$10,606.99	$12,272.01	
Tyson	$32,889.00	$14,816.49	$18,072.51	
Underwood	$29,312.00	$13,205.06	$16,106.94	
Unger	$26,481.00	$11,929.69	$14,551.31	
Wendt	$19,733.00	$8,988.38	$10,744.62	
Williams	$10,277.00	$4,681.17	$5,595.83	
Yarborough	$29,016.00	$13,071.71	$15,944.29	
Yelman	$31,862.00	$14,353.83	$17,508.17	
Young	$25,623.00	$11,543.16	$14,079.84	
Zingerling	$47,633.00	$23,858.67	$23,774.33	
Zoe	$23,187.00	$10,445.74	$12,741.26	

COUNT: SUM: SUM: SUM:
63 $1,668,072.00 $762,722.81 $905,349.19

Figure 18.5 *The Under Each Column option*

The Report Definition

When you click **OK** in the Report Statistics dialog box, the report definition appears (see Figure 18.6). This is much like List view with formulas specifying the contents of the fields. You're now in Report view, and you can start tailoring the report.

Notice the row headers in the figure. You can have several kinds of rows in a report definition. *Title* rows must be at the top. Database generates two title rows in the standard report: the one containing the title from the New Report dialog box in column D, and a blank one for spacing. *Headings* rows come after the title rows. Again, Database generates two rows: the one containing the names of the fields in the report, and a blank one for spacing.

The *record* row contains the formulas for the fields to be included in the report. The *summary* rows set up the labels and formulas for the statistics. These formulas use the standard Works functions, such as **COUNT**, **SUM** and **AVG**. Database inserts a blank summary row (for spacing) after the record row, then as many additional summary rows as needed to specify all the statistics you have requested.

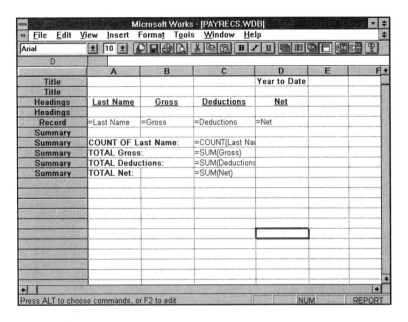

Figure 18.6 *Report definition*

Previewing the Report

You can't really judge what your report will look like from the report definition—at least not until you're better acquainted with the relationships between the definition and the printed result. In the meantime, you can easily see the results with Print Preview. You'll probably find that there are many changes you want to make.

Tailoring the Report Definition

Much of the tailoring in a report consists of the same formatting tasks that you do with Word Processor and Spreadsheet. You can format the pages of the report with margins, headers, footers, and page breaks. You can format text for font, style, size, and so on; you can also change the text of any labels (such as the headings) and add more labels. You can change the size of the columns and rows, add borders and patterns, select numeric formats, and align the data.

Figure 18.7 shows some of the reformatting that was done to produce the report in Figures 18.1 and 18.2. The title was enlarged to 14 points and centered across columns A through D. The headings are no longer underlined, but their cells are shaded light gray. Also, the text has been changed somewhat ("Gross" becomes "Gross Pay," for example). The summary rows have been moved to the right, the labels have been rewritten slightly, and they have been right-aligned.

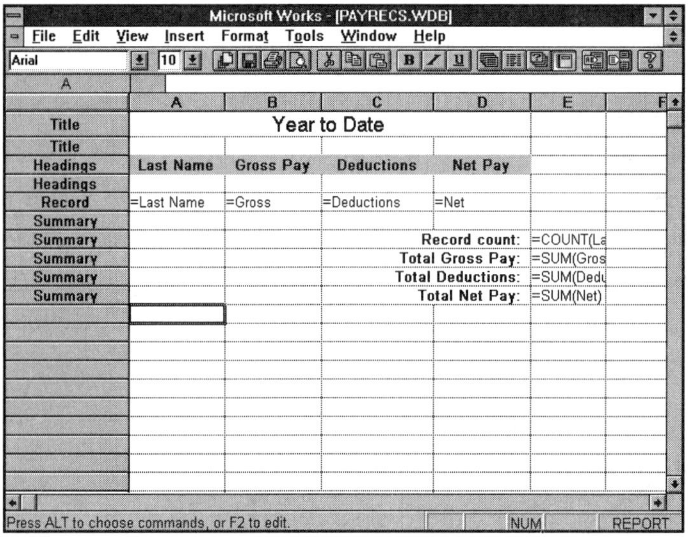

Figure 18.7 *Formatting a Report*

Inserting Rows and Columns

You can insert columns in a report definition just as you do in a spreadsheet. You can also insert rows, although the process is a little different because you have to choose a row type.

❖ **To insert a row:**

1. Select the row that should follow the inserted row. (You can select several rows if you want to insert multiple rows.)

2. Choose **Insert Row/Column**. The Insert Row dialog box opens (see Figure 18.8).

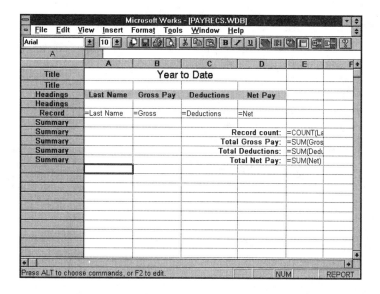

Figure 18.8 *Insert Row dialog box*

3. Double-click the type of row you want to insert. Since each row can appear only in certain positions, if the type isn't appropriate for the position you have indicated, Database inserts the row(s) in a proper position.

The row is blank when it is inserted. You can add data to it or leave it blank for spacing purposes.

A fast and easy way to insert extra space between sections is to increase the height of the first row in the next section.

SHORTCUT

You can have more than one record row in a report, if you want to print multiple lines for each record in the database. Figure 18.9 shows an example, where each record takes four rows: a blank row and three data rows. The headings have been set up to show what is in each row. (The data in the rows has been staggered so that everything in the top row is left aligned, everything in the middle row is centered, and everything in the bottom row is right aligned.) Shading and borders have been used to clarify the display as much as possible. Figure 18.10 shows sample output from the definition in Figure 18.9.

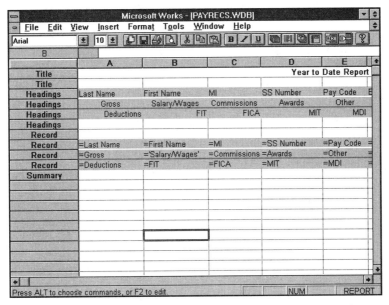

Figure 18.9 *Definition with more than one row per record*

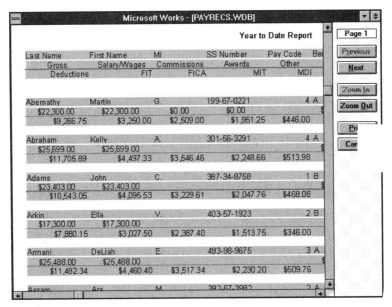

Figure 18.10 *Sample output with more than one row per record*

Printing more than one row per record can cause a problem with page breaks. There is no way to prevent Works from breaking the page in the middle of a record—after the second row, for example. You could copy the report output to a Word Processor document, as you'll see later, and insert page breaks there, but you can copy only the text, not the shading and borders.

Grouping and Sorting

The **Tools Sort Records** command is used both to sort the records and to group them. Figure 18.11 shows the dialog box that opens when you choose this command. As you can see, you can establish up to three sort criteria. You don't have to actually select any rows or fields before opening the dialog box. You choose the fields in the dialog box; all unhidden records are sorted.

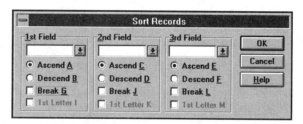

Figure 18.11 *Sort Records dialog box*

If you check the **Break** box underneath a field, Database groups records according to the values in that field. For example, suppose that you set up Benefits Code as the first sort field and check **Break**. All the records with Benefits Code A will come first. At the end of the A group, Database prints subtotals for that group. Then it starts the B group. Each time the code changes, Database ends the current group and starts a new group. Figure 18.12 shows an example in which you can see the bottom of group A, all of group B, and the beginning of group C.

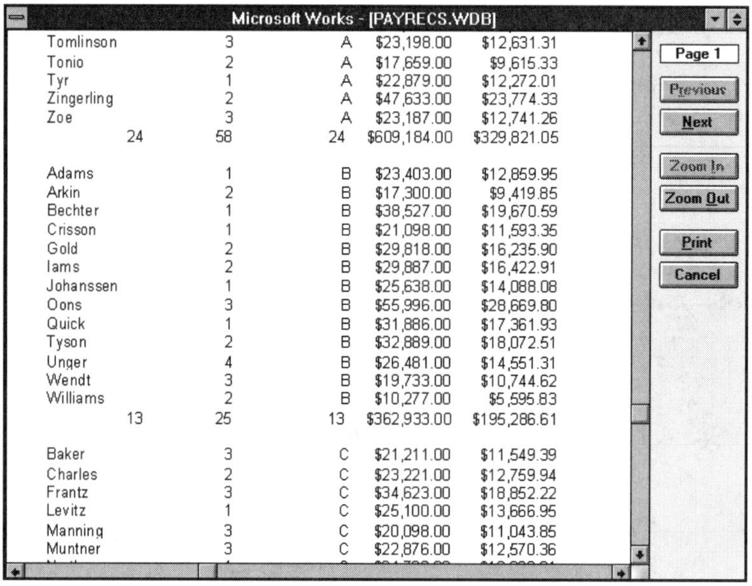

Tomlinson		3	A	$23,198.00	$12,631.31
Tonio		2	A	$17,659.00	$9,615.33
Tyr		1	A	$22,879.00	$12,272.01
Zingerling		2	A	$47,633.00	$23,774.33
Zoe		3	A	$23,187.00	$12,741.26
	24	58	24	$609,184.00	$329,821.05
Adams		1	B	$23,403.00	$12,859.95
Arkin		2	B	$17,300.00	$9,419.85
Bechter		1	B	$38,527.00	$19,670.59
Crisson		1	B	$21,098.00	$11,593.35
Gold		2	B	$29,818.00	$16,235.90
Iams		2	B	$29,887.00	$16,422.91
Johanssen		1	B	$25,638.00	$14,088.08
Oons		3	B	$55,996.00	$28,669.80
Quick		1	B	$31,886.00	$17,361.93
Tyson		2	B	$32,889.00	$18,072.51
Unger		4	B	$26,481.00	$14,551.31
Wendt		3	B	$19,733.00	$10,744.62
Williams		2	B	$10,277.00	$5,595.83
	13	25	13	$362,933.00	$195,286.61
Baker		3	C	$21,211.00	$11,549.39
Charles		2	C	$23,221.00	$12,759.94
Frantz		3	C	$34,623.00	$18,852.22
Levitz		1	C	$25,100.00	$13,666.95
Manning		3	C	$20,098.00	$11,043.85
Muntner		3	C	$22,876.00	$12,570.36

Figure 18.12 *Sample breaks*

Figure 18.13 shows the report definition for the report in Figure 18.12. Notice the Summ Benefits rows. The name of the row comes from the word Summary and the name of the field providing the break point (Benefits Code). The first Summ Benefits row was added by Database when the **Break** box was checked in the Sort Records dialog box; Database inserted its default formulas for the subtotal line in this row. You'll usually want to add at least one blank Summ row, as shown in the example, to provide some spacing after the subtotals line. (When a Summ row has been inserted by Database, the Insert Row dialog box (see Figure 18.8) includes that type of row in its list box.)

You might not want to include all the subtotals provided by Database. It automatically counts all text fields and sums all numeric fields. The results of the default subtotals are shown in Figure 18.12. As you can see, there is a count under the Last Name column and the same count under the Benefits Code column. If none of the fields can be blank, all the counts will be the same for a group, so there's no sense in printing more than one of them. In the same example, the second column is a pay code, and summing it makes no sense. You can delete any formulas you don't want from the Summ *breakpoint* line. If you don't want any subtotals, delete all the formulas, in which case you'll get a blank line between the groups.

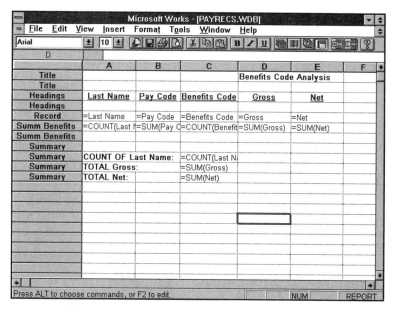

Figure 18.13 *Sample report definition showing Summ Rows*

In many cases, you want to group records by the first letter of a name or ID field, not by the entire name. Go back to Figure 18.1 for an example. Notice that the records are grouped according to the first letter of the **Last Name** field. (The subtotals were removed.) If you just check **Break** in the Sort Records dialog box, Database will print a breakpoint every time the name changes. For the most part, that means a breakpoint after every record. To break only when the first letter changes, also check **1st Letter** in the dialog box.

Figure 18.14 shows the complete definition for the report in Figures 18.1 and 18.2, including formatting and breaks. Notice the Summ Last Name row to group the records by the first letter of the last name without inserting any subtotals.

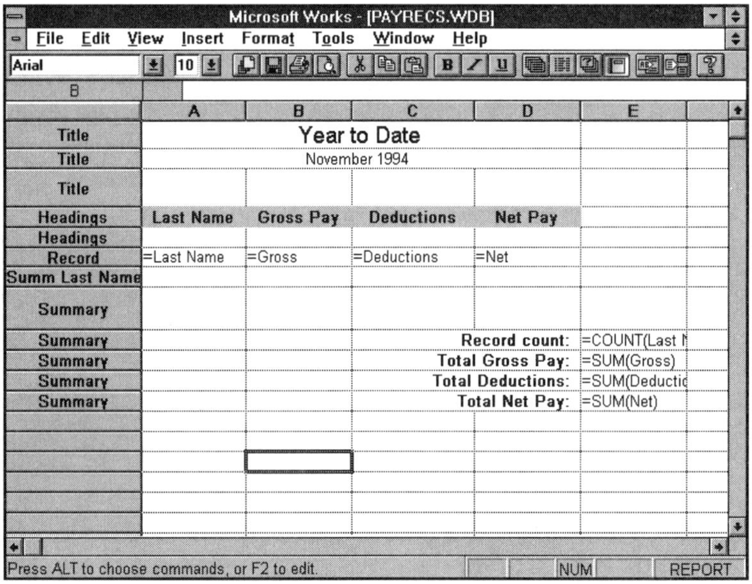

Figure 18.14 *Sample report definition*

Managing Reports

When you're satisfied with the way your report looks on-screen, you can print it by clicking the **Print** button while Report view is on your screen. Database automatically prints all unhidden records when you use a database report. To include only part of the records in the report, switch to List or Form view and hide the ones you don't want. You can hide them via a query and/or individually using the **View Hide Record** command.

Integrating with Word Processor

Like Spreadsheet, Report view doesn't let you embed or link anything into a report. If you want to add a graphic, such as your company logo, to the report, you must copy the report output to a Word Processor document.

❖ **To copy report output to a Word Processor document:**

1. Choose **Edit Copy Report Output**. Works generates the report on the Clipboard. The message bar reports progress as the report is generated.

2. Open the Word Processor document and position the cursor.

3. Click the **Paste** icon. The entire report is inserted as normal text at the cursor position.

If the report contains shading or borders, they are not included. Character formatting and alignment are copied, but centering across several fields is not.

Working with Report Names

Each report you create is automatically saved as Report1, Report2, and so on, with the database it belongs to. You can return to a report, rename it, delete it, and so on.

❖ **To return to a report:**

1. Choose **View Report**. The Report dialog box lists the reports for the current database.

2. Double-click the desired report. The selected report definition appears in Report view.

❖ **To rename one or more reports:**

1. Choose **Tools Name Report**. The Name Report dialog box opens.

2. Click the report you want to rename.

3. Type a name in the **Name** box.

4. Click **Rename**. The new name replaces the former name in the list box. The dialog box stays on the screen so that you can rename other reports.

5. Repeat Steps 2 through 4 for each report you want to rename.

6. Click **OK** to close the dialog box.

NOTE

Edit Undo can't undo report rename actions.

❖ **To delete one or more reports:**

1. Choose **Tools Delete Report**. The Delete Report dialog box opens.
2. Click the report you want to delete.
3. Click **Delete**. The report is deleted from the list box. The dialog box stays on the screen so that you can delete other reports.
4. Repeat Steps 2 through 3 for each report you want to delete.
5. Click **OK** to close the dialog box.

WARNING

Edit Undo can't undo report deletions.

Sometimes it's easier to create a new report by adapting an existing one than by starting from scratch. The following procedure shows you how to make a copy of an existing report.

❖ **To duplicate one or more reports:**

1. Choose **Tools Duplicate Report.** The Duplicate Report dialog box opens.
2. Click the report you want to duplicate.
3. Type a name for the duplicate in the **Name** box.
4. Click **Duplicate**. The new report appears in the list box. The dialog box stays on the screen so that you can duplicate other reports.
5. Repeat Steps 2 through 4 for each report you want to duplicate.
6. Click **OK** to close the dialog box.

After you make a duplicate, you can tailor it as needed to create the report you want.

Summary

This chapter showed you how to:

❖ Create and print reports based on your databases

❖ Create a standard report, add statistics to it, and tailor it.

❖ Examine the output from a report by using Print Preview

❖ Print the report

❖ Copy it to a Word Processor document

❖ Save, rename, delete, and duplicate reports

The next part of this book deals with the fourth and final Works tool: Communications.

PART V

Communications

CHAPTER 19

The Communications Tool

I f you have a modem, it probably came with the necessary communications software. But if not, Works provides a complete Communications package that integrates with the other Works tools so that you can send messages and files to other computers, over telephone lines or directly.

In this chapter, you will learn to:

- ❖ Use the modem to dial numbers from any Works tool
- ❖ Create and use Communications documents to connect with other computers via modem
- ❖ Connect directly with another computer via cable
- ❖ Send text to and receive text from another computer
- ❖ Send files to and receive files from another computer
- ❖ Create and use scripts for repetitive communications tasks

453

Dialing Numbers

If you have a modem, you can dial a telephone number from any Works tool. Just select the telephone number in a Word Processor, Spreadsheet, or Database document and choose **Tools Dial This Number**. This is not a Communications feature. Once the number is dialed, you have to pick up the phone to talk to the person (or answering machine) on the other end. Works tells you when the number has been dialed and you can pick up the handset.

Creating a New Communications Document

A Communications document contains all the information necessary to establish a connection with one of the people or systems that you communicate with. You might, for example, create a Communications document for your on-line information service (CompuServe, Prodigy, America OnLine, and so on), a separate Communications document for each bulletin board system (BBS) that you use, and separate Communications documents for each friend whom you communicate directly with (without going through an on-line service or BBS).

A Communications document contains information such as the telephone number to dial, the speed at which to transfer information, what type of terminal you have, and so on. If you had to create a Communications document from scratch, you would have to know a lot of details about Communications and about the computer you are trying to reach. Fortunately, Communications will usually do most of the work for you by making a lot of assumptions.

Start a new Communications document by choosing the **Communications** button in the Startup dialog box. The first time you click this button, the Modem **Test** dialog box appears (see Figure 19.1). Click the **Test** button so that Works can find your modem. Until you do this, you can't use Communications with your modem.

N O T E

If Works can't find your modem, you need to resolve the problem before you can use Communications. Your hardware dealer should be able to help you.

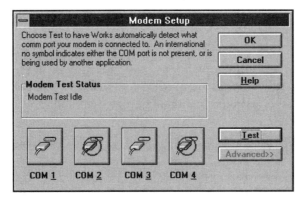

Figure 19.1 *Modem Test dialog box*

Using the Easy Connect Dialog Box

When you complete the modem test successfully, the Easy Connect dialog box appears (see Figure 19.2). In most situations, you should be able to fill in the phone number and a name for the person or service you are calling, and that's it.

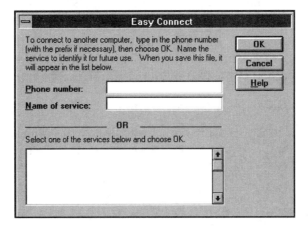

Figure 19.2 *Easy Connect dialog box*

Typing the Phone Number

You can type the phone number with or without hyphens, but don't use parentheses. In other words, type a long distance number as 18005553000 or 1-800-555-3000, but not 1 (800) 555-3000. Be sure to include all the digits you would dial if dialing the number manually: your long distance service access code (if appropriate), the area code (if appropriate), and the phone number itself.

Include a comma in the number to pause for a moment. If you are calling from a switchboard system that requires you to dial a 9 (or some other number) and wait for a dial tone before continuing, type the 9 followed by a comma, as in the following number:

9,1-800-555-3000

If one comma doesn't generate a long enough pause for your system, type several commas in a row.

N O T E

Assigning a Name to the Communications Document

The name that you type in the **Name of Service** text box will appear in the list box the next time you open this dialog box. It also appears on the Phone menu. You can select it in either location to reconnect with the same service or person.

Click **OK** to actually dial the number and see if you can connect with the desired service. Later topics in this chapter deal with what you should do after you have made a successful connection. If you make a connection and don't know how to proceed, choose **Phone Hang Up** and read the rest of the chapter.

Saving the Communications Document

Assigning a name to the service is not enough to save the Communications document on disk. Be sure to choose **File Save** and enter a filename to save your document.

If Easy Connect Doesn't Work–Doing It the Hard Way

The Easy Connect dialog box makes a great many assumptions about the Communications parameters needed to establish a connection with the other computer. The assumptions it makes are the most common ones and should work almost all the time. They will most certainly work with the major on-line information services and the larger BBSs. But if they don't work for the service you are trying to reach, you might have to set some of the communications parameters manually. (Note that they are different for each document.)

You must get information on which parameters to set and how to set them from the service you are trying to reach. The settings that you can change are all in the Settings dialog box and are shown in Figures 19.3 through 19.6. You open the Settings dialog box from any of the first four commands in the Settings menu (**Phone**, **Communication**, **Terminal**, **Transfer**). Then you can switch to any of the four pages by clicking its tab.

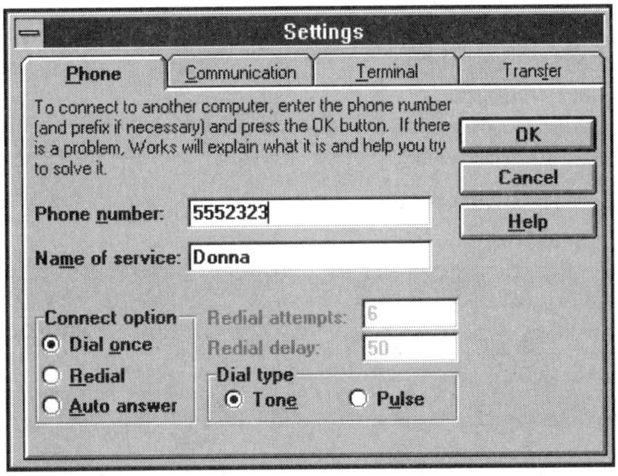

Figure 19.3 *Settings dialog box, Phone page*

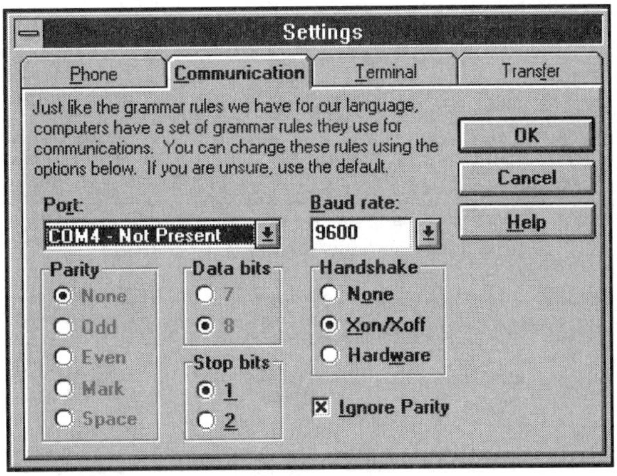

Figure 19.4 *Settings dialog box, Communication page*

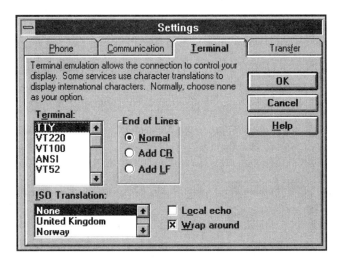

Figure 19.5 *Settings dialog box, Terminal page*

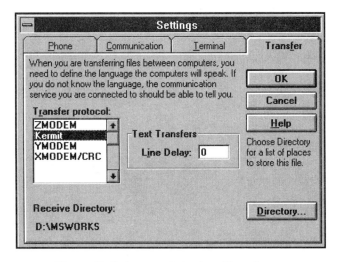

Figure 19.6 *Settings dialog box, Transfer page*

As you can see in the figures, Communications has a vocabulary all its own. The following glossary should help you understand the settings you might have to make.

Connect Option   The default setting, **Dial Once**, means that Communications will try only once to reach the specified party. If it gets no answer or a busy signal, it gives up. The **Redial** setting keeps trying (see **Redial attempts** and **Redial delay**). The **Auto answer** setting sets up your modem to answer any incoming calls automatically.

Redial attempts   If **Redial** is selected, this setting determines the number of times Communications will redial the number. The default is **6**.

Redial delay   Determines how many seconds Communications will wait between redial attempts.

Dial Type   Determines whether Communications will generate touch tones or pulses when dialing. Some areas have not upgraded to touch tone and require pulses.

Port   The place where your modem (and other devices) plug into your PC. A PC can have up to four communications ports, also called *serial ports* or *COM ports*. The modem test determines which port your modem is connected to, but if you have two modems, you can use this setting to choose one.

Baud Rate   This setting determines how fast data is sent and received. Both computer's modems must use the same baud rate. **9600** is the default, but you might have to use a different speed.

Parity   This setting determines how both computers check to make sure no errors have crept into the data during transfer. Both computers must use the same parity setting. **None** (that is, no parity checking) is the default.

Ignore Parity   This setting turns off parity checking. Uncheck it to make the settings in the **Parity** group available.

Data Bits   Modems can send 7 or 8 bits per byte. Both computers must use the same setting.

Stop Bits   Each byte must be followed by a certain number of stop bits so the receiving computer can identify the end of the byte. Both computers must use the same setting.

Handshake   The **Handshake** setting determines how the computers signal each other that they are ready to receive data. Both computers must use the same setting.

Terminal   Each computer must know what type of monitor the other one has, so it can send data appropriately. Works will emulate the standard terminal types shown in the dialog box. **TTY** (teletypewriter) is the default; it lets Works match your terminal to the other computer's.

ISO Translation   If you're receiving data containing international characters such as ñ and ö, you might need to tell Works what country the data is from so it interprets it correctly. The default is **None** (no translation).

Local Echo   If the characters you type don't appear on your own monitor, try checking this option.

Wrap Around   By default, Works wraps line that are wider than the window so that they fit in the window. Turn off this option if you would rather scroll sideways to read entire lines.

End of Lines   If the text you receive is all strung out in one paragraph, choose **Add CR** (carriage return) or **Add LF** (line feed) to start new paragraphs at the ends of lines.

Protocol   Data is transmitted in blocks. This setting determines the size of the blocks and how both computers signal the beginning and end of a block. Both computers must use the same setting. **Kermit** is the default.

Line Delay   Sometimes one or the other computer needs to receive data more slowly. Use **Line Delay** to slow down transmission. A 1 inserts a 1/10th-of-a-second delay after each line of text.

Recalling a Communications Document

After you have created a Communications document, you can recall it by reopening the document in the normal manner. That is, select it from the list in the Startup dialog box or choose **Open an Existing Document**. When you open the document, Works offers to dial the number immediately. You can choose **Yes** to dial the number or **No** if you want to change some of the settings first.

Communicating with an On-line Information Service or Bulletin Board

Most on-line information services require you to open an account before you can sign onto the service. You will probably receive a user ID and a password. You'll also receive instructions about what Communications parameters to use. When you dial up the service, it asks for your user ID and password. Then a menu lets you choose what you want to do. Be sure to sign off from the service before hanging up with the **Phone Hangup** command. If not, you might be charged for extra on-line time.

Many bulletin boards are free and don't require you to open an account. With others, you can register the first time you use the service. But if the **Easy Connect** parameters don't work, you'll have to find out what settings to use. You can usually find out from a published source or by calling the sys-op (*system operator*—the person who manages the bulletin board).

Communicating with a Friend

If you want to connect to a friend's computer via your modems but without going through a service, you'll both have to agree on what settings to use. Then one computer must be set up to receive a call.

❖ **To receive a call for the first time:**

1. Open a new Communications document.
2. Choose **Setting Phone** (see Figure 19.3).
3. Click **Auto Answer**.

4. Click **OK**. The dialog box closes, and your system is now ready to receive an incoming call.

5. Set up the rest of the Communications settings for this document to match your friend's system.

6. Tell your friend to place the call.

When you're done with the call, be sure to save the document so you can switch into auto answer mode easily whenever you want to receive a call.

Establishing a Direct Connection

Communications lets you connect two computers directly, without using a modem. They must be cabled together via their COM ports. See your dealer to get the right kind of cable. You can then transfer data from one to the other. If you have a laptop, you'll appreciate the ability to transfer data and programs between it and your desktop computer without having to copy the data to floppy disks first. (The same is true if you have two desktop computers.)

❖   **To connect two computers for the first time:**

1. Cable the two computers together using an available COM port on each computer.

2. On the computer that will be used to send data, open a new Communications document. The Easy Connect dialog box opens.

3. Choose **Cancel** to close the dialog box.

4. Choose **Settings Communication**. The Settings dialog box opens (see Figure 19.4).

5. Choose the COM port that you have connected the cable to on the sending computer.

6. Choose a baud rate. Since no modem or telephone lines are involved, you can probably choose the fastest rate (19,200 baud).

7. Click OK.

8. Choose **Phone Easy Connect**. The Easy Connect dialog box opens.

9. Delete any information in the text boxes. They should both be blank.

10. Choose **OK**. Communications waits for the receiving computer to be set up.

11. Repeat Steps 2 through 10 for the receiving computer. (Be sure to select the COM port that the cable is connected to on the receiving computer. It might be different than the sending one.)

When both computers are connected, the *OFFLINE* message in the status bar changes to a time counter.

NOTE

12. Type text or send files as desired. (The next sections explain how to do this.)

13. When you're done with the connection, choose **Phone Hangup** on each computer.

If you plan to use this facility more than once, be sure to save the new Communications documents on each computer. Then you can simply open the document instead of doing steps 2 through 7.

It's not absolutely required that both computers use Works Communications. If one computer doesn't have Works but has another communications facility that is capable of direct connection, you might be able to connect to it from Works.

NOTE

Sending and Receiving Text

Once you have established a connection to another computer, whether it's a direct connection, a friend's computer, or a service, you should be able to send and receive text. The messages that you send and receive all appear in the Communications document window. All you have to do is start typing.

Suppose you have connected to an on-line information service and get the message that you have mail waiting. Select your service's commands to receive your mail. The messages are displayed in your Communications document. To send answers, select your service's commands to send mail, then type the messages you want to send.

Suppose instead that you have connected to a friend's computer, and your friend is on-line at the other end of the connection. You can type messages, and your friend can type replies immediately.

Reviewing Text

Messages can scroll by pretty quickly when you're communicating. Sometimes a long message scrolls off the screen so fast that you don't get the chance to read it all. You can click the **Pause** button on the toolbar (see Figure 19.7) to stop transmitting while you read something, then click the button again to continue. But you may not want to do that if you're paying by the minute for the service.

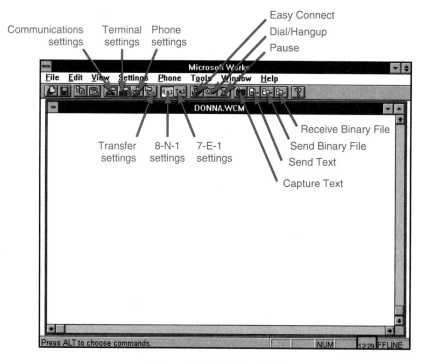

Figure 19.7 *Toolbar buttons*

Communications stores everything that appears in the document window in a memory buffer. It's a fairly large buffer—256,000 lines—so you can probably catch your entire session and review it later. If you exceed the size of the buffer, the oldest lines are overwritten with newer ones. All you have to do to review the contents of the buffer is scroll through the document window. You can do this after you disconnect from the other services.

N O T E If you want to view the contents while still connected to another computer, click the **Pause** button while you scroll around. Position the cursor at the end of the text before clicking **Pause** again to continue communicating.

The text in the buffer will not be saved if you close the Communications document. To save it, you should copy it to another file.

❖ **To save the contents of the buffer in a file:**

1. Select the contents that you want to save.
2. Copy the selected text to a Word Processor document file.

Capturing Text

Another way to preserve incoming text is to capture it right away in a file. Then you don't have to bother copying it to a file. If someone is sending you a long message, such as a complete report, or if you think that your session will exceed 256,000 lines, you might as well capture it in a file.

❖ **To capture incoming text in a file:**

1. Click the **Capture Text** icon in the toolbar (see Figure 19.7). The Capture Text dialog box opens (see Figure 19.8).

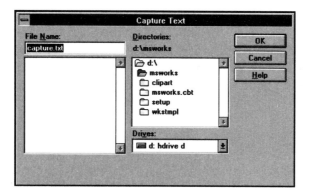

Figure 19.8 *Capture Text dialog box*

2. Type a name for the file in the **File Name** box.

3. Click **OK**. Communications captures all incoming text in the indicated file. You can open the file later and deal with the text just like any other document file.

If you identify an existing file in Step 2, you must choose to Append the new text to the end of the file, Replace the existing file, or Cancel so you can try again with a different file name.

Communications continues to capture text to the indicated file until you tell it to stop or until you close the current document. The **Capture Text** icon on the toolbar remains pressed down as long as the feature is turned on. To stop capturing, click the icon again.

Sending a Text File

Unless you want to interact "live" with a friend or a bulletin board group, you'll usually dial up a service, transmit some text to a forum or a mailbox, then hang up again without interacting with anyone. You can save a lot of on-line time, and therefore expense, by preparing your text in a Word Processor document file before you go on-line.

There are two ways to transfer text from another document, depending on whether you want to send the whole file or just part of it:

❖ Copy the desired text from the other document to the Communications document.

❖ Choose Tools Send Text and select the text file to be transmitted.

Don't bother formatting any text you send this way. Works transmits only the unformatted text.

N O T E

Sending and Receiving Files

When you send a text file using the procedure in the last section, it is displayed as a message on the recipient's monitor, just as if you had typed the text on-line. But you can also send a file and receive files from disk to disk without displaying the contents on either monitor. Sending a file in this manner is often called *uploading* and receiving one is often called *downloading*.

If you want to send information to a friend and don't need to the friend to read and respond to the information on-line, it's much more efficient to send a file than a text message. If you're sending information to someone via a BBS or on-line service, upload a file to them. When you have two computers linked via a cable, you send files from one to the other.

You can send two basic types of files, *text* and *binary*. A text file contains unformatted text, just like you type at the keyboard when communicating. A binary file can contain anything: formatting, shading, graphics, and so on. It usually takes longer and costs more to transmit a binary file.

❖ **To send a file:**

1. If using an on-line service or BBS, select the service's commands to indicate that you want to send/upload a text or binary file and to identify the recipient. The service will usually display some kind of message that says, *Begin sending* or *Start transmitting*.

You'll probably have to choose a protocol for the receiving end and set your own Communications document to the same protocol. Choose **ZModem** if it's available; it's the fastest and the best. Otherwise, try **XModem**, **Kermit**, and **YModem**, in that order.

N O T E

2. Click the **Send Text File** or **Send Binary File** icon on the toolbar. The Send File dialog box opens.

3. Select the file to send. A dialog box keeps you informed of progress.

❖ **To receive a file:**

1. If you are using a BBS or service, choose whatever commands are necessary to indicate that you want to receive/download a text or binary file. The service will usually display some kind of message that says, *Begin receiving.*

You'll probably have to choose a protocol for the sending service and set your own Communications document to the same protocol.

N O T E

2. Choose **Tools Receive File**. The Receiving File dialog box opens.

3. If you are using the **XModem** protocol, you need to specify a name under which to store the file on your computer. (With the other protocols, the file's name from the sending computer is used.)

4. Click **OK** to start receiving. A dialog box keeps you informed of progress.

Suppose you're on-line with a friend and want to send a file. Make sure you're using the same parameters, then choose **Tools Send File** and select the file to be sent. When your system is ready, your friend should enter the commands to receive it.

If you're sending a file from one computer to another that is cabled to it, enter the commands to send it from the sending computer, then go to the other computer and enter the commands to receive it.

You can interrupt a file transfer by pressing the **Esc** key.

N O T E

Scripts

Some Communications tasks are the same every time you use a Communications document. You can record them as a script and play them back whenever you want to repeat the task.

Recording a Script

The most common script is the one that signs you on to an on-line service: It sends your user ID, password, and any other keystrokes that you need to sign on. You can have only one sign-on script in a Communications document. The document might have several other scripts, however.

❖ **To record a script:**

1. Choose **Tools Record Script**. The Record Script dialog box opens (see Figure 19.9).

Figure 19.9 *Record Script dialog box*

2. Select **Sign-on** or **Other**.

3. If you choose **Other**, you must enter a name of up to 15 characters in the **Script Name** box. (The **OK** button is dimmed until you enter a name for the script.)

4. Click **OK**. The message *REC* appears in the status box to let you know that Communications is recording everything you type and every mouse action.

5. For a sign-on script, connect to the on-line service and sign on as normal. For another type of script, perform the steps that you want to record. Communications records the script.

6. Choose **Tools End Recording**. The REC message disappears and script recording terminates.

NOTE

If you change your mind while recording a script, choose **Tools Cancel Recording**. Communications stops recording, and the script is not saved.

WARNING

The script is part of the Communications document and is not saved on disk until you save the document. If you close the document without saving it, the script is lost.

Playing Back a Script

When you open a Communications document that has a sign-on script, the script is automatically played to connect with the on-line service. Other types of scripts must be specifically played back by choosing **Tools *script-name***.

Managing Scripts

The **Tools Edit Script** command opens the Edit Script dialog box, which lists all the scripts for the current Communications document. Select a script and click **Rename** to rename it or **Delete** to delete it. You can also modify the script, but you have to know how to use the script commands. It's usually easier to delete the script and record a new one.

Summary

This chapter showed you how to:

- ❖ Use the Communications tool
- ❖ Create a new Communications document using either the Easy Connect dialog box, or using the Settings dialog box if that becomes necessary
- ❖ Connect with an on-line communications service, a bulletin board system, or a friend with a modem
- ❖ Connect your computer directly with another one via cable and transfer data from one to the other
- ❖ Send and receive text and files
- ❖ Record and use a script
- ❖ Dial telephone numbers (without establishing a communications connection) from any Works tool

Now you have learned how to use all four Works tools—Word Processor, Spreadsheet, Database, and Communications—along with the extra features that make Works so special, such as WordArt and Microsoft Draw. You know how to create documents, integrate data into them from other tools, enhance them with artwork and other formatting features, and save and print the results. You have also seen how to use a wealth of professionally designed documents provided by the WorksWizards and AutoStart Templates. You are fully prepared to use Works in your daily work to accomplish your tasks not only with speed and ease, but also with a bit of flair. Have fun!

Index

A

I

Icon, 4, 8, 13

    Minimized window, 19–20

    Saving icon positions, 25

Importing drawings, 224–225

Importing files, 199–201

Indentation, 131–134

Insert key, 109

Insert mode, 86, 109

Inserting an object in a document. *See* Embedded object, Linked object

Inserting records, 403

Inserting rows and columns

    Database Report, 440–443

    Spreadsheet, 258–259, 295

Inserting text, 109

Installing Works for Windows, 32–38

    Changing, 38

    Complete installation, 35–36

    Custom installation, 36–37

    Minimum installation, 38

ISO translation, 460

Italics (characters). *See* Style

J

Justified alignment, 135–137, 156

L

Label,

    Chart, 336–337

    Database, 383

Labels, mailing, 76–78

Landscape orientation, 300, 391

Leaders, 146

Leading zeros format, 279–280

Learning Works, 47–48

Left alignment, 134, 136, 137, 286

Left tab stop, 144–145

Legend (Chart), 335–336

Letterhead WorksWizard, 67–68

LF (line feed), 460

Line chart, 326–328, 331

Line delay, 460

Line style (Microsoft Draw), 217–218

Line tool (Microsoft Draw), 206–207

Linked object, 363–370, 416–417

List box, 22

List view, 387–389, 398